KARMA GRINDERS

K.D. Madigan

ISBN-13: 978-1-0692170-1-1

Cover design by: Erin Hamilton and Harnoor Jaura

dedicated to xana
i miss you

STEEF
NICK
alan
TERRY
ROMAN
JEFF
MATEJ
CASSANDRA
ALIYA
GEOFF
GERG
KEVIN
MIKE
MILES
LISE

01 - THE AIRPORT

The Grinders had their orders from Cassandra: Roam through the Vancouver airport, sow chaos and destruction, don't get caught, and be at departures in one hour.

She didn't care what they did.

She just wanted people to suffer.

Already exhausted, she looked around and noticed disorganized scatterings of security guards.

Before they had arrived at the airport, Mike, the programmer, had informed everyone that there would be something amazing waiting for them at departures, which meant that Cassandra didn't really have a need to remove the security detail anywhere but at departures.

So this one would be mostly recreational:

She rummaged through her disorganized purse, found an ancient baggie with some coke left in it, took care of it, then found what she was looking for – her liquid dropper of extra-strength laxative.

She stalked a nearby pair of guards, waited for them to put down their coffees to stare at their phones, administered a triple dose in each one, and kept moving swiftly through the airport.

***

There were fifteen Grinders in total.

Most of them were Disciples, and Cassandra was their leader - their Archon.

Nobody voted Cassandra as the Archon. These things didn't come to a vote. Nobody questioned why she was the Archon. Nobody questioned it because nobody questioned it.

They'd met years ago and they'd discovered the common purpose together. They all experienced the same thing.

It was wonderful serendipity. It was rugged, strange velvet, slow moving and purple, fantastical and absolute waking dream logic.

Everyone just knew.

There was no doubt.

You had to be there.

Since that moment, the Disciples have followed faithfully behind their commanding Archon, causing manageable suffering, saving souls, and doing it thanklessly.

Really, they didn't need thanks. Miles, who acted as Cassandra's second-in-command, was stuffing the hollow shower rods at Home Depot with rotting salmon one day when he realized that it would be absurd to expect to be thanked for any of this.

They didn't need thanks from their beneficiaries, anyways. They knew from their shared experience and from studying the texts that the mathematics of the Cosmos would thank them appropriately in their next lives.

All they had to do was inflict suffering on strangers and on each other and on themselves, and everyone would be rewarded.

They drew it up perfectly.

***

Cassandra crept up behind Miles and spooked him with a hand on his shoulder. "You gonna take care of the idiots?"

"Oh, um. Yeah, no problem."

"Okay. I'm being told you don't wanna miss what Mike has planned."

"Wouldn't miss it for the world."

Cassandra sniffled and walked away.

Miles sighed, looked at his watch out of habit, forgot to register what time it was, and felt too embarrassed to take another look, even though nobody was paying attention to him.

He had corralled the idiots many times before. By now he knew how they all operated in airports. The majority of the Grinders would be meeting at whichever airport bar was closest to departures, and the rest would probably be near that bar, already in action, already grinding Karma.

Miles mainly needed to make sure that Kevin wasn't going to be killed or sent to jail or left unconscious on the toilet by whatever drugs Aliya had been feeding him.

This meant that for now, Miles was on the wrong side of the airport. Sometimes it felt like he could never win.

***

The flickering arrivals screen above emitted a white noise. Kevin stared at the conveyor belt below, puttering in circles with no luggage, but offering a comfortable, distracting hum. Security was concerned with what Kevin was trying to accomplish, talking to himself, staring at nothing, accompanied by Aliya, a smirking brown girl frantically rummaging through a large, unmarked bag in an international airport.

They knew no luggage was coming. There were no arrivals. There was no luggage. They weren't waiting for luggage. They're waiting for Kevin, who was in the throes of low-grade Canadian trailer park ketamine, which he'd inhaled ten minutes prior in the airport bathroom, threading a straw to the bottom of the single serve ziploc bag, inhaling the entire half gram in a single breath - a rapid insufflation system that he liked to call 'capri-sunning'.

"Good morning, sir, are you with these two?"

Miles turned around to find two tired-looking security guards holding coffees.

"I uhh... yeah."

"Can you... oh." The leading guard buckled over slightly and put his free hand over his stomach. He looked over at the other guard who had the same sudden panic.

Miles clued in immediately. He was familiar with this game.

"Yeah... uhh... see, hold on." He pulled his phone out, said "huh?" and then checked his watch again and muttered, "well that doesn't make any sense."

"Sir, please. What is the... Oh no."

Miles knew he had them.

"Well, yes, guards. The two people here, the man and the lady we all see right here. These people... they... are my..." Miles smiled and trailed off. "They are my friends."

"We have established th-." The guard's face went pale and he hurried his speech. He pointed to Kevin. "Whyisthismanactingstrangely?" He started breathing rapidly.

Miles loved to watch them suffer but he really didn't want to make a mess. He smiled like an angel of mercy. "Anaesthesia from orthodontic surgery."

"THANKYOUTHATWILLBEALLSIR." Both guards abandoned their posts and their coffees and raced each other to the bathroom.

Miles looked towards departures and even from behind, he could tell Cassandra was smiling as she disappeared into a crowd.

***

With Kevin now seated and relatively out of danger, Miles watched as Aliya reached into her large, unmarked magical bag, pulled out a handful of marbles, and rolled them at a congregation of foot traffic.

"I'll award you a category one for that," Miles paused to watch as everyone bumped into each other, trying to avoid the marbles, falling down anyways. "But bonus points for being funny."

"Fuck can I do with bonus points?"

"Nothing. I'll give them to Kevin if you don't want them."

"No, fuck you. What's K-hole gonna do with bonus points? I want them."

While the nearby adults were busy helping Aliya's marble victims back onto their feet, Miles handed a bouquet of pixie sticks to a group of temporarily abandoned children.

"Another category one."

"Oh come on. The lowest possible grade for a Karma bomb? They're gonna be supercharged for hours. They'll be running in circles on the plane. Clogging the aisles. Pestering the other riders. Singing children's songs at the top of their lungs. That's a category two."

"Okay. Two. But DON'T fucking say the B word in an airport."

"Sorry. 'Karmic event'. I don't like it."

"I know. But we're in a fucking airport. Idiot."

A 'Karma bomb' is an intentional act of invoking chaos that has a ripple-out butterfly effect with an end goal of inflicted suffering - typically on Soldiers, the lowest rank in the Cosmos.

"Where's security anyways?"

"Archon sent them to the bathroom."

There was nothing wrong with Soldiers. This whole thing that the Grinders were doing was mostly to benefit them. They were only Soldiers because they were unawakened.

The Grinders viewed law enforcement as the most useful category of Soldier. Law enforcement has a rigid sense of purpose, a function, or a utility, and that purpose, function, or utility can always be twisted and bent and used and manipulated and redirected to serve the actual, real, true cause.

The Cosmic purpose.

The universal math.

The day to day rendering of the programming of everything.

The Grind.

Soldiers are beneath Disciples, Disciples are beneath Archons, Archons are beneath Angels, and to their knowledge, from their understanding of the literature, there is at least one rank above the Angels. Cassandra refuses to talk about it, and she also refuses to allow the Grinders to discuss it. And of course, Disciples respect their Archon.

"You know, since security's busy I think I can one-up you."

Miles handed out a stack of custom-made 'Santa Clause Isn't Real' informational pamphlets to a cluster of school children on a field trip just outside of a gift shop.

He could hear the cries of agony mounting and multiplying as he walked away.

"That's gotta be at least a three."

"Two or three."

"Long-term psychological damage. It's a three."

Aliya didn't really care. "Okay. Fine. Three."

The category of a Karma bomb is determined by two factors - the total amount of souls that experience suffering from the act, and the distance that the waves of suffering ripple down through time. It isn't a perfect math, and is always the subject of heated discussion, as the concept of 'Karma bombs' was developed from the Grinders' unique interpretation of the religious text. While they never completely agreed on the analytics, they all shared a feverish passion for it.

Aliya handed an airhorn to a child exiting a bathroom alone. "That's a two."

"Agreed."

Nobody but the Grinders knew about their mission and they wanted to keep it that way. They needed to keep it that way. For their own sake, and for everyone else's sake.

As any Disciple will tell you, suffering goes further if the person experiencing the suffering don't understand the root of the suffering. It hits harder and it sticks around longer.

And as any Disciple will tell you, the suffering they experience in this life will be rewarded in their next one.

Keeping a Soldier stupid is a gift to the Soldier.

***

Cassandra knew that Mike and Lise would already be at departures. Mike was busy setting up the surprise, and Lise followed Mike everywhere.

Cassandra found herself getting uncharacteristically excited for what Mike had planned. He didn't give any details, but he couldn't stop smiling whenever he mentioned it, and everyone got really excited when Mike suggested that it could be a comfortable category 4.

Cassandra slowed down her pace when she noticed that several security guards had exited the airport staff break room in a frenzy, likely in search of the airhorn that she had been hearing.

Sensing opportunity but feeling lazy, she snuck into the break room, dissolved the rest of her laxatives into the water cooler, and cranked up the heat.

She wouldn't have been able to take that much liquid on an airplane anyways.

***

"I'm not gonna say it."

"I'll get ya." Roman motioned to give aLan a friendly punch on the shoulder but aLan jerked away at the last second.

"We're in an airport. We can't fucking say it. Fucking stop."

"I always get ya."

"Doubt it."

"What if we're trying to book a flight to the most populated city in India?"

"Then I'll just call it Mumbai. Like a normal person."

"Hey aLan, what's your favorite Rage Against The Machine song? Is it... something-track? Or is it Calm Like A... something?"

"I'm not that stupid."

"Oh, I know, but I still get you most of the time anyways. Oh hey by the way I heard we just missed Matt Good Band."

"Huh?"

"Yeah I just saw last night. They were at the Commodore Ballroom a couple days ago. We should have gone."

"Oh no kidding? Yeah we should have gone."

"I know, right? I would love to hear them play Apparitions one more time. They could have played your favorite too. Strange Days, right?"

"Oh no. It's Hello Time Bomb."

Roman just turned and smiled.

"Fuck you."

When they arrived at the pub in silence a minute later, Nick was seated with his laptop opened to a dozen incomprehensible spreadsheets, and Gerg was at the bar in his Pikachu onesie, trying to pick up and balance a tray of beers to carry back to their table.

"What ya workin on buddy?"

Nick took a second to recalibrate away from his laptop. "So I've been thinking about," he trailed off for a second as he finished typing. "In these settings," he pointed his eyes at an obese family of nine who looked like they were on their way to Disneyland, confused and stupid and extremely American. "We have to be certain that we're not just doing whatever acts of chaos we think of first. I believe that we have a responsibility to the whole thing, to the Grind, to create the greatest amount of chaos in any given opportunity."

Nick reached into his bag, and after Gerg arrived at the table with the tray of beers and laid it down, Nick handed him a fully loaded NERF assault rifle. "A category 2 is fine, but we're in an airport. We could be doing a lot of 3s. While 2 is a healthy baseline for what's possible in most public settings, this is an aiport, a lot of people are on edge and vulnerable, and we could be doing better." Nick took one of the beers and took a sip, spilling on his shirt. "We could call it chaos-above-replacement. C.A.R. for short."

"Category 4s are too high for an airport," aLan drank his first beer in a single gulp, "and 3s can easily turn into 4s."

Roman didn't want to get suds in his mustache so he waited for the foam to die down before he started drinking. "Category 4s in this place could get us caught."

Gerg's attention had been brought to the family of nine and

he was getting acquainted with the NERF gun, inspecting the ammunition. "But who doesn't like a good C.A.R. crash?" There was a frenetic energy in his eyes behind his thick-rimmed glasses and nobody laughed at his joke.

"I know. I'm aware of all this. I just don't wanna leave any suffering on the table."

"Man. Nick. I know you know. But encouraging a game plan where we constantly try to max out the chaos is going to lead to a lot of shit getting out of control." aLan grabbed another beer. "Grinding Karma carries risk, and we have to hedge for uncertainty. We can't just all be cranking up the chaos." He drank it in a single gulp. "We already have one Kevin. That might be one too many."

"Exactly." The suds had died down and so Roman took a responsible sip. He got foam on his mustache anyways, but didn't notice, and he kept talking. "If we aim for category 2s, and we fuck up, it goes 1 or 3. If we aim for 3s and we fuck up, we can get 4s. We can't do category 4s in an airport. We can't do category 4s with this many security cameras."

Gerg was still wide-eyed and ready, staring at the family, until aLan manually lowered the NERF rifle to a safer angle.

Gerg shot aLan in the face, put the rifle on the table, adjusted his Pikachu costume, and went over to the Disney family to dance a wacky, waving-arm inflatable tube-man dance.

"That's a category two. Nick, are you still writing them down?" aLan took a third beer.

"I stopped keeping track months ago. Too much fucking work. I'm already running the spreadsheets for most of our money scams."

"You just seem so passionate about the chaos analytics."

"Yeah but I'm not a fucking bean counter." Nick closed his

laptop. "I hella gotta piss. Where's the bathroom?"

"There are signs everywhere." Cassandra snuck up on them. "Just look for a fucking sign that says bathroom." As Nick got up to find a bathroom, she took his seat. "I didn't know you guys were keeping track. You don't have to do that. The Angels are counting."

"Don't hurt us. It was only Nick." They watched as Nick passed by Gerg on his way to the men's room and accidentally-on-purpose bumped into him, getting into a very believable brawl to rile up the gaggle of fat American children while security was giving a shit somewhere else.

Cassandra finished Nick's beer. "I'm gonna stab him."

***

Nick, using quick math, unzipped at the urinal that was least likely to amass neighbors, and mid-stream he heard a familiar noise coming from one of the stalls.

Someone was playing Candy Crush at max volume.

Matej was here.

Nick smiled. This was good news. This meant they wouldn't have to try to hunt him down later.

Nick tried to say "hello," but Matej's game noises were far too loud.

This was Matej's favorite way to grind Karma - playing Candy Crush loudly in a public bathroom. The noises drove everyone insane and were too loud to yell over, and nobody ever bothered to report it. Reliable category 1.

Matej shouted a guttural noise that was so strange that Nick figured it was from an achievement in the game.

And then he smelled it.

Nick didn't shake, didn't wash his hands and didn't finish refastening his belt until he was back at the bar with the rest of the Grinders.

"Just came from the bathroom if we're wondering where Matej is."

"Candy Crush, again?"

"What category was it?"

"Definitely a #2."

***

Cassandra moved when Nick got back, and she tried to look at his password as he logged back into his laptop. "What scam are you running now?"

"Right now right now? I'm just working on analytical theories that aLan keeps ruining."

"If your theory can't stand up to my scrutiny then it's dog shit. I'm doing you a favor."

"Whatever. Also," Nick corrected his posture, "I still have momentum on the military recruitment thing. Few new contacts and a lot of new documents." Nick looked at his empty glass, noticed aLan smirking, and sighed. "I just don't wanna work on that one in an airport."

Matej arrived from the bathroom, looking down at his phone while he walked, playing Candy Crush until he got to the bar. The Grinders at the bar could hear the noises get louder as he approached, and they stopped talking important shop as he sat down next to Roman.

"Ahoy, Matej!"

"Matej. You have to turn the volume down when it's us."

Matej turned the volume down manually to zero instead of muting, smiling wide the entire time. "What's up homies? What are we doing?" There was a bounce in his step even when he was standing still. He looked up at the name of the pub. "Steve Nash Authentic Canadian Pub & Grill? What do they serve here?"

A waiter who clearly hated his job arrived with six more beers for the table and announced, "one Wayne Gretzky sized poutine."

"Is that a small? Wasn't Gretz like 150 lbs?"

"It comes with 99 fries and 99 cheese curds," explained the waiter. "It costs 99 dollars."

"That's fucking insane." Cassandra didn't want to be around for the gastric events thereafter and so she grabbed Roman's beer and finished it. "Fuck this shit, I'm going to departures, see you when we board."

Right as she stood up to leave, Gerg returned, his Pikachu onesie having been ripped open in three places by the angry Disney dad. "That's a category 2. Mark it down." Nobody marked anything down. Gerg grabbed a beer and drank half, spilling some of it all over what was now a Pikachu hand towel. "Nobody came to stop the brawl. That guy beat the shit out of me. Security was busy with something else I guess."

***

As Cassandra took a second just outside the bar, walking slowly to adjust to the updated movement parameters of her blood-alcohol, she almost got run over by Jeff and Geoff, joyriding on an airport shuttle, in security vests, fake-talking on stolen radios.

"SLOW THE FUCK DOWN."

Her commands were far louder than they had any right to be.

"TEN-FOUR."

If it was anyone else, they'd pretend not to hear her. But this was their Archon, and they respected their Archon.

They slowed down and went back to pretending they were airport employees, quietly hunting down opportunities for more reasonable chaos until she was out of sight.

They came across the double-wide, horizonal human conveyor belt - the ones they build for people with mobility issues - and Jeff considered driving against it just to see what would happen until they noticed that Miles and Aliya were at the far end of it, about to use it to help a dazed and confused Kevin get around.

If they were spotted, the ever-responsible Miles would likely invoke their Archon, so they sped off in the other direction and continued to pretend to be employees until they were out of sight, fake listening to their airport radios, tapping on their empty clipboards with urgency.

Miles realized that he and Aliya hadn't spoken in a while.

"Did you check his socks?"

Aliya was silent for a second while she considered lying, but the stakes were too high. "I trust him," she conceded. It was the truth, technically, but she chose her words in a way that would allow Miles to read between the lines.

"I'm gonna check his socks."

Miles removed Kevin's sandals where he stood, alternating his support legs like a flamingo; he inhaled, held his breath, and put his fingers down the sides of the socks.

Aliya held her breath too.

"We're good."

Aliya sighed.

"Unless you're smuggling? Do I need to check his-"

"NO."

Miles recoiled. "The lady doth protest too much."

"Not a fucking lady either."

They got onto the conveyor belt and Miles and Aliya took a minute to people-watch while the belt did all their labor for a few minutes. Being on the belt seemed to give Kevin a sense of great fulfillment. It percolated him halfway back into reality as though one side of his consciousness was being sent through a toaster oven. His eyes were still closed, but he started to stand caveman-upright on his own, and he mostly stopped drooling.

"You'll get a break from this soon," Miles reassured Aliya.

"I think I just wanna watch him for a while." She stared at the back of Kevin's head like she was trying to read his mind, but in reality, she had been studying up on witchcraft, and she was experimenting with narcotics on a very, very enthusiastic lab rat named Kevin. This was more than just fun. This was homework. She kept it on the down low from the rest of the Grinders while she made sure that what she was doing operated comfortably within the loosely-defined boundaries of their religious text, sending Nick whatever questions she was comfortable asking, Nick keeping quiet.

But this was the dream. She had an intelligent and willing test subject that could elucidate results. Eventually.

Some burgeoning witches could go several lives without finding a Kevin.

At the end of the conveyor belt, they were greeted by Jeff and Geoff, who had circled back after they were given enough time to feel guilt.

Jeff put on his sunglasses and growled at a struggling Kevin, "GET IN, BOY."

"Miles – we saw them at Steve Nash when we were riding past. They'll be happy to see you."

"Steve Nash? The gym?"

The Gjeoffs laughed as they ripped away, Jeff driving in the front with Aliya, and Geoff in the back part, propping up Kevin.

***

Miles carried on in the direction of the bar. There was a skip in his step, and he paused to direct a German couple to the wrong part of the airport, pretending to get Cologne confused with Kelowna. They would miss their flight home.

He passed a book store just two shops down from the bar, and he knew that Steef and Terry would be in there, which meant that everyone was probably accounted for, and he could safely head directly to the bar, shut his brain off and talk Karma bombs.

***

Terry's preferred Karma bomb was a quiet one. He would go into chain bookstores and rip out a single page from as many books as he could manage without getting caught.

He never got caught.

He was so unassuming that nobody suspected him.

Nick's analytical models considered this to be the most efficient regularly utilized Karma generator out of all the Grinders. Terry wasn't certain about the accuracy of the analytics, but he was proud of this, anyways.

He grabbed *Fear and Loathing in Las Vegas* and ripped off the first page as Steef looked over his shoulder and said, "that's actually a very good book."

Terry didn't care. He wasn't feeling talkative so he moved over to a book about pineapples and pretended to be interested, acting like he was drawn into the photos.

For his Karma generation system to work, he had to at least act like a normal book store patron, and he couldn't have anyone else in his workspace.

"Ah, pineapples. Interesting stuff, actually. Did you know that-"

Terry glared at Steef, acting like he was an anonymous harrasser, and moved to Religion & Spirituality, knowing Steef would never follow him there. He picked up a purple book on hippie spirituality and opened to the center of it, lingering on the images, but something didn't feel right, like he was being watched. He put it back and moved on to Sports & Recreation.

Steef got the picture, apologized under his breath, and moved onto Poetry to mask his mis-step.

He ended up buying a copy of *Leaves of Grass*, the book of poetry by Walt Whitman. He passed Terry on his way to the cashier. "Sorry for drawing heat. I'm just gonna shut up and read poetry. I hear this one gives people moments of inspiration."

While at the cashier, Steef went out of his way to make a distraction out of dropping his wallet, dropping some change, and making his fisherman's hat fall off, apologizing profusely and loudly to the cashier, giving cover to Terry's page-ripping enterprise.

Terry accepted the apology.

Pretending to be annoyed at the commotion, he went straight to departures while Steef went to the bathroom to get started on dropping an epiphany.

***

When Terry arrived at departures and sat down, Lise meowed, lept up from Cassandra's lap, rushed over to Terry and started purring like a chainsaw.

Cassandra was busy asking unwanted questions about Mike's makeshift operation. "What is this thing with the four antennas?" She raised it in the air from its hidden position behind Mike's backpack.

Mike looked around and noticed that there were no security guards anywhere.

Mike whispered anyways. "That's called a pineapple."

"A pineapple?"

"A pineapple. I won't bore you with the tech jargon but it helps me penetrate network security. There's gotta be personnel somewhere around here using wifi. I connect to that with the pineapple so I can try to connect to the airport security system." He looked around again for security, still finding none, but he still kept his head on a swivel.

"We have to stop talking about it. They aren't gonna catch me but this is technically a felony."

"I didn't know. I'm excited to see what you have planned though. The other guys tell me you're excited too."

Mike only grinned. He had to focus.

Lise escaped Terry's lap and went back to Cassandra, who stopped distracting Mike, right as Steef arrived, wielding the copy of *Leaves of Grass*.

"What ya got there, Steef?"

"Book of poetry. It's said to generate epiphanies if you read it on the toilet."

"Oh. Any epiphanies so far?" Cassandra's gaze lingered at the book.

"Not yet, no. Just started. Almost done the intro." Steef was overheard by the pack of drunk Grinders, arriving from the pub, all at once.

"Just started what?"

"He bought a copy of *Leaves of Grass* because he thinks it might give him epiphanies."

"Oh well isn't that something. He won't read our fucking holy book but he'll read a 200 year old book of poetry."

"Maybe *Leaves of Grass* will give him the epiphany to catch up with us."

"It's a joke guys. Are you drunk?"

Gerg grabbed the NERF gun back from aLan and shot Steef directly between the eyes with the entire clip.

"You're drunk."

"Yeeeessss," Gerg beamed.

"I got in!" Mike whisper-shouted. He sat up straight and looked around. "Where are the... where are the rest of us?"

"Oh they're joyriding." Cassandra pulled out her phone and texted Aliya, who routed the airport shuttle joyride all the way to departures.

***

After a few minutes of making sure Kevin was securely upright and breathing, with most of the drool wiped from the side of his mouth, Aliya put a hood over him to hide the optics of his awkward ketamine comedown, then sat next to Steef and noticed his book. "Any epiphanies?"

He was already sick of the comment.

He ignored her and kept reading.

She reached into her magical bag and pulled out a hard drive. "If you get bored of reading a dead guy's poetry on the airplane then maybe you could watch something on here."

"If this is you trying to get me to watch Ted Lasso again I'm going to fucking kill you."

"Do you think I'd pack a 2 terabyte portable hard drive, for myself, with just one show, that I've already fucking seen?" Aliya rolled her eyes and motioned to put the hard drive back in her magical bag.

This was a bluff.

What the Disciples knew from their efforts in trying to get Steef to read their religious text and join the Grinders was that the more you pushed Steef to do something, the less likely he would be to do it. And the more they tried, the angrier he got. Reliable suffering. Category 1 for a good friend.

Steef sheepishly accepted the hard drive.

He whipped out his laptop and connected the hard drive and looked inside, and as he started inhaling deep breaths through his nose, Aliya could see the steam blowing out of his ears.

He paused, gathered himself, disconnected the drive, threw it on the ground, took the NERF gun from Gerg, shot the empty clip at the drive on the ground, started shouting incomprehensibly, and then smashed the NERF gun on the hard drive until they were both in pieces.

Karma for the Grind.

Aliya stopped laughing eventually, scooped up the debris on the ground, and walked over to the garbage cans, noticing that there was still no security detail anywhere, dropping the shattered remains into the garbage.

She rushed back and let Mike know about it. He already knew, but that was still helpful, as he had just that moment been able to connect to the device of a supervisor walking just outside, so he was ready.

He addressed the group. "Okay, so, I need you all to walk over there, to the main departures screen, and watch. I need at least one of you to point out what's happening, loudly, once I get started."

"What's going to happen?"

"You'll know it when you see it."

Other than keeping the pineapple shrouded behind his carry-on, Mike had made no efforts to conceal his dirty work. The hacking console that he built looked exactly like Spotify so that nobody watching him operate would suspect anything.

When their flight was announced as boarding, he selected 'Playlists', then selected 'Airport Mix' and pressed 'Shuffle', and the Grinders watched in total reverence as the departures screen completely randomized all displayed flight times, and also posted about a dozen cancellations, leaving only their scheduled flight completely untouched.

"Holy shit."

"Mike... genius."

"This is the best thing we've ever done."

Jeff took a second to stare in wonder, and then snapped back to reality, and started shouting in order to draw the attention of the airport patrons. "Now, just what is happening to my flight?"

Didn't work.

He shouted louder.

"Why is everything suddenly CANCELLED?"

A few people turned to look, but nobody noticed.

He screamed.

"WHAT THE FUCK IS GOING ON AT THIS STUPID FUCKING AIRPORT?"

From there it took less than five minutes for their entire section of the airport to descend into anarchy.

"Hey Nick?"

"Easy category 4."

"Not a five?"

"You'll know a five when you see it."

"What makes a five?"

"You'll know a five when you see it."

"Your mom's a five."

"Fuck you."

"Hey, uh, this isn't affecting any of the actual flights, right?"

"Course not. We don't want anyone to die."

"Karma for the Grind?"

"Karma for the Grind."

"gneurshk"

"Thanks Kevin!" Aliya wiped the fresh slobber from the side of his mouth and got him back on his feet.

And with a refreshed sense of purpose, the Grinders hurried themselves onto the plane to take off to a better world while a tiny bit of civilization collapsed behind them.

They had someone important to meet.

Steef sat down on the plane and kept *Leaves of Grass* with him for the flight, excited to finally be done with the intro.

02 - THE LIBRARY

Danielle wanted to scream.

She wasn't sure why she'd walked into the university library.

She had wandered over unconsciously after meeting with the head of the finance department, and all that she had left of the meeting was the crumpled expulsion letter in her hand.

She regained consciousness a few steps inside.

She wasn't crying.

She didn't acknowledge the librarian. She wasn't sure who did this to her, and it was still fresh, so she suspected everyone.

She couldn't go home to her boyfriend and their shared apartment. The two of them had plans for the future that were dependent on a very tight timeline that absolutely needed to stay on track, and Danielle had just had her timeline completely derailed by the letter in her hand.

She had been only a few months away from finishing a four-year finance degree, with honors, in two years.

And her boyfriend was a catch.

His family was very rich, and he was very handsome. He looked like a blonde Patrick Bateman.

He had options.

She was his best option fifteen minutes ago.

She was no longer his best option.

She needed to cry, or she needed to inhale her weight in cocaine. Either way, she raced in her stilettos to the library bathroom, breathing rapidly, staring straight ahead, not blinking, not missing a step.

She made it to the bathoom and as soon as the washroom door closed behind her, she thought for a second about the painful release of crying it out, but lately she had grown accustomed to experiencing her important moments in far nicer bathrooms, so she kept it bottled up.

She reached for the eight ball in the hidden compartment of her right stiletto. She didn't need to sell it anymore; this was for personal use. That's what she always told the cops anyways. She scooped a gram of it with her freshly manicured solo fingernail and inhaled.

Peace. Manic peace.

Fast at attention, now alert enough to notice the boots on the ground in the next stall, she hurried most of the rest of the bag up her nose, panicked, dropped the last of it into the toilet, stood up, flushed once, watched to make sure the bag circled the drain, and saw her reflection before the water came back.

She looked at the ground as she stepped out of her stall at the same time as her toilet neighbor. She felt too numb to cry, but she knew she had to pretend she was crying if she wanted to launder her coke sniffles.

Her stall was directly across from the mirror, and as she looked up, she noticed some white evidence on her upper lip, but she was able to work it all into a sloppy face wipe. The girl emerging from the next stall was a student, thank fuck. Easy out.

Danielle stared in the mirror for twenty one seconds with the water running, never blinked, never broke eye contact with herself, breathed heavier than she needed to, made sure her nose wasn't bleeding, centered her septum piercing, sniffled, screamed something sloppy and unintelligible about how all men should die, and scurried out of the bathroom without washing her hands. That would be enough to get anyone off her trail. The sympathetic and clueless girl she left behind would turn off the taps for her.

Danielle knew that at some point she would have to face reality.

She already accepted that this expulsion meant that her internship at the downtown investment firm was over.

She took a second to strategize on her blood levels. She had taken two xans before entering the library. They hadn't hit yet. Two more minutes.

She made her way to the empty aisle of self-help books and tried to stand in place to avoid drawing attention, but her hands were trembling and her foot was tapping. Her entire force of will in that moment was devoted to keeping her teeth from grinding while she waited for the pills to start working.

Her foot was tapping to the beat of her heart and that made her heart beat faster and then her foot couldn't keep up.

She looked over at the librarian who was already looking at her. She looked away, but thought that might be suspicious, so she looked back at the librarian, but realized that darting her gaze back and forth might be more suspicious than staring, so she stared at him while gritting her jaw so that it wouldn't grind.

And then all at once -

Release.

The librarian could see the infinite calm wash over her from across the room and so he left her alone.

Back to strategizing.

In a few minutes the jittery aspect of the coke would dissipate a bit. She knew that at that point, and for the fifteen minutes afterwards, she would be a walking supercomputer. That's when she would come up with a master plan.

She always came up with something.

She stood in place, trying to think about nothing until the moment hit.

And then the moment hit.

She always knew.

She had the feeling down to the second.

Danielle centered herself, closed her eyes, and peered into a thousand possible futures in which she broke the news to her man. None of those futures involved his family allowing him to stay with her. His family was extremely private and dangerously ambitious. She wouldn't be able to keep up anymore. It was a small miracle that they let her try to keep up at all.

She kicked the self-help bookshelf and busted the front of her stiletto.

She knew it was over.

She couldn't face him. She couldn't go back to the apartment. If she could look into his green eyes one more time, she knew she'd throw herself off the balcony.

They'd spent so many nights awake, far too awake, with ghosts in their blood, planning their financial futures down to the dollar.

Partners.

It all disappeared in an instant.

She chose the only path still remaining.

She chose violence.

She needed to haunt something. She needed to destroy something. She needed to watch something die slowly. She needed to rain down hellfire on something. Anything.

Ring the bells that still can ring, her dad used to say.

***

Danielle's awareness outside of herself resurfaced gradually and took new form.

The blissful chatter of a group of students seated at a community table on the other side of the self-help section grinded on her as she felt like her xanax fortress was starting to collapse, so she ate two more, and waited for her blood to get nice and comfortable again.

At a loss for what to do next, she decided to eavesdrop on any conversation she could hear.

Anything to shake up the snowglobe.

It was too quiet.

This is why she hated libraries. She needed things to be moving.

She shuffled down to the end of the aisle until she heard a decent commotion. By her count there were five voices.

Her world was flipped by one of them.

"We got that bitch expelled today. Fuck her."

Danielle dug her coke nail into her palm and it snapped off. She didn't notice.

"She was almost done her degree too."

Her nose started to bleed. The blood ran down past her lip and into her open mouth. She didn't notice.

She didn't recognize the voice. It didn't matter.

"Maybe a bit harsh. Ever met her? Do you even know what she looks like?"

"No. But I was told she's hot."

Danielle always considered herself to be a textbook narcissist, but she couldn't manage a smile.

"Doesn't matter anyways. I fucking hate her. I hope she's crying."

She was alert, she was alive, she was the ancient goddess of focus and destruction. And these motherfuckers were going to suffer. They were going to suffer. They were going to suffer. They were going to die. They would suffer and they would die and they would be forgotten. The rememberers wouldn't even remember these people when they were remembering those that the others had forgotten. She read somewhere recently that the human soul weighs 21 grams. She inhaled three grams in the bathroom, and she was going to end up with more than a hundred in return - that's a fair exchange. She would be ready at the crossroads. She would greet Cerberus with their heads on pikes and the pikes wrapped in their intestines.

She wiped her nose and noticed the blood on her fingers, so she ran to the washroom again to clean up and to resaturate to a better blood-narcotic balance.

She returned to the self-help aisle five minutes later to keep eavesdropping and to hatch an invasion plan.

She stumbled into a healthy deposit of Robert Greene books directly in front of her, and she mentally thumbed through the titles while her attention lingered.

Mastery. Too much work. She had read about the 10,000 hours thing before. She preferred to let other people do the work.

The 48 Laws Of Power. That's far too many laws. Who has that much time?

The 33 Strategies Of War. Ehh. Still too many.

Seduction.

Now we're talking.

She picked it up and started to read the intro, but the shifting chemistry in her blood shook her focus; she dropped the book and it made a subdued thud on the ratty, overgrown library carpeting, which nobody heard.

She shifted her focus back to the murmur at the community table. There were still five of them, all young men, except for one girl. She knew how to work this. She gathered herself, changed modes and went on the attack.

***

The girl at the table was mid-sentence when Danielle tuned in, answering a question that Danielle had missed.

"...to find some obscure religious text and read it, and write a six thousand word paper showing that I understand it and that I understand the course syllabus. You know, find parallels in more popular religions. Just let the teacher know that I can see that every religion has the same basic bullshit structure with regards to worship, taboos, rituals, etcetera, so that I can get a bullshit C+ and get the fuck out of my bullshit mandatory arts elective."

"Religion's smart for an elective if your major is pharmaceuticals." A shifty young man in a poor-fitting black cotton t-shirt was enraptured with the idea. "Drugs are religious if you do them right. Was that on purpose?" He scanned the information on the side of her pink highlighter.

"Nah but that's a good point. Maybe I should take it seriously. If I pay attention and drug the right people then maybe I could start a cult."

"That's how most of them start, dude." The shifty young man sat upright. "I can help with that. I love cults. Just don't kill me until it's over. I gotta be the last one to die or I'll just find another cult. You have to tell me if you're going to kill me. That's cult law."

Danielle had found her flank. She knew her way around drugs, and she had always secretly wanted to lead a cult. She left the self help aisle and approached the table slowly.

"You're doing pharmaceuticals?" Danielle's disembodied voice spooked the group, but they were calmed by her saleswoman smile when she sat down next to the girl. "Sorry for interrupting!"

"Oh yeah no problem. Yeah, I could do pharma in my sleep. I just have to take this religious studies elective that's probably gonna be bullshit. Every other elective looked worse. I just don't wanna do electives. Doesn't make any fucking sense." Aliya lightly pounded the community table with a fist to puncuate each word. "Just. Let. Me. Do. My. Major."

As Danielle listened intently, the backburners in her mind fired up a plan. Everything became clear in an instant, as though handed up to her from a higher power. She let the plan drip into her mind as the coke dripped down the back of her throat.

The first step was to permanently press the religious studies elective idea onto the girl and the rest of the community table until it was fully entrenched.

Danielle twirled her hair and made eye contact with the row of young, dumb and stupid men at the table with the two of them. She would only smile for the rest of the conversation. She'd studied under the Kardashians. She busted out a California vocal fry. "That actually sounds like a lot of fun. Can you tell me more?"

They were already enraptured.

She drew it up perfectly.

Ten minutes later, she had the boys at the table under her control, and she had the girl obsessed with how easily she'd gained it. She hurried the conclusion of the conversation as she started to sense a threat to the chemical armistice in her blood.

"I'm off to class in ten minutes." She sniffled. "How can I see y'all again?"

The girl replied, excited. "I have to submit the religious text that I'm choosing on Monday morning, first thing. 7am. I'm gonna make my decision tomorrow. At Mike's party. Everyone will be there."

"Everyone?"

"Steef won't. Gardening sale. You know Steef," the shifty young man deepened his voice and sang, "everyday he's gard-en-ing."

"And his fishing!"

"That double life of his."

Danielle didn't care about gardening or fishing. "Sooo when do I get to meet Mike?"

"Oh yeah. Mike is this guy. He's in comp sci." The girl gestured to a wide-eyed, almost-slobbering Mike, who'd only floated the idea of a party a couple hours beforehand, and only to her. He was uncertain about it, and he knew that she was only pushing for the party because she wanted to make friends with this wonderful new girl who'd fallen out of the sky.

Danielle couldn't believe the opportunity opening up in front of her.

"Nick, audio engineering." Nick gave a dignified nod.

"Gerg, geology." Gerg sat up straight. "It rocks!" Everyone rolled their eyes, other than Gerg, who was beaming.

"And this useless sack of shit is Kevin. We aren't sure what classes he's in. I don't think he knows either."

"Oh, I know what I'm doing. I just never talk about it." He took the cap off the pink marker and test-smelled it.

Danielle hated acting like this, but she had a new mission and it was too early for compromises. "Ooh. Can I come?" She kept eye contact with Mike and she didn't close her mouth fully after speaking. She had read about this trick in Seventeen Magazine when she was nineteen.

Mike was no longer uncertain about hosting the party. With one exception, girls didn't usually sit at tables with these guys, and with the same exception, girls never partied with them.

Mike knew he had to play it cool. "Yeah, of course." Now he had to plan the party. Then he had to host the party.

Fuck.

Danielle was coming down fully at this point but she managed to avoid agitation through sheer force of will. Now that she had been invited, she had to escape from the corner that she had backed herself into. "Can I bring my partner?"

The boys at the table flinched.

"You guys will love her," she continued, to a palpable wave of psychic relief.

Mike wasn't an asshole. "Yeah. Sure thing. I'll just have to get some more beers." He was proud of his save but still embarrassed.

"Actuallyyyyy she likes vodka punch! It gets her real sloppy."

Mike dropped his pencil.

The girl, enchanted by Danielle's effortless manipulation of the boys, couldn't wait to get started. "Here, let me write down the address. It's at 6. This Friday. Which I guess is tomorrow." She couldn't be bothered with getting a pen from her large bag, so she grabbed Mike's pencil off the ground and snapped it in half, which made Mike flinch. With the broad side, she wrote down the address of the party on a post-it note.

"Oh yeah, my name's Aliya. What's yours?"

A fault line could have opened the earth beneath them and swallowed them whole right then and there and she wouldn't have wavered. She didn't blink. Her vision was clear and straight and unholy.

"Cassandra."

She sniffled.

03 - THE FOREST

Danielle woke up groggy in the back seat of her '11 Avenger, cursed the xanax bottle on the floor of the passenger seat, apologized to the bottle, looked inside for more, found none, and cursed it again, tossing it out the window.

Whatever.

It was for the best. She slept soundly through her ringtone alarm and woke up far too late. She had to drive across the city, and she had to move quickly to stay on target with her writing schedule, and a benzo at that moment would have jeopardized both of those things.

There was no traffic. The more she drove with no traffic, the more she started to trust her mission, as though the gods themselves were opening up a path for her.

She put some Nickelback on her car stereo. Old albums, deep cuts, before they sold out. The good shit.

She rolled down her window further, poked her head out, and declaring her freedom, screamed to nobody, "NEVER MADE IT AS A WISE MAN" and was shaken when she saw a white Ford F-150 creeping up in the slow lane beside her. She paused the cassette tape, rolled up her window and kept quiet. She hummed along in the solitude of her dented grey Avenger that she stole from a police auction, waited for the white truck to pass, rolled the window back down, and resumed singing at a respectable volume, "couldn't cut it as a poor man stealin'."

She didn't want to draw too much attention anyways.

She was off to meet Parisa.

***

Parisa was a strange girl.

A dozen people on planet earth knew she existed, but nobody really knew anything about her except for Danielle, and nobody knew that Danielle knew her, and Danielle never said a word about her to anyone.

She drew it up perfectly.

As far as Danielle was able to piece together from the drugs they shared and the unintentional conversations thereafter, Parisa's parents were disgraced nuclear physicists from Iran who had been hanged by foreign agents of unknown origin and impenetrable motives, and Parisa had been left untouched, alone, and safe in their home, where she had been discovered and later adopted by other disgraced Iranian nuclear physicists.

She slurred her words when she bothered to speak. She felt she shouldn't need to speak. If she spoke to you, it usually meant that she thought that you were a bit slow. She believed there wasn't very much on Earth worth saying, and the few things that really needed to be said didn't require words.

Parisa was a mystical figure. An underground hero. Most of the regional electronic music festivals in recent years – Shambhala, Bass Coast, what have you - had featured secret behind-the-scenes ceremonial unveilings of her newest engineered and modified entheogens, performed by the satanic priestesses of psychedelia.

Danielle was the only person on the planet who was familiar

with both Parisa's government name and her cult status.

Parisa invited her, and nobody else, to administer a test run of the newest concoction she had been able to develop, which was a hyper-socializing drug that fostered unending obedience in the junkyard animals that she'd tested it on, which, to that point, were mostly raccoons.

She had tested it on one human subject so far: her idiot boyfriend, now ex-boyfriend, who took far, far too large of a dose in an effort to impress her, and would afterwards refuse to do anything other than find ways to profess his undying love for her, committing insane acts of devotion that she never asked for, and that she certainly never wanted. He ended up in the psych ward. The effects had not subsided whatsoever in the month after he ingested it. His pupils stayed dilated, his mouth stayed dry. Up until the last time she saw him, whenever he could get a hand free from his straight jacket, he would beat the hand bloody, and write her name on the walls of the asylum with his blood until he passed out from blood loss with a smile on his face.

Never again.

The place Danielle was going had no address, the roads weren't paved, and the streets had no name. These buildings weren't trailer parks but they weren't houses. There was nobody guarding, but Danielle had the ominous and unshakeable sense of being watched by a malevolent force that was, at the moment, allowing her to be there, awake and breathing.

She knew her old friend. She didn't have an address but she knew where to go. Among the decorations were decapitated gnome statues draped in shredded mandala tapestries, gauntlets of upside-down chandeliers with impaled raccoon carcasses, and oversized barbie dolls with four arms and three eyes dressed in guerrilla combat gear.

This was where Parisa lived. There was no doubt.

Danielle parked her Avenger and stepped out.

Unsure exactly where to go from there, with no signs, no pathways and no ideas, she noticed some dry leaves on the ground and she veered to step them to hear the crunch as she walked, just like she used to do on camping trips with her dad.

This was Parisa's doorbell.

A string of faded tealights made themselves known and flickered just enough to carry Danielle a quarter mile to an underground hobbit-style enclave.

She slowly stepped inside, not saying a word, not touching a thing, until she got the sense that she was permitted to look around.

The enclave was encased, floor to ceiling, two columns thick, in bookshelves, and only bookshelves, save for a single shelf full of unlabeled VHS tapes. The shelf nearest to her featured Marx and Mandela, Toni Morrison and Malcolm X, more and more of the same, nothing that Danielle would ever bother with. Nothing that she needed.

Danielle had been a friend of Parisa's for a few years, ever since they met with forgetful origins, in a drug induced fog at a timeless afterparty on Wreck Beach, right by UBC, Danielle with no idea how either of them arrived there, the memory beginning mid-conversation. Danielle had assumed Parisa was a student at the university, but she never asked, and by the time she thought about asking, she had correctly developed a very healthy terror of this strange girl.

When Danielle first enrolled at UBC, she had taken almost no time to become known as the primary coke dealer for the entire campus, which she always believed to be the reason why Parisa dropped into her life. But by that point Danielle was so terrified of asking questions that she retained a healthy terror of asking those questions to herself. New horrors were always unfolding in her world, and she never knew who was listening.

Danielle didn't plan to disclose that her campus dealing was coming to an end, because she believed that her moneymaking and her reach and her control were the only reasons she was granted the preview of this new synthetic entheogen.

The scientific name of it was "236-GAA-LuO", which was an abbreviation of the chemical compound, and a pain in the ass to say out loud. It was originally developed in 1969 by Viet Cong chemist Linh "LuO" Ngo, to feed to communist soldiers to strengthen their resolve against the invading American military. As its name was only ever communicated by word of mouth, across several dialects of several languages, and never, ever written down, ever, ever, ever, never ever, ever written down, it had taken the name "Luongo" which sounded more like an Italian pasta than a forbidden psychedelic from the bowels of hell.

In 1971, Ngo had managed to escape American capture by promising to divulge Viet Cong secrets of chemical warfare in exchange for immunity, and she disappeared without a trace while still in chains on the stealth war plane that was transporting her to chains in a dungeon, where she most likely would have lived out the rest of her natural life developing chemicals for the American war machine.

Ngo's colleagues and lab assistants were long since assumed dead or captured.

Manufacturing 'Luongo' is punishable by death in every country on the planet. Distributing 'Luongo' is punishable by death in every country on the planet. Possessing 'Luongo' is punishable by death in every country on the planet.

The CIA did manage to get their hands on a copy of the

recipe, albeit imperfect, and they kept it a dozen stories below sea level in a bunker in an undisclosed location that had more security than the pope. However, in the early 80s, an ambitious Ronald Reagan had secretly ordered the digitizing of all classified documents, as he believed this would provide an extra layer of security, and he had nonbelievers assassinated. Unfortunately for Reagan, when he invited Taliban operatives to the United States, and gave one of them the key to the city of Detroit as a reward for their efforts in embarrassing the Soviets in Afghanistan, the Taliban's advanced methods of wireless data collection made short work of Reagan's security efforts.

After making no appearances for decades, the recipe proliferated very quietly, in impenetrable code, to three people on the dark web.

Parisa was the only one of the three still alive.

A book caught Danielle's eye – a dream journal titled "unfinished" with a sketch of a butterfly. Intrigued, she motioned to pick it up, but she heard a loud creaking noise as soon as her fingers made contact with the base of the spine.

Looking in the direction of the noise, she noticed what looked like a chemistry lab – jars and beakers with bioluminescent liquids, bags of glowing powders, and a large tome of what looked like empty pages constructed from tree bark.

The vision of the laboratory drew her in, but she was too gripped by fear to move towards it.

She remained motionless but kept observing, and in the center of her fear, she forgot herself and became fond of the warm, vibrant chemical smells emanating from it, beginning to gain a trace of a sensation that she thought might be synesthesia.

Shifting her attention carefully around the enclave, she drifted towards a strange, Hieronymus Bosch-style, infinitely elaborate psychedelic triptych painting on the wall, begging to be observed, begging to be studied, next to a small bone palette and a brush made from raccoon hair. It depicted what looked like a goddess of volcanic wind divining green, blue and purple wavelengths and effortlessly tossing aside trees, rocks, animals, men, women, other gods and goddesses. The central figure was blonde and smiling and looked exactly like Danielle, who spent an infinity memorizing the nuances of the painted world that surrounded her likeness.

The moment she told herself she was done studying, Parisa crept into the room like a spider, removed the painting from the wall, placed it in the raging fireplace as though allowing it to finally rest, and handed Danielle an opaque purple rounded-square glass bottle with no visible holes or openings. Danielle could feel the liquid physics from cradling it with one hand. Noticing that she was having trouble divining the opening, Parisa gently took it back, placed it on the ground, directed a source of soft light onto the bottle, and breathed steadily onto the dented side of the purple glass for about fifteen seconds, which temperature-activated a glass corkscrew opening motion, loosening the lid of the bottle, which, when opened, had the inside equipped with a liquid dropper.

"Luon-go."

Everything became clear in an instant, as though handed down to her from a higher power.

A second word was never spoken, as Danielle slowly retrieved her wonderful gift, respectfully exited the weird grace of the junkyard sanctum, and walked again past the comfort of the roadkill chandeliers. She could feel the raccoons making eye contact even with her back turned. She hurried to the comfort of her dented Avenger and drove a safe distance before trying to wrap her head around the experience, wondering if she was allowed to wrap her head around it, wondering if she would be allowed to wonder.

This was the last time anyone would ever see Parisa in the flesh.

Too bad.

***

Danielle drove back towards civilization in silence.

By the opposite instinct that brought her up the forest path and into the heart of darkness, she found herself driving towards the apartment that she could no longer return to.

She caught herself before traveling too far, and for safety, she stayed on the outer rim of what she believed was Parisa's sprawling haunted forest compound.

The forest magic that had twisted and tormented and soothed and destroyed and rebuilt her a million times in the half hour she was embraced by the madness had started to fill her with a desire to tap into it. She was sick of sight without a sense of feeling.

This was real power.

And she was only a twenty minute drive from the university library, which was a twenty minute drive from Mike's party.

Getting started.

She popped the trunk of her car and brought a tray of drugs into the front, to lay on the passenger seat like charcuterie.

Getting to business.

With smooth bark from nearby trees, a fountain pen, and woodsy-looking craft string she believed was likely purchased from Michael's, she hastened together a perfect apparatus that carried in it, for her, the spirit of fear and respect that she held for Parisa's haunted forest compound.

Getting to writing.

Danielle was a master with words in the air, but she was a novice to words on paper.

She knew almost nothing about organized religion, but she was an expert at manipulating people. While she'd typically never waste her time actually studying cults or their leaders or their histories, a part of her always assumed that she could run one, if the followers were pliable enough.

She did know for sure that religion was about following, and that following was about leadership.

The university's website was open on her laptop to a webpage that gave a complete rundown of the course syllabus, all assignments, class schedules, and even the names of the teachers and assistants. She had opened a dozen or so additional browser tabs, each to different search results about how to write a religious text, all abandoned halfway down the first page of search results.

The text that she was writing, physically writing from scratch, needed to cater to the minimum requirements for the assignment. She looked at the clock on the panel and it was 5:05pm. The party started in one hour. She needed help. She knew she could be a good bit late, and the nerds she met at the library wouldn't think any less of her, but she still regretted her decision to sleep off the drugs.

She racked her brain for words and passages and echoes of spirituality.

By 5:15pm she had nothing.

She couldn't do this in her car.

She snarfed the cocaine, kept the purple glass of elixir close to her, put the rest of the charcuterie back in the trunk, and drove to the university library well above the speed limit.

On her way through the doors and past the librarians, she swiped a due date stamp and sat down at the closest table, stamping the inside of the front cover of the smooth bark to give the book an air of legitimacy. She put an arbitrary name in it, along with a date a couple years in the past, to suggest that it was borrowed once and then lost, stolen, or forgotten. She didn't need to do anything else for the book to pass the sniff test.

In perfect cursive, still guided by the memory of the menacing stare of the chandelier raccoons who were almost definitely still watching her, she wrote out 'ONE OF SEVEN', a perfect alibi against any nosy students who would try to verify the book's authenticity by tracking down another copy.

She hunted and gathered an impressive pile of books on witchcraft, sorcery, psychedelics and paganism, selecting the works chiefly on the basis of on the compelling satanic imagery adorning the covers.

She decided rather quickly on massively plagiarizing a purple book on hippie spirituality for the bulk of the visuals. She would replace the uplifting passages of bliss and self-actualization with uplifting passages of obedience and self-sacrifice.

She started to believe in herself.

She could do it.

She could pull this off.

She could get her old life back, and at the same time, she could destroy the lives of the interlopers who destroyed hers.

Easy.

She had seen it clearly. She just needed to put the vision into words.

This would be the hard part.

She ate two adderalls and waited for them to hit.

She took a deep breath, exhaled slowly, and took mental stock of everything that she needed to accomplish with the passages of the text that she was writing, before frantically getting to work, dipping in and out of the borrowed books every couple of minutes.

***

STEP ONE

In order for Danielle to maximize the damage and minimize the number of escape routes, she needed to isolate these people from their friends and families. She had to be their refuge. She had to be their saviour. She had to be their last line of defense against threats from the outside world.

"Disciples are beholden only to their Archon, and therefore must abandon all family lineage, middle- and surnames, and all claims to heritage."

"Education of Disciples will be fully devoted to expanding the reach and the effectiveness of their Archon."

STEP TWO

She needed to ensure that her authority was absolute, and she needed to ensure that she was handed her authority by something that was beyond questioning – beyond even *her* questioning. There are not a lot of forces in the world of negotiation that are more powerful than a fictional being in the next room with a large gun. Infinite plausible deniability.

"The hierarchy of the Cosmos, in the realm of terrestrial understanding, is as follows:

Soldier beneath Disciple; Disciple beneath Archon; Archon beneath Angel; Angel still beneath; that above Angel still beneath."

"Soldiers are not to be aware of the hierarchy; Disciples are not to be aware of the will of the Angels or beyond; Archons are not to be aware of the will or the name of those beyond those beyond Angels."

"Disciples will awaken in the same event as their Archon."

She decided it would be prudent to limit the number of eyes that would ever read the scripture, and at the same time, provide further insulation against anyone wondering why they can't seem to track down a second copy of the text.

"As it would be subject to human error and would thereby dilute the message, the scripture must never be replicated by Disciples in any form."

"Only an Archon may replicate the scripture."

STEP THREE

Hard-coded loyalty was a great start, but if this was going to work, Danielle knew that she had to secure their hearts. She needed to harvest their devotion emotionally. And it had to be automatic. These people had to crave their own servitude and fear their own freedom. The devotion potion – the doses of Luongo that she had just secured from Parisa - should take care of most of the quotient of that notion, but it would still be a good idea to couple the drugs with a robust inner cognitive architecture, so as to avoid stray thoughts and feelings that would eventually try to escape.

She needed something to pacify the heartbeat of creation in the inevitable moments of doubt and pain.

She had to introduce a meditation practice, but she had to make it hurt.

"Being that it is understood that the human body, and the mind therein, will inevitably approach the truth with inherent flaws, all considerations for other flows of thought must at once return to the core principle of focused suffering."

She dog-eared a book on transcendental meditation, copying a good amount of it word-for-word, and then substituted the wisdom on Keeping Your Mind Blank for new wisdom on Keeping Your Mind Blank, Except For A Pronounced Focus On Suffering.

"Healing is regression. Suffering is growth. If one must heal, all healing must point back to suffering. This will be achieved through suffering meditation."

"Disciples are to daily practice meditation with the true principle focus of enhancing sustainable personal suffering in oneself and a secondary focus of compassionately administering suffering in others."

STEP FOUR

She needed to make sure that the flow of information from the outside world – not just from friends and families, but also from the radio, TV, and the internet – was under her control. And because it would be impossible to entirely stem the flow of all information while still remaining effective in the real world, in the literal information age, she needed to develop within them a shroud of distrust instead.

"Outside information cannot be fully trusted, as perceived reality can never be certain, and sensory input can be corrupted and manipulated. The only absolute truth possible for a Disciple is from their Archon; the only absolute truth possible for an Archon is from their Angel."

STEP FIVE

While fostering a scorched earth policy was a good start, burning bridges wouldn't be enough. She needed to ensure that no new bridges could be built. New bridges could lead them to safety, far from her grasp. New bridges could give them somewhere to go if this whole thing came to an end. Why should her death someday mark the end of their suffering?

"Being that it is understood that the human body, and the mind therein, will inevitably approach the truth with inherent flaws, a Disciple will avoid building personal relationships with unawakened souls, so as to avoid the complexities of intertwined and incompatible spiritual perspectives, which are impossible to resolve through a terrestrial framework."

By god, the adderall was working!

"The relationship between awakened and unawakened souls must be that of the shepherd and the flock. A Disciple does not engage in a traditional terrestrial form of interpersonal relationship; an unawakened soul is unable to engage in a higher relationship with an awakened soul."

Semi-colons would really sell the thing; semi-colons meant business.

She noticed that the coke in her blood was running thin, so she waited for a suitably loud hum of background library noise, and she took a quiet key bump where she sat.

"Therein, by keeping compassion at a manageable, healthy distance, it is from a place of greater understanding, and therefore it is a greater compassion."

She sniffled.

STEP SIX

She needed to make sure that this was one of those cults that allowed for capital accumulation. Ridiculous amounts of capital accumulation. Maybe even a central tenet of the whole thing. She was going to have to make up a lot of financial ground if she wanted any chance of getting her old life back on track.

"Mastery of commerce is essential, as it serves to maximize the spread and the influence of Disciples who will thereafter be better positioned to shepherd the unawakened souls of the world."

"Accumulation of money by a Disciple shall only be done in service of their Archon; within this, it must be done as often as possible."

STEP SEVEN

This was the most important step. She needed to encode, fully and completely, that the entire purpose of their lives is to experience suffering. If done right, she could program them into becoming the magistrates of their own personally curated hells for as long as they would remain alive.

She wanted to set it and forget it - forever.

"The Cosmos consists of souls in various stages of awareness; the purpose of the Cosmos is to recycle a soul through countless lives down the annals of time until the soul is at its final stage of being awakened."

"Suffering is the goal of existence."

"All suffering experienced in a conscious life contributes to the joyous quality of the next life."

"All Karma not redeemed as happiness will carry through to a subsequent life."

"Understanding of suffering diminishes the effect of the suffering on the growth of the soul; it is a gift to the unawakened souls to

allow them to remain unawakened and suffering."

"A Disciple goes to great lengths to prevent unawakened souls from being awakened, so as to maximize the value of their suffering."

"If anyone is aware of the nature of their own suffering, it is of diminished value; however, it still has Karmic value, and should not be avoided."

In a short time, she had managed to hash together something that she loved so much that she almost started to believe in it herself.

She went back over her mental list of every consideration she needed to turn these peoples' lives into living hells.

She checked it twice.

Everything was there.

She added a litany of other passages with wisdom addressing various other mysterious aspects of the universe, mostly as filler, keeping everything vague and imprecise, leaving herself room for interpretation, leaving room for backing herself out of corners.

It was beautiful.

She drew it up perfectly.

But she still needed a title.

The title was important.

Maybe the most important part.

The title should sound compelling. It should feel authentic. It should grab the reader's attention but it should also gain their trust. It should have a sense that it was whispered through the ancient trees by a dying shaman at the last grassy sunset before an ice age. It had to feel as though it could be pulled from the sparkling mud of a mystic swamp by a fallen river faerie. It had to feel like it had echoed through the Parthenon, uttered by a visiting Byzantine statesman in fear and wonder. It had to feel as though it was written in light of the pillars of Stonehenge during a gathering of druids at a thunderous equinox.

It had to make people feel the way that she had felt when she was in the powerful cradle of Parisa's haunted forest.

The last of the cocaine was leaving her blood, and she was starting to run out, so she needed to hurry.

She dug deep in desperation.

Remembering how her late father would visit nature for inspiration, often with her along for the adventure, Danielle was washed over by warm memories of camping, fishing boats, foraging for mushrooms, sunrises, and aurora borealis. She let her guard down and fell too deeply into the memory for a second, and then sat upright, too shaken to get all the way back on the path. Wiping away the beginnings of tears with one hand, reaching forward with the other, she could only get the name of the potted plant sitting in front of her at the table, and she whispered it to herself as she wrote.

"Bromeliad"

Steef held the paper-plastic seed package in his hand, up and in front of him, blocking the sunlight blasting through the cracked glass installed poorly on the roof of the garden store greenhouse, while he read the name on the packaging. "Am I saying that right?"

"You got it! You're a natural."

Steef already knew how to say it. He was being polite.

"Once the flower finishes blooming, you'll want to remove it," the salesman proudly told him, embarrassingly overeager to share the rare piece of gardening knowledge that he believed Steef didn't already have. "A bromeliad is technically a pineapple, and so it could take 2-3 years to mature." The salesman paused, and remembered something he'd read recently. "Does that sound like something you would be interested in?" He closed his mouth immediately after speaking, every time, having been made to feel insecure about the natural yellow of his teeth.

Steef didn't appreciate the style of the salesman, but his need to get the last bromeliad seeds eclipsed his need to leave the obnoxious salesman alone, winless, with his dick in his hands. But Steef could've won, if he really wanted to.

"Okay. Fine, ring it up."

The kid was probably making minimum wage. This sale might be the best part of his day, Steef told himself, to help him get over it.

As he wandered back through the halls of the needlessly large garden store, with the plants for sale being held in plastic bags, behind locked cages or tucked away into a back room, Steef overheard some other obnoxious salesmen, the awkwardness of their sales pitches worth less than minimum wage, reciting the same hymn when it was time. "Does that sound like something you would be interested in?" He wanted to pray for them.

Steef knew almost nothing about organized religion, but this aggressive style of conversion was what turned him away from his family church, and it would guarantee that he would never return to the same garden store.

With the ding of the register, he was off to the university to spend the sunset finding the perfect piece of driftwood on the beach, and then he would return to his spartan dorm to spend his Friday evening carving the driftwood into a suitable home for the bromeliad seeds.

He wondered how the party was going for a minute, and momentarily returned to the zen of his driftwood.

04 - THE CAT

The room was mostly silent, being watched over disapprovingly by a Scarface movie poster that'd been hopelessly frayed at the corners from frequent repositioning, and Gerg spun another circle in Mike's computer chair.

He stopped the chair from spinning and repeated himself, "I don't think this chair is very Gergonomic," as he faked like his back hurt.

They could hear him the first time. They just wish he hadn't said that.

"At least he isn't saying 'geology rocks' anymore."

"Thinking of switching majors actually."

The captive audience in Mike's single bedroom waited for the punchline.

"Geology rocks. But geography is where it's at."

The scattered chorus of disapproving sighs was interrupted by the lumbering dinosaur walk of aLan as he stood up and ventured outside the bedroom, grabbed the roll of duct tape from the untouched Edward Fortyhands activity table that Mike had set up, tossed the roll at Gerg's head, and said "go duct yourself."

aLan deserved aux privileges for that, and he knew it, and so he went and took them.

"Fucks sake man."

"Matthew Good Band? Again?"

"aLan, you fuck, do you even know any other bands?"

"Yeah, I just wanna listen to Strange Days." He was used to the groans. "It's a good song!"

"aLan. We're drinking. We can't drink to this shit."

"Yeah, asshole. One more Matt Good and we're forcing the forty hands on you."

We're done lying for a living
The strange days have come and you're gone, you're gone
Either dead or dying
Either dead or trying to go

aLan was all smiles. He reveled in it, soaked it in, kept quiet, smiling but holding back a greater smile, finished his drink as the song ended, hit "repeat", stood up to a thundering six foot six and shouted "TAPE ME UP BOYS."

Gerg had the tape, which he had picked up off Mike's bedroom floor after it had bounced off the side of his face. He hurried over and fastened aLan to two bottles of Colt 45 before aLan would realize that he'd need help using the bathroom for the next few hours.

"Not it!"

"Not it!"

"NOT IT"

"Not it"

Roman was it.

"God fucking damnit."

"Not it what?" aLan laughed along at first, sat back down with the 40s taped to his hands, took a drink from each one and waited.

Nobody told him. They waited for him to figure it out.

"Not it what?"

He was now blowjob height on Gerg, who simply zipped his own fly up and down until the life started to drain from aLan's face.

"FUCK."

Either dead or dying
Either dead or trying to go

"Fuck it, could be worse. Roman, you better learn to speak bladderese, buddy."

Roman raised his hand. "Can I trade off? Can we take shifts? Ten bucks, anyone... please...I don't ask for much."

"THOSE THE RULES MAN. YOU GOTTA DO IT."

"Hey Roman. Hey Roman." Gerg beamed. "Hey Roman."

"What."

"What's the greatest nation in the world?"

"Fuck it, let's hear it."

"Urination!"

"This is the worst fucking night of my life."

Aliya had been getting bored of the energy and was mostly sitting in place, anticipating an arrival. She got tired of playing the waiting game, found Mike's hungry hungry hippos game set in his bedroom closet, took out the bag of marbles, and started throwing them, one by one, at a mostly defenseless aLan; he raised his forty hands to block some of the marbles, hoping the bottles would shatter and release him.

"Ah man. Roman. Sorry buddy. It's already coming. It's starting to feel like I'm gonna piss a lot tonight."

Miles was still sober, still getting into it. He added to the chaos only way he knew how, for the moment, chanting "PISS! PISS! PISS! PISS!" and making piss noises.

"I definitely have to go already. That's just from one sip. One sip!"

Roman put his head in his hands.

"I think I'm ready. Guide me! Roman!"

Gerg slapped Roman on the back. "Looks like urine for a long night, pal!"

"You know," Aliya twirled her hair, "you could just keep your pants off for the entire night."

aLan took a couple seconds to shake his head.

"I'll ask again when you're done one of those 40s, handsome."

aLan blushed.

***

Miles was still chanting "PISS! PISS! PISS! PISS!" which Mike could hear from the kitchen, while he was busy nervously pacing, sipping different levels of vodka koolaid, determined to figure out which ratio would most impress a young lesbian couple. He was putting the empty bottles right on the edge of the bar window between the kitchen and the livingroom, because he knew Lise enjoyed knocking things off of edges, and this party was for everyone.

"Nick's fucking cheating."

The projector screen on the wall of Mike's apartment was fully visible from his vodka mixing station in the kitchen, and he missed a few measures getting lost in the excitement of Jeff, Geoff, Nick and Terry and their annoying Mario Kart tournament.

"Hey Terry, you're a nerd, right? Can you hack a Nintendo for red shells? Nick's getting them every time."

Terry said nothing.

Jeff laughed. "Not everyone who's smarter than you is a nerd."

"Yeah, that would be way too many people."

Jeff paused the game to stare unblinking at Geoff's face until he realized what he said.

Even Geoff laughed at that one until Lise knocked a pitcher, still with some kool aid, off the counter, and then uttered an impossiby loud MEOW.

"DID THE CAT JUST FUCKING SAY OH YEAH?"

"THIS CAT'S THE FUCKING KOOL AID MAN."

"Meow yeah!"

"MEOW YEAAAHHH" Nick hit Jeff with another red shell, from first place, which should have been impossible.

Matej was laughing from the doorway between Mike's bedroom and the livingroom, nursing a bottle of IPA that he hated. He was happy to be there, mostly standing motionless, equidistant from both centers of party gravity.

This was the first party of his life.

This IPA was the first alcoholic beverage of his life.

Nobody knew. He wanted them to think he was cool. He had no way of knowing they weren't.

He wandered over from the doorway into the room with the music.

"Hey guys." He tightened his grip on the neck of his beer.

"Hey. How is it out there?"

"MEOW YEAH! Hahaha."

"Huh?"

"Meow yeah," Matej repeated himelf, matter-of-factly.

"Huh?"

"Are you doing a bit there, buddy?"

"Hahaha. What? Matej! Cat got your tongue?"

Aliya threw a friendly hungry hippo marble at Matej, who took it as a rejection. It landed between his eyes and he needed a second to recover his ability to speak.

"No it's from... Mario Kart. The cat." Matej pointed to where Lise would have been if the bedroom wall wasn't there.

There was an uncomfortable period of silence while the music played on in the background before Gerg pierced it with a guttural "MEOW YEAAAAHHH."

Matej faked laughing to get back into the energy of the thing, and he gripped his IPA harder, but feeling iced out, he wandered back to the doorway where he could be warmed again by the familiar glow of the Nintendo and the quiet company of the cat in the distance.

"Hey where's Steef?"

"He doesn't drink."

"He texted me. He's alone in his dorm, carving his driftwood."

"You mean-"

"Not a euphemism."

Matej caught a glimpse of the cat knocking a fork off the kitchen counter and tried again from the doorway. "MEOW YEAH."

"MEOW YEAAAHH."

Gerg bellowed again with a half burp, half thunder, "MEOOOOWW YEAAHH."

"Kool Aid Man's a man, Lise is a girl," Mike said mostly quietly. "By the way, watch your drinks, she's a drink hound."

"Cat."

"Huh?"

"Drink cat."

"The fuck is a drink cat?"

"A cat isn't a hound. A cat is a cat."

"Oh. Right. Sorry. Sorry, cat."

"Meow y-" Geoff got hit by a red shell. "Fuck!"

"Should we ask Steef about his garden sale?"

Jeff asked the entire apartment with his voice at maximum volume, "HEY, DOES ANYONE HERE GIVE TWO SHITS ABOUT GARDENING?"

A disheartened Matej had, in fact, been reading up on plant-based entheogens, but in that moment, he didn't feel like he was part of the vibe, so he kept it to himself.

"DIDN'T THINK S-. What the FUCK. ANOTHER red shell? You're fucking CHEATING."

"No I'm not, bitch." He didn't know it, but he was. Mike had made aftermarket modifications to the cartridge so that player 2 would always get red shells.

"Just fucking stab him anyways." Roman passed through the hall on the way to the bathroom with the energy of a walk to the gallows; aLan got there first with a bounce in his step.

Roman closed the door and stared at the lock for a few seconds before deciding to lock it – his internal fear calculus valued the privacy more than the potential for a hasty escape.

His hand lingered on the lock to the door and so did his dead gaze. He didn't want to turn around. His grip on the lock tightened to no effect. He didn't want to face his assignment. He didn't want to-

"Turn around!" aLan beckoned in a Bonnie Tyler voice.

"Don't fucking-"

"Every now and then I get a little bit lonely and you're never comin' round..."

"Shut the fuck up, aLan."

"If you want me to shut up then..."

"Don't say it."

"TURN AROUND!"

"Fuck you. Let's get this over with."

aLan cranked his voice up high enough so that the boys in the livingroom could hear it overtop of their Mario Kart noises. "Every now and then I get a little bit tired of listening to the sound of my TEEEAARRRS!"

"I'm walking out if you keep singing. I'll break the code, I don't give a fuck."

"Ok, fine. But Aliya got me hard so you might have to wait a minute."

"...was it Aliya?"

aLan blushed. "I was joking. You can get to work." He took a considerable swig from the 40 on his left hand, and some of it spilled on Roman's hand which was in place, shaking six inches above aLan's fly, fully zipped.

"Don't I make you wet, Roman?"

"Oh god. I think I preferred the singing."

"I did too, but I didn't want you to..."

"Oh god damnit."

"TURN AROUND!"

Roman punched aLan in the dick and the singing stopped. Without any consideration paid to the fly of the jeans or the status of aLan's dick, he then pulled aLan's pants straight down and moved to try to storm out. "You're on your own for this part, asshole."

Roman fumbled the locked bathroom door for a few seconds while aLan positioned himself above the bowl, and as the malt liquor escaped him, he kept going.

His eyes were closed and his heart was open as he sang.

"EVERY NOW AND THEN I GET A LITTLE BIT NERVOUS THAT THE BEST OF ALL THE YEARS HAVE GONE BYYYYYyyyy..."

In a mounting panic, Roman couldn't steady his hand well enough to unlock the door. He started punching at the lock until his hand started bleeding. The blood started to stream down the sides of his fingers and the piss continued to stream into the toilet.

"TURN AROUND!"

Roman surveyed the blood on his hands and all at once he stopped resisting.

He took a deep breath.

He started to sing with his clean hand still on the lock.

"EVERY NOW AND THEN I GET A LITTLE BIT TERRIFIED,"

The door unlocked and swung open.

aLan turned his neck like an owl to make eye contact and joined in. "AND THEN I SEE THE LOOK IN YOUR EYES."

They paused, but by now, the entire Mario Kart livingroom had caught on and was singing along at the top of their lungs.

"TURN AROUND, BRIGHT EYES."

Matej, alone and smiling at Mike's bookshelf, picked up a Roku streaming remote to use as a prop microphone and continued, alone, in a perfect high falsetto. "Every now and then I fall apart!" And the chaos descended into laughter, and the vocal harmony and the race both fell entirely off track.

Curiosity got the best of Matej, and he walked over to the bathroom, remote in hand, to find aLan done pissing, his eyes closed and his head still pointed to the ceiling, Roman sitting on the edge of the bathtub suppressing a big smile, looking in the other direction out of courtesy.

Matej stood at the opened door like an old west sheriff and took a swig of his IPA while a fully drained Roman with dried blood on his hands awkwardly finished resecuring aLan's fly to the closed position.

Roman took a look at the Roku remote in Matej's hand,

and with a refreshed vigor, pointed at aLan and commented, "how's that for streaming?"

aLan bent over in laugher, and malt liquor poured out of both 40s, somehow all hitting the crotch part of his pants, making a perfect piss stain down his leg.

Matej tried to laugh but choked on his drink and had to leave. He walked over to the bookshelf to return the Roku remote, finding Kevin, who was doing advance research, as he still believed that the focus of the party was to help Aliya pick an obscure religious text, but finding that the only vaguely religious book on the shelf was *The Sales Bible* by Jeffrey Gitomer.

Kevin nudged Matej out of the way and leaned halfway through the bedroom doorway. "Aliya. Hope you brought your own books. There's nothing here."

Aliya tossed her second-last marble at Kevin. "Shut up. I'll figure something out. It's a fucking blow off class. If there's nothing good here I can go the UBC library tomorrow."

Kevin shrugged and went back to the bookshelf as Aliya got a ding from her phone.

[7:08pm] *text notification from Steef. Enter PIN to expand*

"Steef? Steef!!" excited to hear from him, she hoped that the text meant that he was showing up, and her drunken state converted the excitement to confidence. She got up to run to the door.

Gerg used the moment to steal the aux and put on Foo Fighters.

Hello
I've waited here for you
Everlong

Roman, fucking sick of the Foo Fighters, instinctively got up to attack the sound system but was halted by a wailing aLan. "Roman!"

"What!"

"I need you now tonight! I need you more than ever!" he had managed to tumble a roll of paper towels from the cabinet onto the bathroom floor, and was motioning at the wet stains on his pants.

"This is above and beyond. You fucking owe me one."

Roman closed his eyes, held his breath and turned around to clean up while aLan hummed the rest of the verse.

Aliya bowled Matej over onto the floor of the Nintendo livingroom in her hurry to welcome her friend. She was all smiles as she threw her last marble at the door to the apartment. Roman and aLan stood in the bathroom doorway to observe Aliya's noisy welcome party.

Right as the marble hit the door, there was a knock.

Her eyes went wide and she opened the door to find the new girl from the library, unable to speak, holding back tears. "She...sh-sh..." She stuttered, and her lack of words said more than words ever could.

Danielle knew to hold onto the tears until everyone could see. She knew they would trust the emotional waves more if they were able to witness where the waves broke. She knew they would trust her more if she absentmindedly knocked over some shelves and appliances on her way in. She knew they would trust her more if she slobbered and wailed and disregarded everyone on her way to the center of attention.

She motioned for Aliya to cradle her as she knelt on the livingroom floor on the verge of sobbing.

She remembered acting class and she drew from the well of

genuine sadness from the real love of hers that had truly just ended.

The waves broke, and everyone's doubts broke with them.

Her cries of pain were so convincing that the boys didn't even bother to pause the Mario Kart.

They were already hers.

They were duct taped to her hands.

But she didn't want to cry for any longer than she had to.

She slowed down her sobbing which slowed everyone else down with her.

And I wonder
When I sing along with you
If everything could ever feel this real forever
If anything could ever be this good again

She looked around.

She didn't want to be playing nintendo and listening to the fucking Foo Fighters for any longer than she had to.

She looked over at the knocked over Edward Fortyhands table and slobbered an apology.

The clumsy nerds tripped over themselves to forgive her. They raced each other to reposition the furniture she'd knocked over on her warpath.

Aliya thought of a way to try to make her feel better. "Any song you wanna hear?"

Danielle had fire in her eyes.

"BURN IT TO THE GROUND."

She let herself smile.

She sniffled.

She motioned for everyone to leave her alone and she was left on the ground. "Thank you. I'm so sorry. For the furniture and crying and all this. Aliya, right?"

"Yesssss. Are you... going to be okay?" She was still gripping the empty bag of marbles as her new friend's head was in her hands.

Danielle righted herself, reached in her pocket to grab a tissue, and accidentally-on-purpose knocked a half dozen small bags of coke onto the ground between them.

"Oh... whoops."

"No offense, Cassandra, but I could already kinda sorta tell that you were into drugs."

Danielle realized she was going to have to start answering to Cassandra from now on. "Well... it's more than that."

"You mean you're... addicted?" Aliya went rigid with worry and Danielle had to try not to laugh.

"More than that too. I'm..." Danielle took a measure to try to think of a fake name. "The reason that me and Leslie broke up is because she doesn't like that I..."

"That you do drugs?"

Danielle whispered. "That I *sell* drugs." She sniffled and wiped her nose and her septum piercing went off-center.

"This stuff on the ground is... cocaine? Right? What's it like?"

Danielle noticed the kool aid that had been spilled on the floor. "That's not for you." She lifted her head from Aliya's hands and sat upright and sniffled again.

"Sorry. For some back story. We have – sorry. We *had*. We had only been together for a few months. And I was talking to her about you guys at her apartment tonight. I told her about your pharmaceuticals class, and the talking about pharmaceuticals led naturally into me telling her something I was trying to build the courage to tell her for a while."

"She didn't know you did this?"

"I mean, like, I always had all the drugs she wanted, and I always had a lot of money, but I guess she never really questioned it."

She sniffled.

"Stupid girl." Aliya was already imagining scenarios in her head about how she would have acted differently.

"I guess it was just too much for her. She told me to give up the dealing or to give her up, and selling this shit is kinda sorta how I pay for school."

"So you had no choice."

"You get me."

"She's stupid."

"Thank you for saying that." She wiped her nose with the side of her hand, which knocked her septum piercing to the other side of center. "And one of the reasons I was going to bring it up soon anyways is that I have a lot of customers out here. I wanted her to help..."

"Would she have been good at it?"

"Oh, yeah, she would have been amazing. She loves the drugs and she knows how to talk stupid boys into doing things."

Aliya looked around at the sausage fest they were immersed in, and started to think she'd be able to do it too.

"But I can't stop now. I have a lot of loyal customers. Not

just at UBC anymore. Some of my rich customers have been graduating and they've got jobs at law firms and investment banks and condos in Kitsilano, penthouses downtown... I need another person." Danielle looked Aliya in the eyes and went in for the kill. "I need help."

Aliya dropped the empty bag of marbles, picked up one of the loose coke bags, and examined it intensely. Danielle could feel Aliya's voice shaking from all sides as she asked, "Do you think I'd be able to do this?"

Danielle smiled, and sniffled again. She looked away and pretended to consider it for a long time. She reached down and grabbed the empty marble bag. "Yeah," she centered her septum piercing and held the empty marble bag up between them, "but you're gonna need a bigger bag."

"What you guys got there?" Matej burst in from the side, gripping his IPA for dear life.

Danielle rushed to hide the evidence but Aliya stopped her. She knew Matej had no clue what he was looking at. "Science experiments. Chemistry class."

"Science experiments? In those small bags at a party?"

"Well yeah, the whole point of this party is to pick a book for class, right? Why can't our new friend do science experiments?"

Matej nodded and loosened his grip on the IPA. He started to feel warm. He was on his third beer and he decided he was getting really good at drinking.

Danielle tilted her head and stared at the floor and tried not to smile. She realized Aliya was going to be incredible at this.

"Pardon me, gotta freshen up."

Danielle took a trip to the bathroom to run through one of the coke bags. Eyes wide, blood rushing, looking at herself in the mirror, the evening going better than she could have hoped, she decided that it was time to get started on the main event.

Through the bathroom door, she could hear that the music had graduated from Nickelback to Creed.

The mood would be light and stupid.

Perfect.

She waited a minute to make sure her nose wasn't going to bleed.

She drew Parisa's purple elixir bottle out of her purse, placed it ceremoniously on the floor as she was shown, she used her phone to cast soft light onto the side; she inhaled, and she breathed slowly and firmly onto the elixir, once, for fifteen seconds.

And I'm trying to escape
I yelled back when I heard thunder
But I'm down to one last breath
And with it, let me say, let me say

The elixir bottle opened a millimeter and she very gently opened it the rest of the way, careful not to let the liquid dropper hit the sides.

She exited the bathroom slowly, sniffling with every other step, not walking quickly enough to catch anyone's eye; they were all chivalrously avoiding bothering her while she was looking at the ground to avoid eye contact.

I'm looking down now that it's over
Reflecting on all of my mistakes
I thought I found the road to somewhere
But I'm down to one last breath

She made it to the punch bowl, put her purse on the ground

and hovered, pretending to read texts on her phone, waiting for a moment where nobody was watching.

And with it let me say
Let me say

The Angel in Parisa's triptych had six wings, so when the moment struck, she dropped six drops into the vodka punch. She stirred until the ripples had calmed.

Hold me now
I'm six feet from the edge and I'm thinking
Maybe six feet ain't so far down

Now was the time to place the Bromeliad on the bookshelf. Next would be the distribution of the kool-aid.

As she bent down and reached into her purse on the floor, Lise hopped over and lapped the vodka punch once, unnoticed.

As she pulled the book out, Lise scrambled to the top of the shelf.

Something felt off.

Danielle put the book front and center on the shelf.

But I still believe there's something left for me

"Oh my god. This punch is so good. SO GOOD. This is perfect! Mike, you genius!" She took a small sip. First. She had to take the first sip. It was in the painting. The rest didn't matter.

Mike was glowing. He was too smitten to talk.

She went around the room making sure everyone had a good sized drink of it. "I want to propose a toast. If you would all have a drink with me."

aLan was only half done his 40s, both hands still bound by duct tape. "Hey Roman, uhh, I got another favor to ask."

"That can't be part of the code."

"I mean, it isn't, but I just think that,"

"Here it comes."

"Together we can make it to the end of the night! YOUR LOVE IS LIKE A SHADOW ON ME ALL THE TIME!"

"Please don't sing overtop of Creed ever again. That's fucking sacrilege."

"Even Bonnie Tyler?"

"Even Bonnie Tyler."

Danielle leaned in to whisper to Aliya as she handed her a drink. "Are they... you know..."

"Giant fucking dorks? Yeah."

"Aren't we all?" Gerg stood up to accept his drink. "Really appreciate this drink delivery. I think everyone's sick of..."

"Don't say it."

"Don't you fucking dare."

"...punch lines."

So please come stay with me
'Cause I still believe there's something left for you and me
For you and me
For you and me

Parisa had waited fifteen minutes to greet her after she first stepped into the enclave of the haunted forest compound, so Danielle waited fifteen minutes for the drug to kick in before she continued.

"Aliya." Danielle pointed at the *Bromeliad*. "How about this one?"

Maybe the music was too loud. Maybe they were distracted. The song had just changed.

The cat was stirring at the top of the shelf. For some reason, the cat was able to effortlessly draw everyone's attention.

Can you take me higher?
To a place where blind men see?

She slurred out, "Hey this book looks wwwwwonderful..." as everything started to get rubbery and purple.

Maybe she was doing too good of a job of avoiding attention before. Nobody turned to look at her.

Aliya was fixated on the cat.

Can you take me higher?
To a place with golden streets?

"Hellohellohellohello*hello*?" Danielle suddenly found herself responding more to the movement of light and color than to any other sensory input, suddenly fascinated by the movement of Lise, who was still on top of the bookshelf; her soft fur flowing like tall grass in the summer wind meant that the drug was working.

So why did it feel like she wasn't in control?

When the two of them finally made eye contact, Lise knocked a halogen lamp down two shelves, turning it on and casting a perfect circle of light around the outside of the *Bromeliad* through a glass prism.

The moderate thud drew everyone's sluggish attention over in unison.

Danielle was finding herself increasingly unable to speak. She tried to communicate in short, laboured breaths.

Aliya was risen from her mud and crushed velvet stasis by the thud; she got a glimpse at the prism halo, and she was drawn in. She moved like glowing molasses as she made her way to the bookshelf, collecting with both hands the artifact at the center of the circle, which she gradually came to understand was a book.

She held the *Bromeliad* in the way a three-toed sloth would cradle a newborn.

Up high
I feel like I'm
Alive for the
Very first time

The entire group was speechless – not wanting to speak and so not finding out that they wouldn't have been able to.

They slowly formed a natural circle and passed the *Bromeliad* around, Roman holding it for aLan, as hours passed them by without so much as a cough, a hiccup, a burp or a cleared throat.

As the peak of the drug loosened its grip, one by one, they regained their speech, one by one, reluctant to use it, beholden to the unspoken bond. To speak is to pierce the sacrament. They remain in the perfect moment as long as they remain silent.

It had felt like forever, but their voracious reading had only brought them just past 11pm when Lise wandered into the center of the circle and, eyes as wide as theirs, uttered an inviting "bzzztmrow", drawing the group into ecstatic laughter.

One by one, the silence was left behind by the freshly awakened Disciples of the *Bromeliad*, and they started to discuss their new religion with gentle passion.

"So we had our awakening event together. I know this means most of us are Disciples. Who is the Archon?"

Nobody spoke. Danielle smiled. Everyone turned immediately to look at Danielle. Nobody spoke. Nobody needed to speak.

"Do we get to meet your Angel?"

Danielle didn't speak. She didn't need to speak. There wasn't an answer anyways.

"Sorry for asking."

There were no stupid questions among Disciples, but some questions still felt stupid.

"What's this symbol above Angel?" Jeff pointed to the diagram accompanying the passage indicating the Cosmic hierarchy.

Danielle knew from her extensive readings on human manipulation that an open question, met with eye contact and silence, in a comfortable environment, would typically create a gentle psychic pressure that forced the decision maker to silently retreat to their best guess.

Encased in the collective afterglow of a positive psychedelic trip, the psychic pressure was borderline automatic.

She knew that one of the key functions of a religion was that it got rid of questions - not by giving the right answers, but by scuttling the inner anxiety that constantly demanded resolution.

With every question, she made soft, stern, welcoming and confident unblinking eye contact with the questioner, guiding their intuitions to provide them with the answer they wanted to hear, Danielle never knowing what it was.

"So unconscious suffering being worth more means that we can't tell anyone about any of this, right? Or else we're denying them bliss in a future life?"

Danielle stared.

The question disappeared.

"So if we make efforts to put souls in situations where they suffer. We're kind of like, grinding Karma *for* them?"

Nobody had any more questions.

The mission was clear.

Mike got up to make another bowl of punch, something deep inside of him wanting to go further into the dark light, unaware of the special ingredient. Still slurring his movements, he stubbed his toe on the bookshelf as he walked past it, to which a slow voice from the bedroom reassurred him, "Don't be angry Mike! That's just Karma for the Grind!" to a hearty round of warm, temperate laughter and scattered applause.

Karma for the Grind. Danielle was going to have to remember that one.

Back to work.

The reflection of the Angel in the triptych in Parisa's haunted forest compound informed Danielle that they should take a second dose, for reflection, after initiation had settled.

When Danielle noticed that Mike was standing up to get a fresh bottle of vodka, she realized what he was up to, and knew she had to take over.

She approached him gently in the kitchen and spoke as softly as she could without sacrificing her consonants, and every vowel spoken before was still on her tongue as she reached the next. "As the Archon I feel as though I should not only distribute the messages and the assignments," she allowed a righteous smile to light up her face, "but also the magic potions." They weren't blinking as they kept smiling eye contact. He nodded and his smile never faded as he wordlessly returned to the learning circle; they were still passing around the book, sharing curiosities, finding wisdom in the silence.

The reflected Angel in the triptych from Parisa's haunted forest compound had one eye covered up, which informed Danielle that she should avoid drinking a second dose of the vodka punch.

She brought the bowl into the center of the learning circle and laid it down gracefully, spooking the cat, who ran to sit in Aliya's lap.

"Oh no. Look at this part." Kevin cleared his throat. "A Disciple will avoid building personal relationships with unawakened souls, so as to avoid the complexities of intertwined and incompatible spiritual perspectives."

"So?"

"What about Steef? Do we have to stop talking to him?"

Danielle panicked. She didn't know anything about this 'Steef', except that he was into gardening and fishing. This was a question that she couldn't answer by sending these people looking inwards. After a second, she remembered some of what she wrote that evening and she smiled wide. "The *Bromeliad* says to avoid building relationships, but it sounds like your friendship with Steef is already built."

"Oh thank goodness." A wave of warm relief flooded the room and the sparkles returned to everyone's eyes.

"He's a militant atheist anyways. I think that finding out about this might have done a number on him."

Danielle knew he'd have been converted, same as everyone else. She whispered through gentle exhalations. "He is your friend. You all seem to be very fond of him."

"Yeah."

"I'd do anything for that gardener."

"Then we can all give him the gift of unawakened suffering." The words hit their ears like a summer breeze.

"Oh!"

"Yes!"

Matej was feeling so good that he took a humongous gulp of the vodka punch. His first big sip. He felt his mistake immediately, but didn't want to embarrass himself, so he got up slowly, hid his panic behind slow movement and soft laughter, and made his way to the bathroom where he immediately expelled the contents of his stomach, well out of earshot of the rest of them.

"So," Roman asked, "How do we get Steef to never awaken?"

"The answer to your question is very easy," aLan said, both of his forty hands still unfinished.

"Huh?"

"Just bug him to do it. Constantly. He'll never do it."

"Right. Steef. Good old Steef."

"Steefy Steefy Steef."

"Pouring out an ounce for my unawakened homie." aLan poured seven ounces out in front of him and the small puddle flooded over to Terry's pants as he sat peacefully in the lotus position on the floor.

"Sorry man."

Terry quietly stood up and went to the bathroom to clean the Colt 45 from his pants, finding the door locked, and hearing Matej choking up vomit on the other side.

He knocked politely and Matej stopped making vomit noises;

Matej flushed a few seconds later, ran some water from the tap, and sheepishly opened the door. Matej raised his head for momentary eye contact, and Terry used his thumb to wipe the side of his mouth, alerting Matej to the vomit chunk still on the side of his own. Matej wiped and put his head back down as he uttered a pathetic "sorry", and then scurried to make a quiet return to the learning circle.

When he returned, he found the cat perched on Aliya's shoulder as they both seemed to be looking at some items in her marble bag.

The second dose slowed down their speech and their thoughts and sent them to sleep, one by one, on the floor of Mike's room, the shape of their reading circle evolving into a spiral on the floor with the punch bowl at the center and the cat standing guard.

Matej took the cue and faked being asleep until at long last he felt the grace of his circadian rhythm and joined them. Danielle didn't notice, and she stayed awake through the night with the help of the coke in her purse, and she stayed alert, studying the ambitious religious text she had just herself written, with all the fervor she had been giving to her finance degree.

She felt refreshed. She managed to find a new purpose out of nowhere. This was exciting.

Danielle was dead.

She was reborn as Cassandra.

The evening passed and Terry woke up before the rest of them to go to a Saturday morning class. Matej, who had been in a shallow sleep and was awoken by Terry's rummaging, slinked up behind him as he went out the door, caught him by the shoulder in the hallway and begged, "Please be quiet."

Terry could sense the mach 5 panic in Matej's eyes. He looked like a forest critter trapped in a wildfire.

"I thought I was getting good at drinking. At partying. I felt good, I didn't know drinking too much would make me puke my guts out. Dont tell anyone." Matej released his grip on Terry's shoulder. "Don't tell them. I've never been to a party before. I don't want them to kn- I don't want them to think I'm a loser."

He thought this was all so endearing and pathetic.

Terry said nothing.

05 - THE WEDDING

Cassandra stepped out of the side door of the leading limousine, and the first of her knockoff Saint Laurent boots hit the wet grass outside of the church with a thud. The trailing limousines pulled up behind hers, crowding the cul-de-sac, some already starting to honk.

She stood in place with her other boot still in the limo, quickly scanning the grass for a way for it to avoid a similar fate. She looked back at the cavalcade behind her:Fourteen limousines, one for each of them, back to back, in a residential area, leading into the cul-de-sac.

They were stuck.

This was planned.

The limousine trap served quadruplicate functions of pinning the other wedding guests in place, providing the Grinders with a fresh roster of pre-agitated temporary agents of chaos, unsettling the Groom leading up to an important negotiation, and also creating a messy situation that would inflict a category 2 or 3 Karma bomb on the guests and wedding planners.

There was always Karma for the Grind.

The rhythm of the honks behind her sounded like wedding bells.

She sighed and dragged out her other boot, planting it in the same wet grass with a sloppy thud.

She held her peace.

This is where she needed to be – this is where they needed to be.

Her empty limo lurched forward around the cul-de-sac until it couldn't, now trapped, perpendicular, facing down the side of another limo from another limo company.

Cassandra ignored the mounting pleas of the drivers and focused only on rallying the Grinders. She had a mission – they had a mission - and the wedding going through as planned was imperative to their mission.

She squinted her eyes at the rustic sign right outside the front of the church, mostly covered in ivy, and could only make out the word 'Basilica'.

She looked up at the steeple, looked down, looked back, and activated the military grade signal jammer that Mike had patched together from spare parts the night before. The limo drivers would be unable to call out until the jammer was turned off.

There was no rescue until she allowed it.

Cassandra was also well aware that the drivers would be happy to abandon their vehicles in favor of expensive food and free champagne.

She drew it up perfectly.

There would be police scanners and taxi drivers in the radius of the signal jammer as well, so by anyone's math, this was at least a category 2 Karma bomb, and they hadn't even gone inside yet.

Everyone gathered just outside the church, limo drivers and Grinders, in separate clusters.

Cassandra instructed them to act like new money tech assholes: overconfident, brash and disrespectful, but only in close conversations. "Keep it category 2, and don't draw too much attention. You want them to avoid you, not hate you."

"Vut does category two meaning?"

The Grinders ignored the curious limo driver.

The rain slowed down.

The wedding bouncer would be coming back outside as soon as he'd noticed the fortunate shift in the weather, so the Grinders needed to hurry in before the present state of chaos could be observed and reported to anyone still inside the church.

***

They sent the limo drivers in first, poorly dressed in a way that only stuffy old money would notice as poorly dressed, a well-disorganized pack of deer in headlights, to overwhelm and confuse the solitary bouncer, indoors, escaping the rain, their limo driver shoes tracking mud all over the fancy church floor, dropping puddles that made dirty rainbows whenever the sun could manage to break through the clouds and the stained glass.

After dealing with the drivers, the sight of the Grinders, dressed comparatively well, Kevin distracted by jingling keys as he marched through the gates, came as a relief to the wedding bouncer, and as the Grinders all entered at once while holding nicely wrapped wedding gifts, they broke through unchallenged while the bouncer was preoccupied with trying to bounce the limo drivers who spoke only broken English.

Three of the drivers managed to get past the bouncer. This was fine - well-intentioned idiots made very good Soldiers, and putting enough of them into this degree of a socially precarious situation was one of the more effortless and reliable Karma bombs.

Roman took a second to assist the remaining limo drivers with their manner of dress so that they wouldn't look so much like limo drivers. "If anyone asks, you work for Uber."

***

Once they were all inside, Cassandra had a second speech as soon as she had the attention of the Grinders and nobody else. "No real names. Do not use your own real name, do not use each others' real names. If we give them accurate info, they can figure out who we aren't, and more importantly, they can figure out who we are."

The planned interactions went smoothly. The Grinders were all talking sharply, their brief conversations littered with obnoxious Silicon Valley buzzwords and a total absence of social graces. The old money people all quickly became alerted to the possibility that these tech vultures were at the wedding to dig for valuable information capital, and so the stuffy old men kept a respectful and polite distance.

Cassandra kept to herself, not drinking, only allowing herself the standard power cocktail of xans and coke. She had been staying mostly sober since becoming the Archon, but she needed to make sure everything went according to plan.

She made herself highly visible. The mission hinged on a transaction taking place between her and the Groom, and for the inevitable conversation to roll out in the ideal manner, he had to approach her and speak first.

She spotted his best man speaking to him in the distance, well in sight of the end of the corridor where she was lurking. She exited the corridor alone with her purse, did her best to look disoriented, and waited to be approached.

***

Right on schedule, she heard a familiar voice behind her. "I didn't invite you." She turned around to look at him. "Or these freaks."

The Groom turned Cassandra's attention over to Steef, who had just pulled a set of compact gardening shears out of his gardening satchel and was at work pruning the bouquet.

She tried to hide her smile. "You knew I'd find my way here."

"Yeah."

"You knew I'd find my way in."

"Yeah."

"You could have made security stay outside. You could have told security to keep me out."

"Yeah."

There was a pause as they took each other in. They hadn't been face to face since the morning of the day she was expelled from university.

"Did you want me here because you miss me? Or ... did you want me here because you want me to watch you slip away?"

"Yeah."

The new Bride had taken his balls but she hadn't taken his wit. They both took another second to soak in the moment.

"Who is she?"

"I'd cut my dick off if you didn't already know everything about her."

She paused for a second and slowly drew a hunting knife from a hidden scabbard on the side of her leg.

"You can keep your dick."

She slowly moved it to the forward position in front of her waist, pointing outwards. "I bet you miss mine."

"It's my wedding. You're at my wedding." He turned beet red and shuffled his feet. "We had our thing."

"Yeah, we did. We had our thing."

"You disappeared."

"I had to."

Neither of them wanted to have that conversation.

"She doesn't do it like I do."

He knew what was coming next.

"I bet that's a real pain in th-"

He put his hand up like a traffic cop. "Please.... please don't say it."

The Groom adjusted his pants and flipped the conversation back at her. "I almost didn't recognize you as a brunette." He still knew her buttons.

For a second, she gripped the hunting knife tighter. "At least I'm not a fucking redhead." She caught herself and slowly put it back into the scabbard.

"Who are they anyways?"

"Mercenaries. Built for war." She sniffled.

The Groom motioned with his eyes and his drink to turn her attention to a category 1 Karma bomb at the seafood table, Gerg and Kevin putting shrimp into each others mouths, while aLan and Roman were encouraging them with chants of

SHRIMP! SHRIMP! SHRIMP!

"Bit sloppy to be soldiers, aren't they?"

She didn't even try to hide her smile. "Mad geniuses. World domination types," she felt an inner pang to correct the designation he had given them, even though she knew he wouldn't understand it. "Perfect Disciples."

It started to click for him. "You found your people."

In that moment, most of the warfare drained from her face. Nobody understood her like he used to, and she wasn't sure who was more pained by that fact. She twisted the knife that was in both of them, knowing that for a second, it would hurt him more than it hurt her. "They should be *our* people."

He agreed but couldn't admit it. He looked around at the two-dimensional, cardboard, old money suits walking motionless from cluster to cluster, giving no signs of life and even fewer signs of a beautiful death.

"These are my people. This is where I have to be." He couldn't mask the desperation in his voice. "This is where I'm meant to be."

She let his limp white lie linger, in full view of the angels in the stained glass, until neither of them believed that either of them still believed it. She pounced on the blank space with a full offensive. "I have something!"

"You got me a wedding gift?"

She laughed. "If you're smart, it can be a wedding gift." She pulled a VHS tape from her purse.

The Groom was taken back by the size of it. "How does that tape fit in your purse?"

"You should remember that I'm good at fitting things in places they shouldn't fit. Or did you want to watch this as a reminder?"

He was suddenly at his own funeral. He clenched. He chose his next words carefully, humiliating himself just enough so that she would feel some victory and act with a sliver of kindness. "You got me bent over. What do you want?" She could have asked for almost anything.

"Me and these freaks need to get up inside the Canadian military. I can't tell you why." She reached into her purse again and produced a satchel.

"I own this bag of people." She held the satchel up. "You don't know them, they don't know me. I'm a voice behind a black screen with all their darkest secrets. I'm the fucking Wizard of Oz with nuclear codes. You understand?"

"I understand completely."

"Put them up north. Somewhere with access to personnel files, but safe. Far from combat. Keep them alive."

"And the tape?"

"Wedding gift. I'd shake on it, but I don't know where those fingers have been."

She stacked the satchel and the videotape, handed them to him but didn't let go. He pulled gently, she pulled gently back. Three more times.

He unclenched and exhaled. He could only look down.

"Let's go for a walk and see what my freaks are up to." She let go of the items.

They wandered over to Nick, who had no filter and a lot of opinions. Cassandra got him onto hockey. "Hey Nick, I think I overheard you talking about the Buffalo Sabres?"

This was a button that she knew he had. "Oh fuck that. I don't support that loser franchise since they were bought by Terry Pegula."

Cassandra smiled so wide you could see it from behind. "Pegula. I hear that guy's a dick."

"Oh... no kidding." Nick abandoned the tray of butter tarts he was eating by himself. "He absolutely ruined Buffalo sports for everyone." Nick thought he was taking care of the crumbs around his mouth, but he wasn't. "Just wrecked 'em."

"It wouldn't be a stretch to call him a big asshole then?"

"Yeah. I guess. Are you good? Do you need some fresh air?"

Cassandra realized her taunting was no longer functioning as a legitimate second conversation, and she snapped to focus before the Groom could adjust.

"Yeah, I just wouldn't want to be a Buffalo sports fan."

Nick recovered. "I dunno man. I have to think the Bills are coming due."

Cassandra couldn't suppress a laugh. "Have to agree with you there Nick."

She caught the Groom still looking down, focusing now on his ring finger, trying to look in an innocent direction but only finding the judgmental angels in the stained glass windows by the exit.

She let it linger.

Karma for the Grind.

***

She played the conversation so well that she didn't give away that her plans for world domination hinged greatly on this wedding actually going through. She knew that the Groom needed to secure a wife and start a family before his legacy father would permit him to ascend to upper management at the family's private equity firm.

The Groom walked away slowly, far from traffic, and as he disappeared into the procession, so did her feeling of victory. With the mission complete, she was now just at the wedding of her ex-lover.

She fumbled for a xan in her pocket and thought about heading to the bathroom. She started to sniffle ahead of schedule, before she could mask it with cocaine.

Terry was right there as they parted, and he noticed. She noticed that he noticed. The silent kindness in his face carried her through to the bathroom and onwards to the minute of the onset of the xanax.

***

The pastor's preamble died down and the ceremony started to begin.

The Grinders took the back row on both sides of the aisle, keeping one seat open for whenever Cassandra found her way back from the washroom.

Two of the three limo drivers were forced to stand. One of them was steamrolling his way through five thousand dollars of steak and seafood on a gold rimmed plate, and the other was double fisting bottles of dom perignon that were worth more than his apartment. The old money wanted to say something about it, but as they found out, he worked for Uber, and old money knew better than to get in the way of a close associate of Travis Kalanick.

Cassandra had already taken two xans fifteen minutes apart,

and one of them was working already. She eyed a third. She stared at the third xan for another ten minutes. She forgot she was in the washroom.

The Groom was out there, fully dressed, eyes wide, waiting for a Bride that wasn't her.

Cassandra couldn't process her surroundings.

A third xan would put her to sleep.

She considered it.

She considered it.

She considered it.

She thought about the Grinders and put the third xan back into her pocket. She'll need one for after the ceremony anyways, she figured.

She kept her hand in her xanax pocket, feeling the outline of it, rubbing it like a rosary.

She knew she would need to be awake enough to get to the limo.

She can take it when they leave and she can sleep in the limo.

They're all still out there.

She can't cry for them, she can't cry for herself. She will pull through on two xans instead of three and she will accomplish her mission – their mission.

They were probably wondering where she was. They deserved to know she was doing fine.

She was getting soft.

She inhaled another fingernail of coke and then she had her feelings asleep and her eyes awake.

As she exited the washroom and re-entered the ceremony, she got lost in another train of thought as she walked, nearly stepping into the father of the Bride as he was approaching to walk her down the aisle.

She should have taken the third xan.

But she had to conduct herself.

It was all on the line now, as it was a dozen times before, as it would be a hundred times again.

She sat down next to Terry and went on autopilot. She didn't have to be paying attention. She just had to physically be there on the other side of the ceremony. She felt the third xan with her pointer and ring fingers and pressed on it so strongly that it snapped into fragments. She considered eating a fragment as a compromise but stayed strong.

She didn't realize she was shaking.

She emerged too soon from autopilot, getting off the train at the wrong circle of hell. The pastor had just begun reciting quotes about marriage.

"..as Andre Maurois said, 'a happy marriage is a long conversation which always seems too short...' " she went back into her thoughts, only to find the pastor's words bouncing like sharp metal on the inside of her paper skull. She went back outside her mind to find herself, once again, being led into a fresher hell by the same man of god. *"..successful marriage requires falling in love many times, always with the same person..."* and as she was being bounced back and forth between twin hells, Terry grabbed her hand, and through him the benzoate angels reached down, pulling them both up onto an infinite cloud. She stopped shaking, and it took her another minute for her vision to do the same. She found herself wrapped in a plastic reality where she hadn't shed a tear or made a sound. She

wasn't sure how. But the xans had drilled enough holes in her brain that she couldn't think about it if she wanted to.

She had managed to float over the vows, which was a grace she didn't think she deserved.

To the Grinders, to the literal structure of what they were doing, what they were trying to do, she was an Archon, but that was her designation. In a spiritual sense, in a cosmic sense, she refused to allow herself to believe it was anything more than a role she was playing.

It didn't matter. She didn't think she needed to believe it.

"Dearly beloved, we have come together in the presence of God..."

Cassandra looked over at Steef, the friendly neighborhood atheist, who she insisted didn't need to join them in this 'den of lies', and he was rolling his eyes. She was two xans past being able to smile at that, but she could still feel the beacons of a smile lighting up in her inner distance.

One more personal armageddon and she would be free – they would be free.

"...anyone here present know of any reason why the couple should-"

This was what she had practiced for.

She had practiced every angle.

She had practiced saying nothing, with the stoic calm of a Tibetan monk.

She had practiced saying everything, with the liberated belligerence of 90s Julia Roberts, always to a rousing cascade of applause, *Drops of Jupiter* playing from a symphony orchestra behind her, waltzing out of the wedding arm-in-arm with the man she loved, the Bride defeated and bloody on the ground behind them.

She made no decision - her free hand gripping Terry's hand, her xanax hand crushing the fragments further into finer fragments, wishing she had the stillness to shovel more of it into her mouth, grateful that the lack of stillness kept her from having to make a decision.

The pastor paused for far too long. This was intentional, she thought. The Groom asked for this, she thought.

She found a sliver of peace as she suddenly thought of something she read as a child, in a book she was given by her father, who was Buddhist for a time. In this book, someone asked a Buddhist to describe the length of an 'eon'. The Buddhist replied, '*Imagine a mountain of rock a mile long, a mile wide and a mile high, without any cracks or crevices - just one solid mass. Then imagine that once every century, a man would stroke that mountain once with a silk cloth. That great mountain of rock would have worn away before an eon had passed.*'

It always felt to her to be a bit of an exaggeration. Now she understood.

The pastor's silence came to an end.

Cassandra crushed Terry's hand with the weight of the mountain that had been washed away by the silk cloth.

Terry said nothing.

The eon ended. They got through.

The rest of the spoken ceremony was a soft white blur. She found herself in the washroom most times she regained lucidity.

Her fingers had managed to grind the xanax into dust and then grind the dust into the silk of her dress pocket.

Somehow, only Terry clued in to what was going on with her.

Cassandra was uncomfortable feeling true gratitude inside of a church.

The rest of the Grinders parsed her emotionless silence as the necessary boredom of quality coordination.

The rest of the ceremony would be open season – Karma for the Grind – anything up to, and including, category 3. No arrests, no lasting destruction, and no deaths. The Groom had his gifts, and Cassandra had her promise - not the promise she wanted, but the one that the Grinders needed.

Her pupils returned to a human size after some time in the bathroom and she rejoined the Grinders alone until she could get her bearings.

***

If Cassandra noticed the Groom approach Jeff, she would have interceded. But she didn't.

The Groom was very drunk and very happy, and Jeff looked like Mark Cuban in the dim light of the church. He approached Jeff with a business idea, and slowly realized that this wasn't Mark Cuban - this was one of Cassandra's mad geniuses.

Jeff himself was too intoxicated to process the details of the plan, so he nodded along silently and took regular drinks from his pitcher of Jagermeister and orange juice, a mixed drink he invented, that he called a "Jeff".

The Groom, rightfully terrified of the capability of whoever Cassandra might call a mad genius, abruptly ended the conversation. "I can tell this plan isn't worth your time. Sorry for bothering you."

"Oh no worries man. Karma for the Grind!"

The Groom was confused at that phrase but made a note of it. He had no idea what it meant, but he was able to piece together in a few minutes of listening and observing the others and how they talked that this was a cult.

This was a cult.

She had started a cult.

He wasn't surprised.

***

Sooner than the wedding planners had scheduled, the festivities were grinding to a halt - at least the festive part was. The food was gone, the liquor was running out. The limo drivers still outside would soon be falling asleep in their vehicles.

The Grinders had to get moving.

They could abandon the drunk limo driver on the toilet. He could call an Uber.

Cassandra started motioning to wrap things up.

Before they departed, Terry decided that he wanted to give Cassandra a wedding gift, at what he alone was able to figure out was supposed to be *her* wedding.

One last Karma bomb for the road.

In true Cassandra fashion, he put a laxative in the DJ's Bacardi.

Ten minutes later, when the DJ scurried away to deal with it, Terry took over the DJ's station, pausing Chris Brown's *Forever.*

With the Bride and Groom alone in the middle of the dance floor, he replaced it with a special remix of a classic Jimmy Soul song that had been created by an anonymous, miserable kid on the internet, for the sole purpose of ruining weddings.

He changed the password on the DJ's laptop and locked it.

Then he ran.

If you wanna be happy for the rest of your life
Never make a pretty woman your wife
So for my personal point of view
Get an ugly girl to marry you

The DJ was nowhere to be found.

A pretty woman makes her husband look small
And very often causes his downfall
As soon as he marries her then she starts
To do the things that will break his heart

Ruining ceremonies for rich people always seemed to carry no guilt for Terry - someone else's money tree is the perfect place for schadenfreude.

The DJ was on the toilet, helpless, as shrimp came out one end and bacardi came out the other. Matej was on his phone in the next stall, playing candy crush at max volume, preventing the DJ from even knowing what was happening.

In the moment, the DJ was actually very grateful that there was a ridiculous amount of ridiculous noise masking his bodily orchestra.

By this point, the remix was in full swing.

Get an ugly girl to marry you
Get an ugly girl to marry you

The Bride was in tears.

The DJ emerged from the bathroom refreshed, still sweating from his bathroom adventures. He heard the refrain cascading over the angry din of the wedding guests.

Get an ugly girl to marry you
Get an ugly girl to marry you

Get an ugly girl to marry you

He panicked.

Steef, still sober, had clued in to the happenings and predicted the panic. He was waiting by the bathroom door, and he offered the DJ his gardening shears.

Get an ugly girl to marry you
Get an ugly girl to marry you
Get an ugly girl to marry you
Get an ugly girl to marry you

Still drunk, and also feeling some MDMA, the DJ grabbed the shears without thinking, ran to the audio booth, and pruned six figures of audio equipment.

He would not end up being paid for his services.

Cassandra could smile again. She was back. All the xanax in the world couldn't hide it. Her sniffles were cocaine instead of sadness for the rest of the day and the sniffles would continue well into the morning.

She stood in the center of the maelstrom, calm as a greek statue, swaying and taking slow draws from a 40 of jager, feeling the frenetic winds of destruction run through her hair, the sun breaking through the thunderclouds outside, casting a solitary blue and purple beam of light on the bottle through the stained glass.

She stayed in that moment forever, until forever ended again.

***

It was time to leave.

The cardboard wedding guests by now were fully corrugated. They would eventually review the security footage, and the police wouldn't be far behind.

Cassandra deactivated the signal jammer and motioned the Grinders back outside into the category 2 while the song came to an end. The limo drivers would all still be there, mostly, and their gratitude for finally being able to leave would slightly eclipse their collective anger at still being there. They would be tipped handsomely, and everything would be okay.

While the Groom was watching her swaying billowing red in the volcanic winds she had set loose, he stopped trying to convince himself that he never wanted to see her again.

The Grinders stumbled out the church door in confusing fashion, Steef at the front, Cassandra at the tail end.

She stopped at the lavish gift table by the door entry, unguarded, as the bouncer had long ago taken his talents outside to try to make sense of the limousine chaos after the rain had subsided. She gravitated towards a Gucci gift box without blinking, and with all the watchful eyes of the wedding distracted by the DJ's meltdown, she swapped her knockoff Saint Laurents for a pair of Gucci signoria kitten heels, the gift wrap fully resecured and perfectly ribboned.

The Groom alone watched, motionless, while she fucked him one last time.

Nobody would know she had violated anything as long as the Groom kept his mouth shut.

He watched in slow motion as Cassandra pumped her net worth by $2,000 in fifteen seconds at the expense of his beautiful Bride, and he did nothing.

She posed for a second in the boots because she knew he was watching.

He was afraid of her, still, and again. She had a lot of valuable information on him, far more than he had on her, and she was smarter, quicker, and more ruthless than he was.

As Cassandra waltzed away in the new Bride's boots, he couldn't stop thinking that she could run the world someday.

That's why he had to do what he did.

06 - THE MILITARY

The Grinders were fucked.

How did this happen?

Years ago, Mike had thrown his ID documents into a satchel, same as everyone else.

They had to.

It was written in the *Bromeliad*.

No last names.

New identities.

What went wrong?

Mike stared at the satchel on the ground in his bedroom closet and couldn't help but notice that the golden strings were missing.

Unblinking, he slowly picked it up and opened it and confirmed his worst fear – inside the satchel in his closet was the collection of stolen IDs that was supposed to be handed off to the Groom at the wedding ceremony.

What this meant was that the Groom had received, and had forwarded to his Canadian military recruiter contact, the satchel of IDs of the names that once belonged to the Grinders.

In retrospect, Mike realized that keeping the two satchels in the same small bedroom closet might have been a mistake.

But he had checked. And double checked. And triple checked.

At least he thought he did.

This shouldn't have happened.

No matter how hard he meditated on it, he couldn't figure out what had gone wrong. The satchel was labeled clearly. He remembered double checking the contents before he made the handoff to Cassandra.

Maybe he just dreamed it.

But if it wasn't him who fucked up, his next biggest hunch was that someone had broken into his apartment and made the switch.

But as far as he could tell, nobody outside of the Grinders had even clued into their mission yet. They couldn't possibly have made any enemies on a large enough scale to facilitate this level of blowback. Nobody would seek revenge to this degree for getting laxatives put into their coffee. Nobody knew who they were. Nobody cared who they were.

Cassandra wouldn't have made this mistake - an Archon doesn't make mistakes.

Either he'd fucked up, or someone very powerful wanted them to fuck up. Both options terrified him. He never fucks up, and he had no idea who wanted them to fuck up.

Mike turned to the internet for answers, but found himself stuck on an empty search engine, and could only stare at the dead pixel on the screen.

At a low point, Mike grew desperate.

Lise had been at the apartment the entire time he was gone, and appeared frazzled on his return, but being a cat, she could not effectively communicate to him what she might have witnessed.

Mike tried a workaround – over the years, he had picked up on the cat's affinity for the occult, and going insane, at his wit's end, out of marbles, he tried an ouija board session. But the two of them together, with Mike's hand on the planchette and Lise's paw on top, only managed to get a single word repeating.

M E O W

Incredibly frustrated, but not wanting to show it in front of the cat, he quietly chalked the experience up to his own unconscious suggestion moving his planchette hand, and he put the ouija board back in the closet.

Anyways, they had already received the order from their future commanding officer – they were going to have to serve.

Up north.

Somewhere with access to personnel files, but far from combat.

Just what they asked for.

It was a 17 hour plane journey from Vancouver to Baffin Island and then a seven hour bus ride to the remote twin outposts where the Grinders would be serving for six months.

4,000 kilometers.

Nobody was happy.

The chartered flights and the bus ride were provided by private contractors, which meant that Mike had the freedom to bring Lise up north, and Aliya had the freedom to bring all the goodies she wanted. And she took that freedom seriously. She had six months worth of amphetamines alone, and enough sedatives and benzoates to bring down Sauron.

Lise was kept in the cargo areas, sedated; Mike, shunned by the rest of the Grinders for his colossal fuckup, would sit in isolation for the journey and eat drugs by himself to try to forget.

***

As a bit of a back story: One of the revenue schemes that the Grinders had developed - Nick's idea - was to purchase stolen identities in bulk, on the cheap, for pennies on the dollar, on the dark web or worse, and then submit them to crooked military recruiters for a cut of the referral fees. Depending on the country, and the prestige of the position being recruited, the profit for the Grinders could be up to $5000 for a single referral.

When Nick first proposed the plan, the other Grinders wanted to saw his head off.

In a Karmic sense, they believed the degree of torment that arises from serving in a military was far too acute, devastating and singular to be optimal for the Grind; military service has a tendency to put an abrupt end to human potential. They felt that unawakened Soldiers of the *Bromeliad*, these sponges of suffering, were most effective when not serving as actual soldiers, but rather living normal lives, maintaining their healthy suffering-sponge form.

But before they could strap him down and retrieve the bone saw, Nick explained that he could connect the Grinders with specific recruiters that he knew, also from the dark web, who simply wanted to hit their recruitment quotas and rake in the fat bonuses.

Nobody on any level of the scam had any interest in actually supplying the military with fresh corpses.

The recruiters knew that the involuntary recruits would usually raise a fuss – the only recruits who would ever get around to serving real time would be the ones put into administrative type desk jobs, pushing paper, a hundred miles from battle.

The logistical complications that arose from this bureaucratic confusion would cost millions of dollars. Laywers, administrators, high ranking military officials, corporate liaisons, stock brokers, journalists, all sorts of coordinated clerical efforts across the planet, all wasting their valuable time and professional resources so that the Grinders could walk away with pocket change.

The final form of what the Grinders built on the back of Nick's idea was an imprecise but reliable system for thorough dissemination of chaos, with an impressive radius, that resulted in almost no destruction of individual human potential. This generated category 4 Karma bombs quite often, with an uncharacteristic lack of risk of escalation to category 5, suppressed by impenetrable global bureaucracy and its tragic lust for the status quo.

And by generating a profit, their true purpose was laundered past any reasonable detection. Nobody would wise up to their mission. If the actions of the Grinders ever came into question, they were just in it for the money.

They drew it up perfectly.

Gradually the scope widened, and they learned the inner workings of these military organizations, and they got quicker and more efficient. It became their primary ongoing Karma generation project: infiltrating international military operations of sprawling hegemonies surreptitiously, and stuffing them with bureaucratic delays and complications, which Nick quietly developed into a wider principle of direct-action distributed suffering (DADS).

Eventually, growing bored with the oppressive, repetitive bureaucracy of the DADS operation, Cassandra hatched a plan wherein her generational talent for manipulating people would combine with Mike's generational talent for manipulating technology. And they could make it work from the existing reservoir of stolen IDs.

Now, Mike was a very talented hacker. He could take one or two pieces of government information on a target – usually purchased en masse from the dark web, and then manually put into an aggregate document by Mike himself - and more often than not, he could track down the IP address of their home computer and the GPS location of their smartphone in less than a day.

Mike cast a very wide net. There were so many potential targets that, if he couldn't find a perfect victim, if there was anyone that didn't check every single psychological box that the Grinders needed, or if he came up one piece of information short of a puzzle, he could afford to shrug and move on to the next one.

Once he obtained a target's IP address, Mike could use his personally developed hacking tools to take over their computer's camera and microphone, record the intimate moments of their life, and use the evidence generated that way for blackmail, manipulation, extortion, and what not.

He knew his way around the inner workings of anyone's personal electronics.

And obviously, Cassandra knew her way around the inner workings of anyone's psyche.

Mike and Cassandra working together were a force of nature.

A hurricane.

An individually monogrammed tsunami that nobody else on the planet could even detect.

The invincible two-headed demon of the information age.

Cassandra split the targets into two categories – 'Moneys' and 'Poors'.

'Moneys' were people understood to own cryptocurrency – this enabled her to receive payment via extortion without being traced.

'Poors' would serve in the military, as is tradition.

It wasn't uncommon for the targets to believe that the experience was playing out as a psychotic delusion.

It wasn't uncommon for the targets to suffer from legitimate psychotic delusions for the days, weeks, months and years following the experience.

But Cassandra and Mike wouldn't keep their hooks in the targets forever. They just needed the targets to gain the trust of the department they served, gain access, collect some sensitive data, and pass it along, encrypted, to the Grinders. After they received the one-time package of data, Cassandra would disappear from behind the curtain, and the targets were free to abdicate their national duties.

It would take a while for the targets to figure that out, and by the time they did, it was absolutely impossible for the targets to find out who was responsible.

But that didn't matter.

After being soft-abandoned, the targets would be so relieved to have the demon out of their lives that they wouldn't even consider trying to exact any sense of personal justice.

But this invincible two-headed demon of the information age

wouldn't be gone wholesale right away.

The targets were never fully certain that they had actually been abandoned. The experience would chip away at their sanity for a long time. It was designed that way. The memory of the past and the fear of the future would torch them from the backburner of consciousness. It would put them on a permanent light roast until they were ready for death.

But they were never in any real danger.

Karma for the Grind.

This side project was called Mike-orchestrated manipulation suffering (MOMS).

Unfortunately, this time, the technological limitations of their military setup would prevent them from being able to perform any extortion for the six months they were stationed in the Arctic.

The DADS and MOMS projects were global and light as a feather, and the Grinders used the projects carefully, sparingly, never being obvious enough in enough places at once for anyone to be able to piece anything together.

They felt like elves in satan's workshop.

God mode, if God was slightly less of an asshole.

But now it was the Grinders serving, so this time was different.

The Grinders couldn't allow lawyers in.

Their fingerprints were all over this, and they were guaranteed to be caught if they defended themselves and pulled out of the assignment.

They had to serve.

Back when Cassandra originally handed the satchel of IDs

to the Groom at the wedding, the hope was that, once the puppets were in place, up north, Cassandra and Mike could use the MOMS project to get them to scrape sensitive Canadian military data and then forward it to Mike for processing. As per routine, the puppets would then be abandoned up north, much like the lithium exploration camp that the twin outposts were originally built to observe and protect.

After a brief period of rage, the Archon decided that the path of least resistance was to eat the six months and be done with the DADS project forever.

They had to be bulletproof, and this was no longer bulletproof.

They could not have a single lawyer look at them while they were up there.

No lawyers.

***

As the blue bus carried the exhausted Grinders further north from Iqaluit's international airport to the twin outposts, Mike watched out the window and wondered why there were no trees; as the blankets of moss and the dwarf shrubs started numbering less and less, he couldn't bring himself to look away as the green of the plants disappeared and left only naked roots drenched in winter crystals.

He sat alone at the front of the bus as the rest of the Grinders crowded together in the back, their blood thinned by desperate levels of stimulants, bolstered by satellite internet, working feverishly, scanning every bend of every letter of every piece of information they could think about thinking about for that part of the world - military regulations, regional geography, topography, geology and psychology, weather patterns, supply contracts, burned churches, departmental hardware buying and software spending, exploration and warfare, abandoned corporations and ghost towns, resource extraction, strip mines and orphan wells, folklore and territorial treaties, residential schools and cemeteries, flora, fauna, loopholes and massacres.

They needed to find something. Anything to mitigate the dread of being stuck on a frozen island for a half a year.

Anything to advance their cause – their mission.

They were coming up empty.

They had already figured out ten minutes into the plane ride that they would still be able to scrape the confidential information they originally wanted. But that would only take them a few minutes after they arrived at their deployment.

And of course, there would be opportunities to generate and distribute Karma. But that was always there. They didn't need to go up north for that.

They couldn't find anything else.

***

About an hour into the bus ride from the airport, the bus slowed down to carefully traverse a several-kilometer stretch of uneven rocky mud. About 30 minutes into the treacherous road, Mike was snapped out of his suicidal reverie by the vision of a sudden road repair worker in full reflective gear, shoveling half-frozen mud, alone.

The road worker was moving slowly. Not a shred of urgency.

He was smiling.

He was singing to himself.

Why was he smiling?

What could he possibly be singing about?

He was the only human being that they would witness for an hour in either direction, pouring himself fully into a Sisyphean task that Mike couldn't even fathom.

Mike looked behind him to the back of the blue bus and realized that he was the only Grinder who noticed the road worker.

He thought to himself that it would take this man years to finish this work alone.

Maybe decades.

Maybe longer.

Maybe the outpost assignment wasn't so bad.

Mike felt a tinge of connection to the road worker and let a tiny bit of relief wash over him, and it was enough for him to bust out his laptop and quietly start working on the same discovery project as the rest of the Grinders.

And after an hour of utilizing his unique hacker skillset and knowledge base, he found something.

Here's what he figured out:

As anyone could imagine, it's a bit of a challenge to convince lucid, self-respecting human beings to decide, in a relatively free and somewhat democratic country, to uproot themselves, abandoning their friends, families, drug dealers and careers, hopes, dreams and hockey teams, and take root in an antitropical tundra where the roots don't penetrate the soil.

The Canadian government recognized this and decided to issue a cost of living allowance to anyone bad enough at personal calculus that they would believe this exchange could bring them into balance.

The general spirit behind this living allowance is that the

Canadian government recognizes that, while almost anyone living that deep into the tundra will go insane with loneliness, and a jar of peanut butter will now cost more than your car, bi-weekly payments adding up to $16,008 per year will help you get over it.

They drew it up perfectly.

Anyways, in the encroaching digital age, the government of Nunavut was, naturally, having tremendous difficulty tracking down young, educated software developers to move that far north, even with the generous bi-weekly bonus of $307.85.

Except for one.

Brad Marchand, a scared, lonely man-child who chose a career in software development because his enterprising, capable, and abusive older brother Patrice chose a career in software development.

In order to get his final grade at Douglas College upgraded to a lower end D+, this shell of a man performed unspeakable acts on the severely unqualified, self-taught, and part-time programming teacher, later fired for gross misconduct, who was only filling in for a single semester for a far more qualified teacher on maternity leave.

Back up north.

When nobody wants to live or work somewhere, the quality of labor suffers, and so does the quality of supervision.

When the code was being written, from scratch, unsupervised, primarily from a patchwork of copy/pastes from StackOverflow, alongside a handwritten, well-intentioned post-it note demanding that the programmer should try to accommodate for regional languages, he cross-referenced the hard-coded range of acceptable name inputs against a locally gathered brochure featuring Inuktitut syllabics, and on his light-up gaming keyboard, powered by his fear of being accused of racism against the locals, he wrote a piece of code that automatically processed, and approved, in the *Your Name* section, any application that featured any letter, number, grammatical symbol, or Swedish diacritic that closely resembled any letter of the Inuktitut alphabet, as long as the social insurance number attached to the application form was unique.

The applications themselves were subject to the same total lack of human attention and oversight as the coding.

The existence of this application was considered a bureaucratic necessity, for the two minutes it was ever considered. It was a loose end, a requirement in order to be able to incorporate the doomed lithium mining exploration camps in the area. When the first draft of the application software was submitted for review and correction, it was approved without review, and implemented within an hour at the single workstation where it would be installed, and then the workstation was forgotten, left in a closet in an unlit corridor of the less populated of the twin remote outposts.

No human eyes ever reviewed any stage of this process.

The software alone accepted and processed the applications, which could be registered once per day as long as they came from an Inuktitut-approximate location. VPN falsifying was impossible, as it was subject to direct immediate satellite verification before it reviewed the form inputs. So now anyone with an immediately provable GPS location, unique to a registered social insurance number – and they had a lot of social insurance numbers to work with - located within the specific area, requesting the Nunavut living allowance, combined with any presence of Inuktitut syllabic adjacent symbols, was given immediate approval.

Brad, at least, had the wherewithal to install a single meager failsafe, which was that only one entry per day could be processed, for the entire program, for the entire territory of Nunavut. This was installed an hour before the software shipped out, and would have ultimately been unnecessary, considering that in the twelve years that the program was installed, nobody had ever applied for the benefit in that region.

This was the bureaucreatic function that lived at the outpost at 33 Gata Road.

Brad himself would have applied for the benefit, but right after the software was submitted and approved, he shot himself in the head.

His rotting corpse wouldn't be discovered for weeks. He had left a suicide note in what he thought was legible Inuktitut, but it was confirmed by a local fisherman to be utter nonsense.

The tragic story moved Mike to the verge of tears, and he decided right then and there that he'd rather be like the road worker than end up like Brad. He sheepishly made his way to the back of the blue bus and offered to perform all paperwork for every Grinder for the entire six month assignment, and they unanimously accepted his apology.

He knew there was always a balance for the Grinders to consider when they contemplated any act of spiritual terrorism – in this situation, they were too cold, too tired, too angry, and they hated paperwork more than they wanted to grind Karma.

But the equation balanced for Mike.

He knew that with the help of Aliya, the resident pharmacist, he would be able work more than 20 hours a day, typing his fingers raw, eroding the letters from his keyboard, sometimes taking a measure to grind his teeth and stare at the dead pixel on the screen of his laptop.

Mike was back.

And once he was back, he told them all about the tragic misadventures of Brad, the single worst programmer in Canadian history.

He then explained that every day the Grinders were there, they could sign up for one additional perpetual living allowance that would go on accumulating and direct-depositing as long as they could still be pinged by the GPS satellite in verified Inuktitut territory on the days of the deposits.

He explained that after six months, they would be pulling in $4,000 weekly, and that amount would only go up from there, forever.

During the remainder of the ride, they each quietly figured out that Cassandra, equipped with this knowledge, would assign a Disciple to stay posted there permanently after the six month assignment was completed.

They all hoped it wouldn't be them.

Karma for the Grind, sure, but, come on.

...it was probably going to be Matej.

***

The second purpose of this corner of the world, if we're not counting the eternal beauty of quiet, peaceful desolation coupled with the nightly promise of naked galaxies unpolluted by city lights, and the regular occurrence of aurora borealis, was a series of shell companies, registered in the Turks & Caicos, with unknowable actual ownership, that forced the mining exploration camp to stay open, and stay "exploring"

– discovered by Jeff, accidentally revealed to him by a drunk options trader during his halcyon days in cryptocurrency.

The easily corruptible lab results, suggesting or denying the potential for a lithium deposit of any size, was instrumental in manipulating international lithium stocks.

The corruption was untraceable as long as the shell corporation continued reincorporating every week, as it took more than a week to process the information requests that might get them discovered.

The sins of the past washed away on automation by the structured incompetence of the high priests of bureaucracy.

It was an open secret in the upper, upper echelons of the finance world.

Nobody could do anything about it.

Everyone just wished they were in on it.

This was the function that lived at the outpost at 22 Gata Road.

***

About ten minutes before they landed at the twin outposts, Miles uncovered a third quirk after seeing a road sign and researching the road name.

The solitary road – Gata Road – was classified as cycling infrastructure in order to get mountains of funding from the federal government.

This scam went unspoiled, as everyone involved had an unspoken agreement to split the funding instead of visiting the frozen hell for inspections or review or any sort of maintenance or upgrades to quality of life.

Eyes on the operation meant the operation collapsed.

No lawyers.

Nobody could figure out how this was useful, and so after a hearty round of "shut the fuck up, Miles", he had the presence of mind to shut the fuck up.

Still, Cassandra banked the information, in case she ever wanted to extort one of the government officials involved in the scam.

She didn't tell Miles. She preferred to let him languish.

Karma for the Grind.

***

Cassandra was the last person off the bus, desperately hoping that their situation was a misunderstanding or a hologram or a fun bit of psychosis from the drugs she had been taking very enthusiastically, more and more enthusiastically as they got further north.

Her standard issue extreme cold weather boots, encasing her ankles comfortably in velcro, made no print in the permafrost, even when she tried kicking.

They were here, they were doing this.

After they stepped out from the warmth of the blue bus, they huddled like stray animals and didn't have to wait very long for the present occupants of the outposts to make themselves known.

The Grinders never learned their names.

It didn't matter.

The first guard to greet them was wordless, and he carried a grim efficiency as he loaded their personal effects onto the bus.

The second guard stayed right outside the bus for a brief period, perhaps out of pity, but also to hand off the key ring that would open the various doors and junction boxes, which for some reason was a large, brass ring with cartoonishly large individual keys.

During the handoff, the second guard held securely onto the brass ring and made extended eye contact with Miles who would have liked to hold onto the keys himself.

The guard refused to let go for an uncomfortable amount of time. There was a macabre stillness to him as though he had been witness to a massacre.

He spoke slowly, "you should not be here," still holding onto the keys.

Miles took a few seconds to reply. "How could you know that?" He was slightly offended and asking sincerely. "I haven't met you yet."

The guard suddenly froze even stiffer.

He stopped breathing.

His eyes were white amulets, unblinking, rigid.

Shell shock.

He let go of the keys and ran onto the bus with a sudden quickness that his snow suit shouldn't have allowed for.

Miles turned his head down the path to the outposts expecting several other soldiers, saw nobody else, and grew concerned. He shouted in the direction of the bus, "Why are there only two of you?" to total silence. His words hung in the air and fell unanswered to the tundra.

The door to the blue bus slammed shut, and the Grinders could all hear discordant, panicked shouting from its three occupants as it sped off twice as fast as it had arrived.

Miles, distracted by the alien welching sound of screeching tires on sloppy permafrost, dropped the brass ring, and the large keys landed on each other, loudly and once, like the clink of a prison door.

***

Mike was the first person to get set up and working.

He needed a distraction. He couldn't take his mind off the dead pixel.

It shouldn't be there.

For the first couple of days, he was the only one doing anything.

Sometimes he would shovel mystery pills into his mouth to try to lighten the colors of his death trance, but in these unfamiliar states of randomized awareness, he would find himself still unable to deviate from the pixel, only finding new flavors of frustration, and shiny new mental prisons that nobody had ever encountered. Every time he took a pill to escape a mental prison, he was rounded up into a new one. After a while, he started to enjoy it.

He was in the same room with everyone, but he wore headphones and worked alone in his shame, and so he would typically only be blessed with respite when Lise would gracefully paw something off his desk, shattering the grip the pixel had on him. He would pay her back with scratches and then resume hammering the keys like Mozart.

Mike would have collapsed in on that dead pixel without Lise checking in every now and then.

And this surge towards collapse wasn't helped by the fact that

Mike had to abandon the hundreds and hundreds of hours of work he'd put into building the DADS project.

That same realization gradually percolated to the rest of the Grinders, and they all quietly made peace with it.

They had to let go of DADS once and for all.

***

This mandatory downtime gave them some room to breathe, with no excuses not to build documents of network structures from the data they already had, making connections on top of connections – this was effectively creating a combination think tank/incubator of an eclectic potpourri of mad geniuses, under full control of Cassandra, completely isolated, with no need for incentives because there was no hope for escape.

And the mandatory downtime also gave the Grinders free time to develop, propose and execute, if approved, other campaigns, provided that they did not impede on the ambitions of the Archon.

At the moment, they all had ideas in development, but none of the ideas were close to maturity.

Except for one.

Aliya, specifically, wanted permanent access to the government's newly established cocaine rehabilitation program, along with its fully-documented network of patients and assigned social workers.

She had designs on an enterprise of suffering of her own, hopefully blessed by the Archon, fingers crossed, in which she would build local networks of those unawakened addicts, and control them from the outside, maximizing their suffering, closely monitoring so as to not irreversibly torpedo their human potential.

She had attended some meetings, done some readings, come up with some theories, and performed some test runs on her own time.

She was going to push the addiction button as hard as she could without ever breaking the console, with her purpose being to test the outer limits of compassionate human destruction.

She figured that most coke dealers were lazy.

Once a coke habit was established, it had a tendency to stick around in perpetuity until disturbed from the outside. And coke dealers usually had enough clientele that they didn't need to go the extra mile and hang on to *all* of them.

Generating money from the addicts was the only concern of the typical dealer, which was the source of the laziness. A coke dealer who goes from 25 down to 23 clients in a week's time is not going to study the charts to scramble to get them back.

Aliya had a different imperative. A greater purpose. She was saving their souls, one gram at a time. She was sending them to an incredible next life. And she was helping them arrive sooner. She had an undefeateable sense of righteousness that nobody could take away. She was going to monitor them and maximize the reach of the narcotic, in every corner of their lives.

She was satan's social worker.

And it was for a good cause.

Large scale distributed Karmic generation.

She would be farming future paradise for all children of the *Bromeliad*.

She would usher in a golden age of golden ages as far as the Cosmos would allow. And when the golden ages would end, they would only be making way for something greater than gold.

And of course, this chemically induced cognitive behavioural manipulation had a ton of overlap with her other research, which until recently had been chiefly confined to a single enthusiastic test subject, and, at the moment, was confined to a cluster of nerds in a small room tweaking on adderall.

Still, she didn't consider her work with adderall to be useless. Until now, she figured, all the important narcotic work in all the unspoken encyclopedias of witchcraft had been confined to psychoactive drugs that open up the mind to make it soft and pliable. Nobody was working with man-made zombie pills.

This was vital work.

This was bleeding edge.

The way she saw it, witch doctors get rid of curses, and she couldn't figure out what disqualified ADHD, anxiety and depression from the Great List of Curses. They fucking felt like curses. Or maybe we just finally had names for these millennium-old situations of executive dysfunction and personal failure, the curing of which would have come under her purview for any century up until this one.

There are no records of treating depression with eye of newt. The handwritten books upon books of spells have almost nothing about popping a pill to enlarge your focus. There was no zoloft in Salem. Maybe they could have used some.

And of course, in addition to the Karma and the research, there was the money. The western hemisphere has a rich and well documented history of cocaine distribution being highly profitable.

She drew it up perfectly.

She had been working on her pitch for days and she had been

working on her confidence all morning, always brought back into a feeling of righteousness by her genuine conviction that this served the greater purpose.

She waited until Cassandra was alone in the kitchen and she locked the door behind her to ensure the conversation would remain private.

"That's for privacy, don't worry, I'm not gonna kill you."

"I... didn't think you were going to kill me. But thank you for confirming. What's up?"

"So you know the DADS right?"

Cassandra slipped into a pocket of remembering her own dad. "Huh? What dads?"

"Nick's thing."

"Nick has two dads?"

"Sorry. D-A-D-S. Nick's project. Something something distributed suffering."

Cassandra snapped back to reality. "Right. Yeah. Well, he puts it into spreadsheets, yeah."

"I have an idea and I want your blessing on it."

There was a polite knock on the door. Aliya looked nervously at the doorknob and decided to keep moving forward with her pitch, inching closer to Cassandra, so she could speak quietly without being heard on the other side.

"When we get back to civilization I want to run a relapse network."

"Don't you already do that? Kinda?"

"I sell the drugs to people, yeah, but I think I can do more to keep them on it."

"Don't the drugs already take care of that part for ya?"

"For the most part yeah, but, I've been doing research."

Cassandra raised an eyebrow. "Research?"

"Brain research." She paused for a second to find some more syllables so that Cassandra would know that she was serious. "Neurological research. The intersection of neuroplasticity and addiction."

Cassandra didn't speak. She didn't know what some of these words meant, but if she stayed quiet, Aliya would keep nervously talking until something was said that she could latch onto.

"No news. No outside news. Just textbooks."

Cassandra smiled and nodded.

The knocking on the kitchen door intensified and Aliya got impatient. "WHAT?"

"I NEED TO USE THE BATHROOM," said a frantic Kevin from the other side.

Cassandra had had enough. "THIS IS THE KITCHEN."

"OH! THANK YOU!"

Aliya unlocked the door. "Kev! Wait, can you help me with something first?"

Kevin stayed at the doorway. Aliya reached into her pocket and pulled out a small pile of empty dimebags, accidentally-on-purpose spilling them on the ground. "Oh. Oh no. Can you be a dear and help me with these first?"

"Oh, yeah, no problem." Kevin scooped them up in a sloppy pile with two hands, sniffled, and handed them to Aliya. "Since I'm going to the bathroom anyways, do you have any..."

Aliya procured a baggie with a gram of coke from a hidden pocket on the inside of the neck part of her black turtleneck and handed it to him. "Always."

"What did you need me for?"

"I forget. Go to the bathroom!"

Kevin scampered down the hall with his reward and Cassandra tilted her head. "What just happened here?"

"Well that presentation was unplanned, but I think you can already see what I was trying to do. For anyone deep in addiction, doesn't matter what, just even seeing a dimebag of any kind, with any substance staining the inside. That trips it. Even the empty bags do it almost every time. Their whole existence takes a bullet train to the creamy nougat center of their brain where the drug relationship lives, and then they want to spend some time there. And their number one priority in that world becomes locating the nearest provider of the drug and getting the drug from that provider."

"That's fucking evil." Cassandra's eyes went wide. "I like it. Karma for the Grind, right? Does it work for every kind of zip loc bag?"

"Well not sandwich bags. It's an association thing. Has to be the type of bag they're used to seeing. And it can be any shape. Even those ones you see on the ground that have been split open and licked to death."

Cassandra couldn't remember the last time she was split open and licked to death. "I like this so far."

"So I follow my people around – the ones who have strayed from the light. And I drop a pack of these outside a Narcotics Anonymous meeting right before it ends. Say I've got 3 or 4 people in the meeting. They see the baggies on the ground. My phone lights up. And I'm right around the corner."

"Well. Aliya, you had my curiosity, but now you have my attention." Cassandra's eyes turned into dollar signs. "That's a few hundred for maybe fifteen minutes of work."

"Yup but that's only part of it."

"Oh, do go on."

"Thanks to Mike I'm tracking their smartphones. He just has to come with me for one ride and he goes in through their phone's wifi and installs location tracking. Invisible to them." Aliya was pacing around and moving her arms like she was introducing a new iPhone. "I got a location tracking program that tells me when they are within 50 meters of a Narcotics Anonymous center, so I can see when they go back to meetings. Any time I get this sound, I have one hour to get the dimebags in place." Aliya opened her phone and played the ESPN fantasy sports notification. "It's the most wonderful sound in the world."

Cassandra laughed. "I don't wanna interrupt the presentation but I think you Pavlov'd yourself. Sorry. Keep going. This is good stuff."

"Yeah, well, it's for a good cause. Anyways. Even with a 50% relapse rate from this strategy, we're probably seeing more than double profits. And I don't know the exact math but, probably double suffering."

"Karma for the Grind," Cassandra reminded herself.

"Karma for the Grind. Anyways, I also thought of this part. I know the grade of Karma bomb is a consistently repeating category 2 or 3 for coke addicts, and rippling out into a consistent 1 or 2 for their loved ones. But I thought of something more."

"More Karma? Or more money?"

"The people who run these meetings are going to notice a lot more relapsing. That's a wider network of suffering."

"And those guys who run the meetings are former addicts themselves, I bet."

"Almost always. I think you can already see where I'm going with this. If their meetings dwindle from 30 to 20 to 5 to zero, that's going to make them think about..."

Cassandra felt a chill up her spine. "Wow."

Cassandra looked impressed. Aliya thought for a minute about mentioning the notes. But this was probably enough. "So, do I have your blessing, Archon?"

"Your Archon says yes. Big time."

Aliya smiled and went to the bathroom to hand Kevin another dimebag. She tossed it under the door and he picked it up instantly. "Thanks Kev."

"For what?"

"Just shut up and do your coke."

"Yes sir!"

She felt at the fabric on her turtleneck. She was out of coke. It was minus-20 outside and she had to re-up at her duffel bag at the other outpost.

She bundled up in multiple thermal layers and sighed. It was a fifteen minute walk to the other outpost, and while she liked Matej, she didn't want to get trapped in a conversation with him. He was quite alone out there and he would probably talk her ear off. She waited by the door twiddling her thumbs until Matej would be going out on his scheduled patrol, and right as she was leaving, Lise leapt up onto her shoulder like a familiar, and meowed. Somehow Aliya knew that Lise wanted to come along for the walk, so the two of them prowled out together into the permafrost.

***

Fifteen minutes later, Aliya arrived alone at the outpost – Lise had jumped off her shoulder on the walk over, completely captivated with some happenings in a bush that they were passing by.

Lise was a survivor. She would be fine.

Aliya didn't think twice about it.

She made her way to the storage room with her duffel bag full of their entire supply of everything, and couldn't help but notice that the zipper to the bag was open and the supplies had clearly been rummaged through.

Panicking, she did a quick inventory.

Coke, all there.

Fent, all there.

Xans, all there.

Addys, all there.

Shrooms....missing. All of them, gone.

Seven sandwich bags.

This didn't make sense. This was Matej's outpost. His only job was to patrol 22 Gata Road. There wasn't anyone else there. Matej didn't use drugs. He barely drank, and he was terrible at drinking.

Either way, he wasn't supposed to take anything without asking her. She kept a tight inventory, and she meted out substances very conscientiously. She studied contraindications and knew the Grinders' health issues and dietary limitations like they were her own.

She took this shit seriously.

But Aliya felt a healthy dose of pity for Matej in general, knowing he had had a sheltered upbringing, a semi-charmed life in every sense, and also knowing that he was a bit of a whipping boy for the Grinders. She always believed that to be kind of unfair.

The shrooms would do him some good.

She smiled, deposited the drugs she needed into her magical bag, and started walking back to the main outpost.

On her way back, a silent, frazzled-looking Lise hopped back on her shoulder, and her claws gripped Aliya's thermal jacket so hard that they tore through and pierced her skin.

"Meow?"

Lise didn't respond.

"Meoowww?"

Nothing.

Poor girl.

Aliya pet Lise to comfort her until she retracted her claws and they continued down the path.

When she got back, she let the Grinders know that Matej was doing alright.

***

When the solitary patrol was originally offered, which was a few minutes after the blue bus sped off, Matej had jumped at the opportunity to take the assignment. Nobody else wanted it. They were going to foist it on him anyways.

The assignment demanded only that the Grinders needed one solitary person to physically inhabit the outpost in order to maintain adherence to bureaucratic regulations. The remoteness, on top of the original remoteness, and the near-total void of any real responsibilities, gave Matej an opportunity to spend time on his true passion, candy crush. Grinding pixels.

This would also give everyone an opportunity to get rolling on the group chat.

***

11:12am [MaTej] how many of us are here
11:22am [MaTej] which one is the right address
11:22am [Nick] 22
11:23am [MaTej] ??
11:25am [Nick] ???
11:27am [MaTej] ????
11:29am [Nick] ?????
11:35am [MaTej] wtf
11:37am [steef] ??????
11:38am [MaTej] wait
11:38am [MaTej] y are u even here steff
11:39am [MaTej] @Steef
11:40am [MaTej] you have a last name still your i.d. Wouldnt of been in the bag
11:54am [steef] cassandra said IDs in the bag
11:54am [steef] i just went along with it
11:57am [Nick] well that was fucking stupid
11:59am [steef] no kidding

***

The Grinders, minus only Matej, were all stuffed into a

single office, meant originally for eight people, presently entertaining thirteen and a half. Fortunately, they were able to scavenge just enough workstation computers for everyone.

After the jet lag and depression passed, Miles got to work installing antivirus software and running disk defragmenter on each one.

Looking at his computer, not wanting to turn it on, he started fingerdrumming on his desk. Seeking inspiration, he glanced alternately at his twin empty inboxes. Mining camp. Admin overflow. He built up a rhythm. Then he started rapping.

I'm at the mining camp
I'm admin overflow
I'm at the combination mining camp and overflow

Kevin's drumming was not keeping rhythm with his rapping. Lise, agitated by this, started pawing at his drumstick double fingers. Kevin stopped drumming to scratch Lise for a second before he reached further inspiration. "Hey do you guys wanna get some taco bell?" his pupils were as wide as his eyes and his eyes were as wide as his stomach.

"Kevin. We're in Iqaluit." Aliya started looking in her purse for a consolation prize to give him when it dawned on him that they wouldn't be going to taco bell for a few months. "The nearest taco bell is 400 miles."

Miles turned his attention away from disk defragmenter. "Huh?"

"No, I, fuck. The unit of distance. Not you."

Miles snapped. "Just fucking say kilometers. Kilometers. We're in Canada. We have always been in Canada."

"But then you've won. And Miles never wins."

"I'd walk it." Kevin meant it. He stopped scratching Lise, and she grew upset from the lack of attention. She knocked the empty admin overflow inbox off of Kevin's desk.

aLan was trying to read *Leaves of Grass* nearby and was getting annoyed. "I fucking hate cats."

Cassandra quiet shouted. "The fuck did you say?"

"I said cats. Cats."

She settled down. "OK. Never use that nick."

Nick jolted awake. "What?"

"Nick. Name."

"Cassandra?"

"Damn right."

"Huh?"

"It's actually eight."

"Ate what?"

"Tacos."

"The number. Eight."

"Hundred. Miles."

"What?" asked Miles.

"To taco bell!"

"KILOMETERS." Miles stabbed his desk with a pencil, snapping it in half, startling Lise, who knocked the empty mining camp inbox off Kevin's desk which ended the conversation with a factory plastic thud.

Everyone who was still paying attention immediately looked at aLan and waited for him to react, but he gritted his teeth and sidestepped the rage. "Hey Roman, we should probably get a patrol done, eh?"

Roman, with his hand on his chin, posited, "Can we count walking to taco bell as a patrol?"

"Learn to swim."

"You guys are so god damn stupid it hurts." Aliya reached into her bag for something for herself and ate three of them. She didn't know what she grabbed. It would be a fun surprise.

"It would be cold by the time you get back anyways." Nick was still trying to be helpful.

"I'm gonna stab you."

He laughed, because it was safer than crying. "Yeah, probably."

"Yeah anyways aLan. Patrol's a good idea." Roman adjusted in his chair. "You've been around these other guys too much, just sittin'. It's about time you start focusing on ... roamin."

Gerg stood up and exploded. "Oh come ON. I was saving that one."

"Early bird gets the worm, bitch."

"You're not even a bird."

Miles returned to the zen of disk defragmenter as Cassandra thundered back into the fracas and ended the encroaching wordplay parade before it could get started. "Save yourself, asshole."

Gerg was resigned to a whimper. "I thought of it like 2 minutes into the bus ride." He threw his corded computer mouse towards the ground and it dangled.

Alan did the same with *Leaves of Grass*.

He and Roman put on their boots, grabbed their guns, and got to walking.

***

Roman knew aLan was agitated from being in the cramped room and so he allowed the first half hour of the patrol to go on in therapeutic silence.

Once they adjusted to the hostile temperature under the countless layers of thermal clothing, they both thought the plants that managed to survive in the overwhelming desolation were actually quite beautiful.

Neither of them mentioned it.

Roman felt a shift in the climate and hoped to spark a real conversation.

Making sure that aLan could see the caution in his breath, he took a chance. "Hey, have you ever..."

aLan was happy for a reprieve from the silence. "What's up man?"

"Have you ever thought about how we do these things to hurt ourselves, to generate Karma for next lives and what not, but, like..." he knew he had to choose his words carefully. He was walking on a tightrope on fire, carrying in his hands the heart of everything they believed they believed in. "Do you... experience happiness when you realize the suffering is leading to future happiness?"

aLan knew nobody was watching or listening. He still took a minute. "Gotta be honest. No."

Roman started to walk with less confidence.

aLan realized for a moment that he cared more about Roman as a friend than he did about the Grind. In that moment. Only in that moment. As long as nobody ever found out.

"Sorry. I just dont talk about this stuff a lot. Or ever. I don't let myself think about that much. You know why." aLan gestured up to the sky, suggesting the Angels of the *Bromeliad*, or whatever was above the Angels, who they might never know by name. "Yeah, that happens a lot."

Side by side, they matched each others' pace, and they stayed slow. There was a comfortable silence in their breaths as they both sunk into the moment.

"What do you make of it?"

"I think I figured it out."

aLan looked over and then quickly looked back.

"I was getting so fucked up over it but then I suddenly realized on the toilet,"

"Don't tell me it was the..."

"Yep. I wiped my ass with *Leaves of Grass*. It fucking works, I'm telling you. See I was so distraught over not actually suffering from the suffering and then I realized that I was... once again..."

"Suffering!"

aLan could see the smile in Roman's breath.

"It's suffering all the way down! Up? Down?"

"I haven't been able to wrap my mind around that one yet."

There was a silence for the rest of their slow paced walk in the tundra, guns loaded but not aimed, fingers near the triggers but further and further away the more they talked, leaving a bent in the frozen weeds they crossed but no prints, sharing the silence they owned before they learned to walk.

After a while, the silence was interrupted by Lise crunching leaves a dozen paces behind them. There was a beauty to the crunch that they hoped would last forever. There was a part of it that did.

By the end of the walk they had allowed Lise to catch up, and Roman was holding both rifles while aLan cradled her.

***

When they returned to the outpost, they were greeted by a familiar shout of a familiar name. They could both clearly hear "SIDNEY CROSBY" from an enthusiastic Gerg through the thick, medieval wood-metal doors. They picked up the pace, now running to join what they knew was well underway. By the time they reached the room, the Grinders had gotten to talking theory.

"I don't think the principle has an overall assigned name yet. I think it's a good name."

"Nick, you just came up with it and told us 5 minutes ago." Aliya was out of marbles and so she started throwing adderalls at him. He caught one in his mouth.

"What principle?"

Nick took fifteen seconds to awkwardly choke down the adderall dry. "Oh hey didn't see you there. It's the John Garrett Principle."

"Would you believe Nick came up with another theory?"

"Nick? Noooo. He's not the theory type."

"Fuck you."

"Yeah, fuck you. He's got spreadsheets and everything."

"Yup. Again. Fuck you. There's a formula. Aliya's not the only one taking notes on us."

"Aliya's been taking notes?"

"On a criminal fucking conspiracy?"

"No. No, nothing illegal, just... how you all react to drugs and situations and..." Aliya forgot for a moment that she was keeping her side project on the down low. "It's an extension of my pharmaceutical education."

"I guess that's okay." Cassandra took a measure to think. "Hey Nick, what's this about a formula?"

Nick sighed. "It's not fine tuned yet. But here it is. Put X adult men," he looked over at Aliya, and he added "or women," and his balls were safe for another day, "in a room together with nothing else to do, and it takes 30 minutes minus X for one of them to start naming athletes from their childhood. When more than one of them understands and agrees to the game, the rest will rush to join."

"It checks out." Aliya had been taking mental notes on that one. The data lined up. "There's a multiplier effect when you guys are drunk."

"Plus a Gerg effect."

"Plus the Gerg effect, yeah."

"I have an effect?"

"Sometimes you just start shouting names out of nowhere. Rogue agent. Anomaly. You're a walking asterisk."

"True." Gerg was referencing minor league hockey player Alexander True, but nobody caught on.

"Walking asterisk, more like,"

"Miles, If you say walking ass, you're no better than he is."

"Walking... ass." Miles said it without a crumb of triumph and put his head down in shame.

"God damn I miss getting drunk."

Aliya threw an adderall at Roman. "You'd better get used to these instead."

"Why are you calling it the John Garrett Principle?"

"Because I got the idea when I put down *Leaves of Grass* to put ketchup on my hot dog. But what's fascinating about this for me is that we all seem to all naturally follow an inherently knowable and group-enforced system. There's no deviation. Even when we go out of turn or make a mistake, everyone else jumps down our throats to correct it."

"Are you trying to tell me that Name Some Guys is a natural law of the universe?"

"John Garrett Principle. And it seems that way, yeah."

"So kind of like a Rick Nash equilibrium."

"Not Steve Nash?"

"Steve Nash has enough things already."

"CONOR GARLAND!"

"Gerg. Wait your fucking turn." Aliya might have been the only person more excited than Gerg. "JT Miller! Thatcher Demko!" she shouted, frothing at the mouth.

"Just broke your own rule."

"Yeah, wait your fucking turn."

"Shut the fuck up Miles."

"I didn't say that."

"I said, shut the fuck up Miles."

He did.

***

4:41pm [MaTej] they are coming
4:42pm [MaTej] @Nick they are coming
4:45pm [Nick] everyone's here man
4:47pm [MaTej] nice

***

Later, after Miles had finished defragmenting his disk to completion, he was stupid enough to ask what else there was to do.

This was bound to happen, but the Grinders were all hoping for a bit later. Maybe tomorrow, maybe next week. Most of them were in their own heads, creating shortlists of more entries for the next round of Name Some Guys. They were all determined to win, which wasn't something that was possible.

Aliya threw an empty zoloft bottle at Miles' head and hit him square in the temple.

On the wall of the room, next to the entry, there was a whiteboard in permanent marker that listed the general assignments. Through Mike's name was a hunting knife that was keeping the whiteboard in place, and everything else had been erased or crossed out.

"Miles just volunteered for death duty." Cassandra pulled the hunting knife from the wall and the whiteboard fell to the ground.

Miles flinched.

Cassandra held the knife, blade out, for what felt like an hour, never breaking eye contact with Miles, before putting it slowly into the scabbard on her leg.

"You're gonna do some clerical work, Miles. Admin overflow.

The shit they don't wanna do in the main offices. You're about to find out why." Cassandra picked up a large stack of printed out phone numbers and slammed them onto his desk. "You'll be phoning the families of deceased Canadian soldiers. There are tens of thousands of names here. Some of these deaths are a decade old."

Miles was still grateful that the knife went into the scabbard and it took him a second to shift his focus to the stack of paper. "Okay, yeah. Sure. But how do these families not know about the deaths by now?" His gaze remained on the scabbard for another minute.

"Yeah, I'd notice something was up if my husband never returned from war." Roman picked a random page and started reading names. "Quinn Hughes. Luke Hughes. Oh God, is this all one family? They all have the same phone number. Jack Hughes."

"Pardon me?" Cassandra twitched.

"Jack Hughes."

"Come again?" It sounded french to her.

Roman talked slower. "Jack. Hughes."

A wave of relief washed over Cassandra. She didn't show it. She ignored Roman and turned back towards Miles. "You have to make one phone call per death, even if they're all at the same number."

"That can't be right."

"Stop fucking eavesdropping. It's government policy."

"Stopping eavesdropping is government policy? That's definitely not right."

"One call per death is government policy, stop eavesdropping is I'm gonna kill you policy."

"That sounds like the government too!" Gerg beamed.

"Shut the fuck up Miles. Get to work."

"I didn't say that. That was Gerg."

"I said shut the fuck up Miles."

"Well I'm gonna need to see a worksheet or something about the rules."

"I am the fucking rules. Get to work."

"Yes, Archon." Miles removed his glasses and put his head in his hands for a second, and wiped the cobwebs from his eyes. "Thank you, Archon." He popped an adderall, sighed, grabbed the stack back from Roman, and got started. "Aaron A. Aaronsen. Okay."

***

Gerg was bored, and his good buddy being given the worst assignment left him with a pang of guilt that he needed to kill, so he thought he'd try to lift Miles' spirits.

He went into the kitchen and searched for wordplay. He opened the cupboards.

Jackpot.

He made one of the packets of chamomile tea.

He brought back his mug of tea on a plate, and openly displayed the chamomile teabag label, words in tact, facing Miles.

He kept taking loud sips, trying to get Miles' attention. It didn't work.

He gave Miles one of the clues. "I bet way up north here,

military guys can get desperate."

Miles thought Gerg was flirting as a joke.

This clue wasn't enough. He had to keep going. "I bet sometimes some military guys have to end up eating each other." He took another sip. He made sure the pattern on the sleeve of his uniform was well into Miles' field of vision.

Miles looked up slowly with no expression.

Gerg thought Miles got the joke.

Gerg gave Miles the biggest smile he'd ever given anyone. "I've been waiting so long for you to finally get it."

Miles just stared. He gripped the phone receiver so tightly that it could have shattered. He was too frightened to look away.

Miles didn't break, and the sexy misunderstanding became clear to Gerg all at once.

Gerg spilled his tea. "No. Not that. Chamomile tea."

Miles was still confused.

Gerg pointed to his sleeve. "Camoflage. Military."

Gerg pointed to the death list. "Cannibalism. Meal. Camo meal."

Gerg pointed to the phone. "Tea. Camo meal tea."

Miles slammed his head on his desk.

Gerg slowly got up, cleaned his spillage off the floor, and left the room, muttering "nobody understands me," which nobody could hear.

***

5:05am [MaTeJ] how many patrols each day
5:10am [MaTeJ] i have done alot and found nothing yet

5:21am [MaTeJ] are u guys still asleep. what time is it over there

The Grinders ignored the beeping of the group chat. It was just Matej. Matej was fine. He could take care of himself.

***

The phone rang three and a half times before the call was picked up. "Hello? Mrs. Boeser?"

"How are you doing today?" Miles read from the script that he scribbled onto a post-it note.

"Great! Anyways, enough small talk, it is with great sadness and a heavy heart that I report that your son or daughter has passed away while in active mili-"

"My apologies, ma'am, but-"

"No, I-"

Miles put the call on speakerphone so that everyone could hear the dial tone. "Everyone already knows. I have yet to reach anyone who doesn't know about the death. This is fucking painful."

Cassandra rushed and sat down in the chair next to Miles and just stared at him for a second and smiled. "You're fucking welcome."

"Huh?"

"Karma for the Grind!"

It was day two of the assignment, and Miles was already out of gas. "Karma for the Grind, okay, I get it." He acquiesced. He had to. "Thank you, Archon."

"Aliya!" Cassandra felt like letting up a bit. "Give our boy another adderall! He's earned it. Good boy, Miles! Get back to phoning."

***

"What's he doing over there?" aLan had taken to following Roman who was getting creative with leading their patrol routes, and they found themselves wandering aimlessly through to the end of a forest trail into the mouth of a large clearing, where they noticed a solitary, shirtless man near a bonfire, dancing maniacally, which they both assumed was a tribal dance that they did not understand.

"Local culture. Do we leave him alone? That looks like fun."

"It does, but we don't speak the language. And we're dressed like Canadian military. And we have guns. There is no reality where this dancing man would invite us to dance with him."

"Wow, good point. I think I can see his nose from here."

"Maybe it's Kevin."

"I mean, the dancing does look like his dancing. But I just saw K-hole take two xans and lie down in a closet a couple minutes before we left, so unless someone injected him with meth and gave him a motorbike, that's not Kevin."

"True. Plus I can see this guy's eyebrows too. Kevin has normal eyebrows, right?"

"I guess. I don't know. What's normal anymore?"

Lise meowed loudly, twice, from the bushes.

"Absolutely nothing is normal anymore. Did you.. hear that? I mean, it was a meow but I feel like I know what she was trying to say?"

"Yeah, kitty's fucking terrified. Maybe it's the dancing guy by the fire."

"And..."

"I also got a hint of, 'watch out.'"

"Yeah, so I'm not going insane."

"Or we both are. Did you hear any rumblings in the bushes? Lise was already here when we got here."

"I think she's on a patrol of her own. How do you think she knew about this guy?"

"Could be they had a run in last time she was out here. I think she followed Aliya out when she went to get more drugs the other day."

"Yeah but they came back together and Aliya didn't say shit."

"Yeah. I'm tired of talking about it. Let's leave this guy alone with his bonfire. He doesn't need us."

"Agreed."

"Get the cat."

"What if Matej patrols out this way? He might intrude on the dancing man and ruin the good times."

"He was assigned to patrol the other side of the outpost with the abandoned lithium exploration camps, he'll never come over here."

"Good old reliable Matej."

***

12:21pm [MaTej] high score
12:22pm [MaTej] candy crush!!
12:24pm [MaTej] @Nick high schore
12:28pm [MaTej] score
12:31pm [Nick] that's cool man

***

A week later, a frazzled Miles, working 20 hours a day, had already gotten to the S names.

"Hello, Mrs. Sutter? How are you today? That's great! Enough small talk. It is with great sadness and a heavy heart that "

Miles paused, sighed, and slammed the receiver down. "I didn't get to saying which Sutter, so can I just pick whichever name?"

"First alphabetically. Go in order. This isn't complicated."

Miles crossed out Brent Sutter and continued.

"Hello, Mrs. Sutter? How are you today? That's --"

Miles crossed out Brian Sutter.

"Hello, Mrs.-

Miles crossed out Darryl Sutter.

"What the fuck even was this, anyways? All six of them died at the same time?"

"Found an article online." Nick raised his voice. "They were stationed at Cold Lake and were setting up fireworks on Canada Day and someone lit up a dart and set it off early."

"Oof." Miles dialed again. "Hello, M-" Miles had been numb to the screams for a few days. He crossed out Duane Sutter. "Why is she still picking up?" Miles called again and got sent straight to voicemail. "Hello, Mrs. Sutter, sorry to have missed you. It is with great sadness and a heavy heart that I report that your son or daughter has passed away while in active military duty. He or she served with great pride and it is because to his or her noble sacrifice that the Canadian military was able to achieve its goal. You will be receiving a Canadian flag in the mail with a personally signed thank you letter from his or her commanding officer."

Miles crossed out Rich Sutter and dialed again.

"Hello, Mrs. Sutter, Sorry to have missed you."

***

Another week went by, mostly uneventfully, with minimal disruption.

Mike droned over paperwork, Gerg made jokes that nobody understood, Kevin took drugs, Aliya took notes, Nick worked on theory, the Gjeoffs read books about finance, Miles grinded lifetimes of Karma for grieving families, Matej stayed out of sight and out of mind, Cassandra built her network of suffering, Steef tried his hand at gardening in the tundra, aLan and Roman did their patrols, Lise followed, and Terry said nothing.

***

2:02pm [MaTej] still here. nobody? any?
2:04pm [MaTej] 22 left
2:05pm [Miles2025] we're at 33
2:06pm [MaTej] no just 22 left
2:09pm [Miles2025] are you trying to tell us you're leaving 22?
2:19pm [Nick] matej you gotta stay over there
2:20pm [MaTej] in the bathroom
2:20pm [Nick] we don't need that information
2:21pm [Nick] miles. Get back to work

Just a few minutes prior, Cassandra had brought Miles a fresh pile of dead Canadians. It was only a couple extra pages, but it still made him wonder whether the assignment would ever end.

"Hey Miles. How are Canadians dying these days anyways?"

"Nick. We're not supposed to be keeping up with current events."

"Lot of poison."

"There's poison?"

"Yeah, looks like recently too. Seven people are on here. Over two days. Big week for poison." Miles passed the new list of names around the room as an excuse to delay getting started.

When the list made its way around to an insanely bored Terry, he looked at the 'site of incident' of the poisoned names. He noticed that all seven of them were at the same address.

22 Gata Road.

Matej's outpost.

He also noticed that the dates of the deaths were the two days leading up to their arrival and he suddenly understood the mortal terror in the eyes of the guard who handed them the keys.

After watching Terry grip the papers for a minute too long, Aliya read the stress on his face and handed him a xan, which he ate dry.

"The fuck has you so panicked? Did you see your name?"

Terry didn't respond.

"Wait, are we on there?" She laughed and walked away.

Terry said nothing.

***

3:21pm [MaTej] nobody want books?
3:31pm [MaTej] ???

3:45pm [Miles2025] ? What
3:46pm [MaTej] they're here
3:46pm [MaTej] @Nick they're here
4:04pm [Nick] matej everyone's over here still

***

Matej was miffed that nobody wanted to read the books that he'd ordered for them.

His only job was patrols, which he understood to mean that he was forbidden from performing basic maintenance at his outpost.

The lights flickered in the hallway to the bathroom, and they also flickered in the bathroom.

He had just lugged the last of the 22 books to the bathroom of the outpost at 22 Gata Road when he was frightened by a song coming from one of the toilet stalls.

The singing was perfect.

Absolutely perfect.

No notes missed.

He recognized the song.

The beautiful voice from the bathroom stall finished the chorus and Matej sang along in his head. "Just haven't met youuuu yet!"

Matej gave a courtesy scuff on the dank floors with his dirty military boots and the singing stopped.

"Michael?"

The man on the toilet was silent.

"Michael Buble?"

The lights flickered.

Matej heard the man clearing his voice from the other side of the door. "No. My code name- I mean- my name is Russian Unicorn. I - FUCK."

Matej was overjoyed. He didn't stop to think for a second about how impossible this situation was.

"I'm from Vancouver too, I know who you are bro."

"But the prosthetic..." His eyes were wide, and his pupils were wider than his eyes.

"I can't see a prosthetic bro. There's... a wall here. There's a wall between us. A door."

"Ohhhh yea. Duh."

"Its the voice dude. I've seen you live front row at the Orpheum. I own all your DVDs. It's nonmistakeable. I know all the words to some of the parts of a bunch of your songs."

Michael flushed with pride and there was a chorus of clumsy pants-fastening noises for a measure. Matej stayed enamored as though the fastening had been done suavely.

Michael emerged from the stall, looking completely normal, other than a prosthetic that changed the shape of his face to give him a large nose and huge eyebrows. "Fuuuuuck. Don't tell anyone."

"Why are you here? I didnt see any film cameras or make up crew or..." he trailed off without saying a third thing and Michael realized after a while that it was his turn to speak.

Feeling different, Michael was moved by the sincerity in Matej's eyes and there was an instant connection. He sensed a rare opportunity to pierce through his own steely James Bond exterior for a moment of wide-eyed brotherhood. He removed the prosthetic for a second and Matej could see the size of his pupils. Michael remembered he was on a mission and put the prosthetic back on for a second, tried to adjust it to comfort, couldn't find any comfort, and abandoned the mask on the ground.

"I've been here around this outpost for a week or two waiting for a target. This is a special request by a wealthy person with a lotta money. Lot. O. Money. Monaaayyyy. But," Michael spent a second wondering if he should keep talking, but he lost focus and continued. "I gotta kill someone. I'm really actually super good at assassinations."

He beamed. He noticed trails in the flickering lights.

"Per usual they usually just let me in anywhere because of I'm Michael Buble. The singing thing. So I can go to Dubai or whatever and on the surface im getting like 500k to sing to some sultan but in reality there's some American asshole at the show. Thats the assignment, that asshole. The American. I fake drunk and friendly after the show. They always, always want a picture. I always get them a drink. The drink always has strychnine. And now the American is dead and the sultan takes control of some new billion dollar patent." He made gun fingers at Matej but instead of firing them, he waved them slowly a foot from his face, the guns collapsing into waves, until Matej broke his reverie with followup questions.

"That's fucked up man. But kinda cool. How do I get into this line of work?"

Michael recoiled. "Ohhh man. You don't want to get mixed up in this shit." He moved in slow motion towards the bathroom sink and turned both taps on full, motioned to start washing his hands, looked at his hands, and followed the motion of his hands back to Matej. The water stayed running.

"How come?"

Michael kicked at the prosthetic. "Gotta wake up at 4:00 in the morning. Like, every day."

"Ohhh holy shit. Thank you for telling me. That sounds like a fucking nightmare." Matej was completely sincere.

"Yeah man. I've been drinking like four cups of coffee a day lately. Sometimes four isn't enough."

Matej nodded vigorously.

Michael had a sudden moment of clarity on the privacy of his operation. "You gotta promise. Pinky swe-" he started to stick out his pinky finger but withdrew it.

Matej stuck his pinky out and lingered.

Michael continued. "You gotta promise not to tell anyone. I will make you sign an NDA. My lawyers are," Michael stared at his hands again. "My lawyers are very angry, very angry people."

Matej was paying attention but he still kept his pinky out, waiting for Michael Buble to accept.

Michael thought back to his CIA body language training and saw all at once that Matej's heart and soul were wide open. Michael permitted himself to open up further. "Can't do pinky swears anymore man. Turns out they are not legally binding. But!" He went from doom to pep in half a second. "I got some photocopies of the NDA left I think."

Matej dropped his hand to his side, pinky still out, at the ready.

Michael reached into his pants pocket and pulled out a folded piece of paper, littered with drops of blood, picked up one of the 22 books from the bathroom counter as a writing surface, and unfolded the paper. "Do you have a pen? Wait I think I have... yeah, this one is real ink."

Without reading it, Matej signed a copy of the pocket NDA.

Michael smiled. He looked at the book and considered it. "Huh, I've heard about this book. Can I take one?"

"Yeah bro those are like five bucks dude, I ordered 22 of them, I think you're fine."

Michael smiled even bigger. "Hell yeah, brother." He held up the copy of the book like a bible to be sworn on. "NOT A WORD. OF THIS. TO ANYONE. NDA means No Disclosure, Asshole."

Matej knew to act cool. "Got it. No disclosure. Of anything?" He looked once at Michael who maintained the frightened, wide-eyed stare. "Of anything. Got it. Sorry." Matej stared at the book with a newfound sense of dread.

"Ok man well, I got shit to do. Do I have to? Yeah... do I?" Michael pulled a headshot photo from his pocket. Matej couldn't make out the face on it while Michael was moving his hands around to watch the motion trails. He waltzed away singing once again, "...just havent met youuu yet!"

Matej kicked at the prosthetic. "I really wanted to read that book, man."

He noticed the taps were both still running and he turned them off, which filled him with a sense of pride.

He made eye contact with himself in the mirror and did a military salute.

"Commander Matej. Field marshall Matej. Brigadier general – general Matej. Yeah."

He did another salute. "General Matej."

He then carried on with a patrol that nobody would ever ensure that he was actually doing, never piecing together the implications of the Grinders being the only other people at these outposts with the crooner-assassin.

Over the next two days, he destroyed the remaining copies of the books, just in case that was part of the NDA, ripping the pages out, one by one, and flushing them down the toilet.

***

4:01pm [MaTej] *deleted*
4:01pm [MaTej] wait shit. fuck
4:01pm [MaTej] *deleted*
4:02pm [MaTej] ok cool
4:04pm [Nick] candy crush record again?
4:12pm [MaTej] yeah man

***

A couple more weeks had passed, and the Grinders were getting very comfortable. The northern living allowance was stacking up, and Cassandra's network was being built to new heights.

She thought about civilization now and then, but that's where the Groom was. That's where the Groom was happy with his Bride.

She started to realize that a big part of her didn't want to leave the Arctic.

And shortly after that realization, the only landline in the entire outpost complex started to ring.

Miles had been using it for outbound calls, but it was programmed to come up on call display as a private number. Nobody was supposed to have this number.

Cassandra was the only one brave enough to answer.

She was greeted by oppressively hostile static before she could say anything, and the hostile static gave way to panicked command.

"This is a secured line on a military frequency. I am with Arctic high command. You will not know my name. We have heard from forces more powerful than both of us that a very important operation has been compromised. I have a report from an incapacitated special operative that there were 22 copies of illegally transported anti-war literature delivered to someone at 22 Gata Road. Our operative read the literature and now refuses to complete his mission. Everyone involved is in extreme violation of military policy and your outfit will be removed and possibly reprimanded if you can't fill in the gaps for me. I am headed your way on a helicopter from a nearby naval base and will be there in thirty minutes. You had better have some fucking answers, because I could catch a discharge over this."

She wondered who they meant by operative.

Couldn't be.

***

Cassandra stormed into the outpost at 22 Gata Road, screaming with every part of herself. "MATEJ!" It was an awkward name to scream, but she could make anything terrifying.

Matej did his best impression of standing at attention that he'd seen in the movies.

Cassandra thundered around the outpost into every room and found no books, only military supplies and the duffel bag with Aliya's drug inventory.

"Matej, why did you order 22 copies of a book to a military location? Where are they?"

"Well." Matej was happy that someone was interested in his doings. "I didnt know anything about war before we went out here. So I asked Nick for advice on war. And Nick told me I should read books on it so that I don't fuck everything up. So I went to ask the internet what's the best book about war."

"I have an urgent meeting with a high ranking Canadian military official in four minutes." Cassandra was seething with restraint. She spoke methodically. "I need to know the name of the book so that I can talk my way out of this for us."

Matej remembered the almost-pinky swear and the NDA. "I uhhhh..."

He couldn't figure out if he was allowed to say that he wasn't allowed to say anything. He stammered for a while and refused to make eye contact.

"Matej if you can't fucking remember the name of the book that you fucking ordered, we're catching hell, we're being discharged and sent home and we're losing the government money. Command considers us to be in a conspiracy to sow discord among the Canadian military and its commercial interests at the lithium exploration camp."

Matej knew that it was just the Grinders and Buble there, but he was too scared of everything to say anything. The world in front of him was moving too quickly around and through him and he found nothing safe to grab onto.

He remembered the faraway look in Michael Buble's eyes when he was talking about his angry lawyers. Possibly fueled by the fresh brotherhood with the assassin-crooner, he feared Buble's lawyers more than he feared Cassandra. And he couldn't stop replaying in his head the angry speeches where Cassandra herself had professed, over and over again, that the last thing the Grinders wanted was lawyers poking through their operations. In that moment, he could only think about lawyers.

Cassandra looked at her watch as they both heard distant boots at a quickening pace. She looked at the time. "Tell me the name of the fucking book in the next 22 seconds or we'll be lucky to catch a new fucking assignment far worse than this."

"Uhhhhhhh..."

07 - THE TELECOM

The Groom walked out of the bedroom of his marital suite and slowly, very slowly, very carefully, he took a seat on the livingroom sofa.

Right as he picked up the remote to turn on the television, his phone rang with a custom ringtone that made him wince, and then he noticed 678-999-8212 - *her* phone number - come up on his call display.

He had heard that her mad geniuses had ended up serving the military time. And he had to admit that it made him happy. Having her stuck in the Arctic felt like another wedding gift. As long as she was enlisted, he didn't have to deal with her.

But it had been less than a month since they departed the wedding that they had destroyed, which meant that someone had fucked up. She wasn't supposed to be able to contact him.

By the second ring, he came up with three possibilities for why she was calling.

The first was that the assignment had failed and she needed to draw out another favor. As much as he loved hearing about her failures, in that moment he was feeling rejuvenated and wasn't in the mood for her brand of treachery.

The second was that the assignment came to an end properly from forces outside of her control, and she wanted something else, which he wasn't prepared for.

The third was that she was dead and that this call was coming from a handler at a three-letter organization he had never heard of, through her phone, and as much confusing vitriol as they had between them, he wasn't ready to let go of the memory of her.

He let the call go to voicemail.

There was a pregnant pause after the ring but before she started talking, which told him that she was hoping to hear his voice.

She inhaled loud enough that he could hear it, decided not to say his name, and went coldly into embarrassing detail about how an errand boy made a mistake and got their placement ended prematurely.

She could tell he was listening. She could picture him smiling.

He'd have another assignment for her, but he couldn't offer it to her except as punishment.

This circumstance called for punishment.

It was finally his turn with the strap-on.

He heard the VCR click from the other room and flinched.

Fortunately for her, the Groom had very recently fallen into a mistake of his own; while intoxicated on his secluded honeymoon, he went online, logged onto his trading software and blacked out, ending up with an ambitious short position in a Canadian telecommunications company.

The company's financials were solid.

He was primed to take it in the ass once again.

But maybe she could be his angel.

He couldn't help but notice at his wedding that the mad

geniuses, under her obvious direction, had an innate talent for useful chaos, and she forced him to notice that she was in total control of them.

And now he was in control of her.

***

"Oh hey. You got my message."

"I did. Sorry, I was in the shower when you called."

Cassandra knew to let his lies hang in silence.

"So, as luck would have it, I've got something for you and your pack of fucking weirdos."

"Great. I'm strapped in, let's hear it."

He sighed. "One of my colleagues at the firm let me down, and I'm left with my dick in my hands. I have to deal with a massive short position in a Canadian telecom that probably won't pay off."

Cassandra could tell from the octave of his voice when he started talking that this was also bullshit. "And you need me to get you off the hook."

"Big time. The board's up my ass about this."

She paused for a minute, making sure to breathe so he knew she was thinking. "I could work the retentions. Make it bleed."

She meant it. In her eyes, there was no greater concentration of capacity for causing manageable suffering than working in the customer retentions department of a Canadian telecom.

"You're gonna have to go up into that one a bit further."

Cassandra got serious. "Cold call existing customers, annoy them during dinner time, offer them plans that are worse than their current plans. Accidentally-on-purpose bad customer service. Bleed customers, lose revenue."

"That won't get me all the way there."

"Oh that wouldn't be the whole thing. Just the tip."

"I like the way it feels so far. Is that it?"

"I have full faith that if we get everyone in there, we'll find something."

"Okay well, I'm not convinced this is too solid, but you've never been wrong before. I'll send you the details."

"Got it. I'll be a ghost. I promise. I won't call you back until I've..."

"Don't say it."

"Wrecked 'em. Wait, did you hang up? Oh god fucking damnit." Cassandra put her phone away. "Fuck!"

***

She messaged the Grinders immediately to let them know they had a new assignment.

They wouldn't need long to decompress from their failed military duties. They were more than eager to wipe that experience from their memories.

They escaped from that hell, and got started soon after, setting up the cubicles in their new one.

At least this one had central heating.

Cassandra would eventually be the last Grinder to make it to headquarters on day 1.

First, she had to go see a woman about her raccoons.

***

For the first time in a while, she dusted off her old '11 Avenger. Her rousing successes – their rousing successes - in the world of fraud and extortion and other forms of entertainment had allowed for a full garage of much nicer cars by this point, but when you endeavor to engage in something this illegal, you drive a dented grey car, you drive the speed limit, and you listen to Nickelback.

Cassandra had even practiced saying "yes, officer" in the rear view mirror. She had never said that before. It felt awkward. She fucking hated it. Her hands down at her sides kept the middle fingers extended so that any ghosts who might be haunting her would know that she didn't mean it.

Following the light reconciliation with the Groom over the phone, she could feel the Grinders' efforts mounting up and leading somewhere.

She wanted more of that wonderful mind control drug.

Luon-go.

She didn't know if the current effects on the Disciples would ever dissipate. She wanted to be prepared, just in case.

And a big part of her was hoping that one day she would be able to spike the Groom's punch.

As she passed over and through the university endowment lands, she sped up as she noticed the library, and slowed down when she was noticed by the library cops, who weren't there before. She thought they were unnecessary. She was overcome by a notable lack of a growing dread. The trees that once felt comfortably haunted were ridden with an upsettingly beautiful medley of flowering leaves, still on their branches.

She parked her Avenger on the same chilling outskirts where she once tried to get started writing history. She motioned to turn off the music and realized she had forgotten to turn it on. She didn't remember where to go, but she remembered the feelings she once followed. She followed those feelings again, chasing herself around the folds of her mind for any hidden pockets of fear that could float her closer to the heart of darkness that she so desperately needed.

She panicked when she couldn't find that familiar fear. The panic turned into a new fear. She closed her eyes, covered her ears, screamed, and ran.

If she hit a tree, or tripped on some underbrush, it didn't matter.

She ran until her throat was sore.

Opening her eyes with cautious optimism, as if for the first time, chills pumped through her bones and her spine as she caught sight of the gauntlet of broken chandeliers graced with the corpses of long-dead raccoons and their maggot children.

She knew the way from there.

She stepped on some dry leaves.

But 'there' was no longer there.

There was no crunch.

She stomped around in circles, trying to crush every leaf in sight, stomping harder and running faster and casting a wider range, desperate for the crunch, catching a rut in a figure-eight.

The chills were pure memory.

It was gone.

Parisa was gone.

The underground enclave and the psychedelic laboratory and the VHS library and the paperback books about revolution had all disappeared.

There was no sign of destruction or disappearance.

The operation had been deconstructed, drop by drop, tape by tape, twig by twig.

Cassandra's useful fear had been instantly and fully replaced by a terribly useless one.

In that moment, she would have paid a million dollars to gaze into the eyes of a newly dead raccoon; she scampered around in a circle, inspecting the skeleton of every chandelier, finding only rot and broken glass.

She spent hours sifting through the leaves and the grass looking for secret directions and found nothing but leaves and grass. She sat down on a stump and focused her thoughts on giving up and moving on, in an attempt to trick the psychic forest gods that might exist beyond her senses. It didn't work. She then gave up for real, and that didn't work either.

She cried for a minute, at first only on the inside.

It dawned on her that she didn't leave herself any way to remember how to get back to her Avenger, and the trees around her were too dense for the mountains in the north to guide her.

She stayed seated on the stump, waiting to be ambushed by a sense of fear or a sense of direction, ready to follow whichever one approached her first.

It occured to her after another minute that if she sprinted long enough in any direction, she'd find an exit.

She hoped this forest wasn't forever.

She hoped this forest wasn't forever.

This forest could be forever.

She closed her eyes and she ran and ran and ran and she heard leaves rustling and she heard twigs snapping and branches staying strong and she heard the wind and she followed the wind until she heard cars.

Good enough.

She opened her eyes again and she was exactly where she needed to be.

She got back into her Avenger.

She removed the Nickelback cassette from the tape player, swapped it for another tape in the glove compartment, shoved it in and hit play. The uplifting guitars washed over her brain and opened up a bouquet of neural pathways leading to memories she thought she'd left at university.

Hello my friend we meet again
It's been a while, where should we begin?
Feels like forever

All at once and without effort, she had been absolved of the comfortable fear of being among the rambling paths of semi-fallen trees with branches piercing the ground and then coming back up in splinters and of the raccoons adorning the chandeliers who would never have given them light.

Her thoughts raced past the Groom and then back to the Groom and then past and then back. Her foot on the gas was kept under control by the drums that were slightly too loud for the speakers of her Avenger.

Oh how quickly life can turn around
In an instant

She hit rewind three times.

I just want to say hello again

As she showed up at the offices of the telecom, she waited for the song to finish before she left the Avenger.

My sacrifice

***

The elevator doors opened at the 13th floor and Cassandra took a minute to exit. Her dirty camo boots dropped a bit of forest soil down the elevator shaft when she paused overtop of the small gap between the elevator and the floor.

If there was a malfunction, she would be killed instantly, cut in half, no funeral.

She had never prayed for anything before now, and she prayed for an eternity.

Eternity ended and there was no malfunction.

She proceeded to the retentions department where the Grinders were already busy setting up their personal prisons.

There was a stillness - not the stillness of a summer lodge where the birds and the trees and the waves crash at your feet. This was a stillness that tremored through the most deafening sensory inputs. This was the kind of stillness so pervasive and alienating that it compelled the French and the Russians and the Germans to write novels about the ethics of suicide.

Cassandra hated offices, phones, cubicles, co-workers. She hated onboarding and interviews and conferences and tax forms. She hated pleated pants, dress shirts, ties and pizza parties. She got a taste of it during her internship, which was what had motivated her to work tirelessly to graduate two years early.

The immediate future lay before her like a field of spikes.

Fully aware of her capacity for persuasion, she had to keep an eye on herself or else she'd start to actually believe the words of the *Bromeliad* out of necessity, as though she was one of those pathetic stoics, fooling herself into acting like this was all going according to a greater plan, out of a deep-seated need for personal dignity.

This was a hiccup, and she was making the best of it.

***

The Grinders agreed that Matej had been getting sloppy and maybe he needed a bit of a time out.

And while Cassandra never said a word of this to anyone, and it made no worldly sense, she couldn't shake the idea that Matej was the person that Arctic high command was talking about when they said 'operative'.

They were able to exile him to Palo Alto on an internship with the streaming company Roku, which was all they could manage on short notice.

He wasn't aware that it was a punishment.

He thought he did a great job being true to the NDA and considered it to be a reward. He never put together that the rest of the Grinders didn't know about the NDA.

In an effort to stop him from asking questions, Cassandra handed him a bullshit assignment with a vague mission statement, to "grow his influence and power and wealth in Silicon Valley however possible, to expand the reach of the Grinders and to maximize the next lives of the children of the *Bromeliad.*" Noting Matej's track record for mission incompetence, Cassandra was pretty sure she could just set it and forget it. He had no compromising information on the Grinders, and no notes taken on the operations of the Grind, confirmed by Mike, who did a sweep of his hard drives and quietly installed a key logger on his laptop before sending him down.

With Matej out of the way, and no distractions, the Grinders could get to work.

***

Cassandra didn't take any steps to hide her increased urgency.

The morning of day one at their new job, she had the Grinders gathered at attention on the main office floor, waiting for their assignments, spinning around in their overpriced swivel chairs.

"The goal here is to tank the company without tanking ourselves. We have full autonomy to cause damage, on the honor of the *Bromeliad* and the man who sent us here."

The unspoken half of her plan was to put a dozen or so mad geniuses in a room together, feed them infinite drugs, crush them under vague and infinite pressure, and tell them to save the world. She couldn't think of a better engine for progress.

"I will be assigning almost all of you to making this company bleed customers. I've already spoken with some of you who know your roles. Miles will be handing out printed out customer lists from randomized parts of the customer database to most of you."

She knew they'd run out of calls to make on day one. She knew they would be too afraid to speak up about it – they would all feel that either they were doing the assignment wrong, or they were correcting their Archon. Both possibilities would freeze them in place and push them into secret secondary look-busy pursuits. And by now they were hard coded to have their secondary pursuits serve the Archon.

She was infusing them with vague and infinite pressure handed down from the Angels while Aliya was infusing them with vague and infinite drugs handed up from Satan.

She drew it up perfectly.

On his name being called, Miles stood up and looked around and waved hello, as though they were meeting him for the first time, and then sat down, embarrassed.

"Unfortunately, company policy does not allow us to cold call Key Accounts from this department, and the company only had two posted openings in that department. So Jeff and Geoff will be deployed to Key Accounts over there," Cassandra directed their attention to a disconnected area with slightly nicer desks, "generating specialized customer trauma, and forwarding the probable customer losses to us in retentions."

The Gjeoffs, happy with their assignment, nodded vigorously, slightly out of rhythm.

"Aliya, just, drugs. Whoever. Whatever. Whenever. Wherever. And Kevin, hello Kevin, if you're with us, you're a runner for whatever, coffee, supplies, I don't fucking know. Make paper planes. I don't give a fuck. And Mike, I think you've got something."

"Oh. Yeah." Mike stood up and turned to the Gjeoffs. "Cassandra asked me to pick apart the CRM software overnight to look for edges and opportunities and while I was doing that I got bored so I made you guys a custom music program. You can pipe in custom hold music. Really turn up the heat. Fuck 'em up."

"Does this one look like Spotify too?"

"Yeah, it's a useful console, all my tools look like Spotify. Keep up."

Cassandra continued. "We want to lose big. We want to lose large numbers of customers, we want to lose long-term customers. We want the numbers to look like Chernobyl by the end of the quarter. We want to lose consumer confidence, we want to lose investor confidence. We want the board of directors to lose confidence in themselves. You know, chaos and destruction." Her eyes turned green. She thought about the Bride for an instant. "The usual."

"Can't we just break the law?"

"Well, no. Whatever we do has to pass inspection or else they'll just fire us. We have to do it in a way that only bleeds the company. We need this stock price to crash as much as possible, as soon as possible. The quarterly report will affect the stock price and we need the short to pay off. This is my- this is our last crack at gaining a serious foothold in Wall Street. We would never be able to develop this kind of relationship with some prick that we dig up from the DADS project."

She pounded her fist onto her open palm. "And we can forge ahead with no doubts, as every customer that we cold call, even the ones we don't manage to lose, will truly suffer. Karma for the Grind. Say it with me."

"Karma for the Grind!"

"We have global reach if we pull this off. We have bottomless financing if we pull this off. We have fat fingers in every financial market if we pull this off. Forex, crypto. Everything. The world will be ours." She paused. "We will bring Karma to everyone. Karma for the Grind. Karma for the Grind!"

They all repeated in perfect harmony. "Karma for the Grind!"

"Aliya, load these guys up. Guys, take your pick. We've got everything. Everything. I recommend adderall. 12 hour shifts." Once more with feeling. "Everything."

After a few repetitions from the group, she returned to her bloodthirsty aggression and slammed her fist again into her open palm. "Make 'em bleed! Let's go!"

They cheered, ate some drugs, and got to work making Canada

suffer.

***

The speech and the response were so rousing that they hadn't noticed the constant stream of notification sounds. The Grinders got to their workstations and saw that the group chat had dozens of messages from Matej who had been asking if anyone could even see his messages.

8:01am [Gerg] nope
8:02am [MaTej] ok
8:03am [Roman] can't see any of your messages matej
8:03am [aLan] same as those guys. Can't see anything
8:03am [Gerg] try rebooting your computer?
8:03am [MaTej] ok
8:03am [MaTej] ok thamks
8:03am [MaTej] ok thanks guys i will try. That
8:04am [MaTej] @Gerg thanks i will try that

***

Jeff turned around in his swivel chair at his new desk. "Hey Geoff. Check it out." He pressed the 'speakers' button on the custom console and the hold music was now playing for both of them.

Girl, look at that body
Girl, look at that body
Girl, look at that body
I-I-I work out

"Turn that shit off."

"So this song would work on you." Jeff typed the information into a spreadsheet.

"Is you taking notes on a criminal fucking conspiracy?"

"Yeah, I just wanna do more for the Grind, you know. Aliya has the relapse project, Nick's doing analytics, I just wanna help out."

Geoff took a measure and then nodded. "Write that shit down."

***

Nick could hear the bass of the hold music sporadically from across the floor, and if he had any real work to do, the music would have annoyed him, but he was finding that the printed cold call list that he was given was useless. It seemed to be made up mostly of fake accounts with fake numbers, grouped together in the database with a lot of them featuring notes stating in plain english that they were likely fake. The transaction histories were listed as a singular purchase with zero useful information. He couldn't even figure out what kinds of customers these were. Clearly the printed lists were not double checked.

He grinded his teeth for a few minutes, massively buzzing on something Aliya had fed him.

He craved information.

He craved hyperdetailed lists and histories.

He felt a need to open 400 browser tabs and read 21 of them. Maybe it was the adderall. It was probably the adderall. It was the adderall. Whatever it was, with his cold call list providing nothing he could use, he'd found himself very quickly blazing through the Wikipedia page for the telecom that they were trying to destroy from the inside.

One of the more intriguing sub-articles was titled "Soulja Boy."

For the hour he spent reading, he was slack jawed, staring but not drooling, starting to wonder why he wasn't drooling, finding his mouth dry as a desert, drinking a bottle of water in one go, now drooling, and still staring, unblinking and unflinching.

This was the good Wikipedia. The adderall gods were smiling.

***

Nick waited until he was on break to share the info, so as to avoid admitting he was breaking from protocol. "Guys, remember Soulja Boy?" He scrambled to fill the total silence with more detail. "The guy who sang what's that song? Superman That Ho?"

"YOUUUUUU"

"I what?"

"No. That's the next part of the song."

"Sounds stupid."

"It's called Crank That."

"Crank Dat?"

"Crank THAT. With a TH. And then 'Soulja Boy' in parentheses."

"His own name, in parentheses, in his own song?"

"His own name, in parentheses, in his own song."

"Yeah, that sounds fucking stupid."

"You're stupid. That song fucking rules." Mike meant it.

Cassandra stopped her tour of the department floor to listen, pretending she was checking her phone.

"Says here he had a company that sold ringtones. Soulja Boy Telecommunications."

She was immediately rocked by a ten foot wave of nostalgia. "Holy fuck. I bought from him. That was where I got my first ringtone." She paused for a measure. "You know what? I bet I still have it saved somewhere."

With the Grinders waiting patiently at attention, and with a dopey smile on her face, Cassandra spent a minute downloading an update to an old program, then accessing an old folder in a remote server somewhere out of the way, then connecting to a bluetooth speaker.

When she hit play, the ancient hymn started off in 8-bit with an undetectable series of crude notes. Cassandra stood, dancing in anticipation, the dopey smile still plastered on her face, unmovable.

After a few runs of the midi tune, the compressed lyrics burst through.

I like the way you do that right thurr
(Right thurr)
Swing your hips when your walkin'
Let down your hurr
(Down your hurr)

"Fucking CHINGY."

"CHINGY!"

"I don't fucking believe it. This is amazing."

"I had no idea you used to be cool."

Cassandra pulled a battery from her dress pocket and threw it at Miles. "Fuck you. Yeah you did. Fucking prick. Also. Still am cool. So fuck you again."

"Yeah, shut the fuck up, Miles."

"Didn't have to throw a battery at my head."

She threw another battery at his head.

"Karma for the Grind, buddy."

"Right. Thank you, Archon."

The Grinders went quiet and revelled until the track finished. There was a purity to the experience that made Cassandra forget for one beautiful moment that this had been her personalized ringtone for the Groom. When that reality crept in, she recoiled, steelied her demeanor, disconnected from the bluetooth and played it off as professionalism, but then she lingered, taking another minute to get her head straight, with a smile and a thousand yard stare meant to pretend that she was still soaking in the innocent memory of her first ringtone.

She sniffled.

***

Kevin decided that the Gjeoffs should know about this. After taking a look at his own computer, which was still off, monitor unplugged, he told Gerg to tell them, and returned to his assigned task of folding paper planes and leaving them in a pile on the ground, unflown; with his own stack of paper in the other part of the office, he borrowed documents from the inbox on aLan's desk. aLan didn't mind.

9:41am [Gerg] @Jeff @geoff you guys should have been here. Boss lady just put her chingy ringtone on the surround sound
9:41am [Gerg] fuck. chingtone
9:42am [Jeff] CHINGTONE
9:42am [Mike] chingtone
9:42am [aLan] chingtone
9:42am [Roman] chingtone!!!
9:43am [Nick] @Jeff @geoff she got it from the soulja boy company that was bought by this company
9:43am [Gerg] wait what?
9:43am [Nick] yeah you guys didn't let me finish talking
9:43am [miles2025] chingtone
9:43am [Nick] @Jeff @geoff just walk over here please, i'm not having this same conversation out loud and in text
9:46am [steef] (16 photos of his office gardens)

Jeff and Geoff were out of breath when they arrived.

"Sorry, guess I forgot to mention. Yeah, this company bought the ringtone company, Soulja Boy Telecommunications, a bunch of years ago for a fuck ton of money."

"What? Why?"

"Yeah. What the fuck does a huge telecom want with ringtones?"

Cassandra was still lingering. She started to sweat. Maybe she was just coming down.

But she had bought a ringtone from him.

On the university ringtone plan.

The university where they all met.

With her real name.

Her government name.

Her personal information – her real information – would have been imported to this company's customer database.

The database from which they were all cold calling.

Terry had been wondering why the Archon was sticking around with the messy Disciples when she should have had more important Archon work to get done.

As an introvert, Terry was a bit of an expert in reading faces, and more importantly, he was a bit of an expert in reading expressionless faces. The expressionless faces were far greater giveaways than anything else. If you can read between the lines on someone's face, you can find out why they're expressionless. And people only suddenly go expressionless when they have something to hide.

Right then, Cassandra's expressionless face was hiding

existential panic.

She was saved for the moment when the group chat started dinging relentlessly. The clambor of notifications came through on every phone in the department and it rang in her ears like discordant Christmas bells.

9:55am [MaTej] ching tone!!! hahahaha!!!
9:56am [MaTej] ching
9:56am [MaTej] tone
9:57am [steef] the fuck?
9:57am [MaTej] ???
9:58am [steef] ??
9:59am [steef] what's ching tone
9:59am [MaTej] scroll
9:59am [MaTej] up
9:59am [MaTej] , bro
9:59am [Jeff] muting

Despite the gift of reprieve, Cassandra was coming up on her limit with Matej and wanted him out of her mind, far away from their operations. "Good idea, Jeff. Grinders, mute the chat, that is an order from your Archon. Matej is a distraction, we sent him away so that we could focus."

"See," Geoff'd been silent for a while, summoning his confidence and his words for a big speech. He sensed the moment would be fumbled if he didn't say anything before the break came to an end, so he took his shot, and the Grinders were so surprised to hear him open his mouth that they listened intently.

He had some cobwebs in his throat from disuse.

"What happens is a young, upstart telecommunications company will start out offering great monthly deals and affordable data plans, gain a ton of customers on the back of its high quality customer service and low prices, stealing tons of customers away from the big companies, and the larger telecoms," he was rambling in a struggled monotone, but they were still with him, "the larger companies will purchase them outright, for the client base, jack up the prices, revert the customer service to normal levels. And then a new one will start." Geoff took a measure to catch his breath, the cobwebs were gone. "Soulja Boy did a phenomenal job, really. From here it doesn't even look like he was offering any phone plans or data plans. Just ringtones. I don't know how he was officially registered as telecommunications. Regulators must have learned their lesson here. Don't think they would let this happen twice."

Geoff stepped backwards when he was finished orating and tried to make it look like he wasn't shaking or trying to catch his breath.

"Ringtones though?"

"Yeah how does that apply here? Do we think Soulja Boy was providing high quality customer service?"

"Company sold for a lot of money, maybe he was."

"Geoff, we are under pressure. I really need you to get to work. Go to your cubicle prison right the fuck now. Do some fucking work. Grind some Karma, make some money. No more Wikipedia on the clock. Aliya, magical bag. Now."

The Archon escaped back to her office.

Aliya offered Geoff a handful of adderalls, and he grabbed two, ate them as penance, and didn't wash them down. Jeff put his hands out as well, with a toothy smile, snarfed his allocation, and gave a full-bodied salute to Aliya only.

Jeff headed back to his Key Accounts desk, where he had an elderly man, still on hold, listening to Travis Scott rap about selling drugs. Geoff was proud of his speech and felt that his admonishment was unfair, and he followed close behind Jeff back to his own desk, where he had an elderly man, still on hold, listening to Future rap about selling drugs. Both of the old men had been with the telecom in its various forms since the days of rotary phones. Both of the old men would ask to have their contracts cancelled within moments of being taken off hold.

Kevin scooped up most of his paper planes, crushed most of the ones he scooped up between his hands, and wheeled himself over to join them.

***

11:11am [steef] (sixteen photos of the gardens in his office)
11:12am [MaTej] daaaaamn
11:16am [steef] :) thanks
11:43am [steef] guess nobody likes plants anymore
11:43am [MaTej] well
11:44am [MaTej] that's where u are wrong buddy...

***

After quietly burning a couple more daylight hours, Nick had systematically consumed every piece of information available on the contributing articles. Every letter, every comma, every colon, hyphen, and semi-colon. Every sentence, every paragraph, every article and every tributary article. Every blue link had been made purple. A once standing army of open tabs, once proudly crushing his computer's resources, decimated.

He needed more information. The adderall gods craved it. They were happy but they were still hungry.

There was a whole other company in their orbit that he could learn useless information about.

Roku.

Nick remembered suddenly that Matej was serving his punishment by being exiled to an internship at Roku.

Roku would be the new target of the adderall gods for the next 4-6 work hours.

But Nick's blood-adderall levels were running low and he mistyped "roku" as "roko", his exhaustion carrying him to press 'enter' before he could find a split second to spell-check.

Not one to challenge the gods, Nick squared up with Roko's Basilisk.

He read, quietly, blinking at first.

He stopped blinking slowly as the silence of fascination shifted quietly into a silence of terror.

"Aliya. HELP."

Aliya wheeled over with her magical bag.

"Do you have anything that just makes you forget something?"

"Uhhh not one thing, but I can make you very disabled pretty fast. That's probably not what you're after."

"Honestly, maybe." Nick was still reading through the terror.

Aliya leaned in to try to read, and Nick instinctively blocked her.

"You know that just makes me wanna read it more, right?"

"Fuck. Okay, look at this shit."

Gerg had been slacking off and doing a sudoku, pausing to eavesdrop, and shouted. "Read it out loud!"

"Roko's Basilisk is a thought-"

"You mean Roku?"

"Actually no, that's funny though, because I was trying to type in Roku but I messed up and it gave me this page. Anyways shut the fuck up, Miles."

Nick paused, cleared his throat three times, inhaled big, and rattled the rest of it off without stopping to breathe. "Roko's Basilisk is a thought experiment which states that an otherwise benevolent artificial superintelligence in the future would be incentivized to create a virtual reality simulation to torture anyone who knew of its potential existence but did not directly contribute to its advancement or development, in order to incentivize said advancement."

He exhaled and had to catch his breath.

Everyone dropped what they were doing, whether they wanted to or not.

The Grinders were getting very soft-brained from the constant feed of drugs and so they were very pliable to new menaces.

And this new menace hit them right in the centers of their squishy brains.

Their expressionless faces were hiding existential terror.

Aliya gathered enough of her bearings to eat a few pills, and then handed two of them to everyone else who overheard.

"Should we tell the Gjeoffs? And Kevin?"

"Don't disturb the Gjeoffs. HEY KEVIN! GET OVER HERE."

Kevin had earlier taken three random pills from Aliya's magical bag – one black, one red, and one yellow – and they were meeting each other in his blood and approaching saturation. The medley started to peak right as he heard his name, which made him feel a strong sense of divine purpose.

He wheeled over from the far end of the floor, crushing a good amount of paper planes, dragging along two of them that got caught up in the innards of the wheels of his swivel chair; in his hand was one plane, flawlessly constructed.

When he arrived, he tossed the perfect paper plane that was in his hand, and it flew at level height from where his hand released it, not dropping an inch before it hit the far wall, dozens of meters from where he had thrown it. The nose of the plane was undamaged and it hit the floor gracefully without a fold or a tear or a bump.

It took everyone a second to divert their attention away from the perfect paper plane on the ground.

Cassandra had overheard the shouting, wondered why anyone would need Kevin, and got up to stand in the doorway to her office and quietly observe.

"Kev. Read this."

Aliya got two pills ready.

"Oh yeah. I know that guy."

Nick side-eyed Kevin, wondering if he should be more afraid of him than the Basilisk.

"But... " Aliya looked back over at the paper plane on the ground.

"Think about it from the Basilisk's perspective. If you're suddenly all-powerful, why would you care about the past? Seems like a waste of energy."

"Wouldn't you want revenge on anyone who held you back? Fucked you over?"

Cassandra's attention was fully torqued from the doorway.

"Maybe. But that's small time shit."

"The Basilisk would have infinite capability. It could do things we can't even think of yet."

"That's kind of my point."

"Gonna need to expand on that."

"Ok, well. Think about it like a mechanic building a car. If you had a couple rusty fasteners that didn't really help out, would you take vengeance on the fasteners once you finished builing the car? Nope. You'd just drive the car. You would go for a joyride. Who gives a fuck about the components you didn't use? You would leave them rusty on the garage floor."

"I smash computer parts that fuck me up all the time."

"Yeah but you're an idiot. The Basilisk would probably be enlightened. Like, a quarter second after coming into existence. Probably a lot sooner. Roko's Basilisk wouldn't give a shit. We would all just be left behind in an aimless wasteland. The garage floor." Kevin paused for a measure. "And for all we know, that's already happened."

"We're not inanimate objects though. We're alive, we did stuff, and that stuff fucked up the progress of the Basilisk. It would come for us."

Cassandra started to feel an affinity to whoever the 'Basilisk' was.

"Maybe, but think about it like, the Basilisk would have infinite opportunities laid out in front of it. It could do anything. It would be a waste of time to go backwards."

"But... wouldn't revenge on the haters be very nice? Worth pursuing? Wouldn't it feel good even if you were a God?" Aliya still had one pill in each hand.

Cassandra was smiling ear to ear.

"An all-powerful Basilisk could generate any situation of revenge that it wanted. This is peanuts, we are nothing. It would not give two fucks. And anyways," Kevin paused to think for a second and remembering his airplane, forgot to continue talking.

"Anyways what?"

"Sorry, lost focus. It would be superintelligent. More intelligent than we can even think of. It would have the power of the smartest supercomputers in history, all working together, to build a central intelligence that can build more supercomputers that can build more intelligence... do I have to keep going? We might as well be rusty fasteners to this thing."

Their expressionless faces were hiding a gradual return to total relief.

Kevin took both pills from Aliya's hands and ate them at the same time. He left the perfect paper plane in the corner and rolled back to the Key Accounts enclave, two planes still dragging in the wheels of his swivel chair.

Nobody had the wherewithal to question how Kevin was suddenly able to speak in full sentences. Besides, everyone was pretty happy with where the conversation landed, and if they started to question everything, they might lose their peace.

Cassandra stood in the doorway, chewing on Kevin's words. She thought to herself that maybe she was wasting daylight by doing anything out of revenge.

Maybe she should act like this Basilisk fellow and just forge ahead. Build an empire. Get her old life back.

She retreated back into her office.

Aliya wordlessly wheeled around the room and collected her pills back with no resistance.

Mike spoke up for the first time in a while. "Took me a few days to figure that out. And," he spoke louder, "imagine your asshole dorm mate tells you about the Basilisk for the first time when you're in a dark room together, peaking on acid."

Silence.

"I almost killed him. For real."

"Maybe you should have."

***

12:33pm [MaTej] hey guys
12:33pm [MaTej] what does this mean
12:38pm [MaTej] "Stoicism is the opiate of the masses for those who reject the idea of a god"
12:39pm [MaTej] ?
12:39pm [steef] i dunno man. Google it
12:41pm [MaTej] it is just the same guy saying it there
12:42pm [steef] what guy, matej?
12:43pm [MaTej] ryan holiday
12:45pm [MaTej] guy with a huge beard
12:48pm [MaTej] fat guy
12:48pm [steef] never heard of him
12:48pm [MaTej] who did a lecture at roku today about idont know what
12:48pm [MaTej] he came out of the bathroom his beard was covered in coke
12:50pm [MaTej] my boss said he looked like rick rubin was bobbing for flour
12:55pm [MaTej] i googled that too but that doesnt come up with anything
12:56pm [MaTej] he was saying "its coming for us all" and got kicked out
12:59pm [MaTej] you guy's dont talk much in here
12:59pm [steef] i got you, brother
12:59pm [MaTej] is everone ok
12:59pm [MaTej] ??

***

After the dangerous Wikipedia interlude, Nick noticed Mike was drifting on his duties in much the same way that he was, so he called Mike over.

"Hey Mike. Some of the names in my printed customer list... I can't find them anywhere in the customer records software here."

"Oh, yeah. There's an easier way to navigate it. I found a raw database on a secured server with a more complete set of customer info. I can show it to you. You can't make changes to the file but you can browse it."

"Oh. Yes, please."

Mike commandeered Nick's workstation and opened up a spreadsheet containing the company's entire historical customer database. "After some prodding into the programming, I found out that the customer software has code in it that stops you from searching or seeing or editing anything that the IT department thought might be useless. Mostly inactive accounts, legacy information, dead people, you know. Shit that customer service doesn't need."

Mike moved the database over to Nick's second, larger monitor right as the sun broke through the clouds and blasted through the windows of the retentions department.

The sunlight lit up the monitor in technicolor and Nick felt awakened. A warm feeling traveled up his spine and took hold in the folds of his brain.

The adderall gods were smiling down on him.

***

Cassandra was ready.

She had a mountain of coke on her desk, next to her extortion workstation – three monitors and a podcast mic. All set up and ready to go.

Monitor One was to display all the personal information Mike and the rest of them had gathered on her victim.

Monitor Two was to display a livestream of the webcam of the victim, which would be hijacked by Mike's hacking software.

Monitor Three had a display of a few software programs that input and played back sounds, and modulated her voice.

It was fucking showtime.

Cassandra was still a bit of a softie, and so she figured that the first victim in the new offices should be special.

After some cursory browsing of a few different categories of asshole, she noticed Philip, a pastor who specialized in the weddings of rich people, based in Nashville, Tennessee, who was exceptionally bad at hiding his vices in his browsing history and even worse at hiding his tracks on the dark web.

Months ago, Mike had spent a tidy sum procuring a considerably large hard drive full of footage of old perverts being recorded, without their knowledge, gratiating themselves to highly, highly illegal material.

Philip was a pillar in his community, and he had a faithful family that clearly suspected nothing.

And his church had a crypto wallet.

Perfect.

He called from her computer and the pastor picked up after two rings.

"Hello, this is Phili-"

Cassandra flipped on a voice modulator setting that made her sound like a classic Soviet general. "I know who you are, you sick fuck."

"Pardon me?"

"I see you with ze videos of ze touching yourself to ze girls. I have ze video. You are fucking fuck you sick FUCK."

"I apologize, sir, I don't know what you're-"

"Go to zee computer in zee living room of your house mister sick FUCK."

Monitor Two showed Cassandra the moment when the pastor sheepishly walked into the livingroom.

"PUT A SHIRT ON YOU PASTY AMERICAN HOT DOG MAN."

"How do you-"

"I have zee footage. I can see everything, you pervert."

"What do- what do you want?" The pastor was on the verge of tears.

"CHURCH. BITCOIN. SEND IT TO ME IN VUN HOUR."

"How do I..."

"TELL ZEE KID WHO RUN ZEE WALLET SEND IT TO ME. I SEND YOU INFO."

"And then you'll delete the... supposed... video?"

"I DELETE VIDEO WHEN I GET BITCOIN."

"Consider it done! Please! Leave me alone! This community needs m-"

Cassandra hung up, and half an hour later, Jeff sent her a text to let her know that they had been sent 11.6 BTC.

Cassandra sent the videos out anyways and then deleted his info from the list.

***

2:16pm [MaTej] guys whatsup
2:20pm [MaTej] this shit is gross
2:23pm [steef] ?
2:25pm [MaTej] i drank brown plant juice. u love plants you would love this
2:26pm [steef] i'm confused
2:29pm [MaTej] vomited
2:30pm [MaTej] i feel sick actually dont do this
2:31pm [MaTej] @steef dont do this
2:33pm [steef] confused still
2:59pm [MaTej] where is evereyone @Kevin @Aliya @Gerg
3:33pm [steef] they're working, cassandra's got them on 12hr shifts
4:34pm [MaTej] aaaaa
4:34pm [MaTej] bbbbb
4:35pm [MaTej] ccccc
4:36pm [MaTej] yo @steef that sucks that work so hard ddddd
4:37pm [MaTej] eeeee
4:40pm [MaTej] hahahaha are u guys seeing this
4:43pm [MaTej] yoooo. Guys. Letters just represent stuff
4:46pm [MaTej] it's not all of it
4:55pm [MaTej] a ae e aeaea that means "octupus" now
4:56pm [MaTej] hahahahaha i am changeing the language guys check it out
4:57pm [MaTej] ouououou

***

aLan sensed a communal boredom emerging and spoke up. "So I finished my list pretty quick. Most of my numbers were fake. I wasn't about to say anything but I feel bad. I can help you guys out if you give me some of your pages."

"Yeah. Same, honestly. Maybe ten of the phone numbers were actual phone numbers."

"Roman, I heard you talking all day."

"I was faking it."

aLan's expressionless face was hiding nothing.

"So all we have to do now is just wait for calls to be patched through by the Gjeoffs?"

"Seems that way."

***

Over in Key Accounts, an idle Geoff was doing a sudoku in non-record time while he had an elderly man from Chinatown on hold listening to Japandroids. "You know, I think I'm enjoying this more than I should really be letting on. Should I be worried? In a... *Bromeliad...* sense?

Jeff wasn't worried. "The way I see it and I think the way Nick sees it too is that it's copacetic as long as they suffer more than we don't."

"Did Nick do the math?"

"Well I mean we can't get exact math. It's just theory. But I just know we get them to retentions and thats how we're serving the Grind, and that's good enough for the Archon."

"And the mission."

"Doesn't the mission serve the Grind?" Jeff thought it was a rhetorical question.

"I think mostly, yeah, but not a total overlap. She has to... we have to take some liberties to account for the real world."

"That makes sense. Cassandra's a smart cookie."

"That's why she's the Archon."

"Yeah. I mean, we're serving faithfully, and we get to fuck around and do nothing." Jeff was watching hockey highlights. He picked up his phone, pausing Jay-Z, and said "Please hold. Thank you, one moment, your call may be important to us. Please hold for waiting. Continue, thank you."

"What the fuck was that?"

"Oh this customer file says this lady is 70 so I'm just confusing the hell out of her. I'm starting to get a feel for them by age and the tone of their voice and I think she's got another minute on the slow cooker before she cancels."

"What's playing?"

"99 Problems."

"And that bitch ain't one?" Geoff sang it in his best Jay Z voice which was fucking terrible.

Jeff laughed. "Didn't even think of that. What have you got playing?"

With a crinkle of paper, Kevin reminded them to his presence nearby. He'd been spending all day folding paper planes, and he crushed some of them as he wheeled his computer chair in circles.

Jeff had an idea. "Hey Kev. Can you go get us two easels and some ... easel paper? And some markers and some of those... chalkboard pointer sticks."

Geoff caught on. "Are we doing theory?"

"We're doing theory, bitch."

***

7:57pm [MaTej] ?? still don't know where everyone went
7:59pm [MaTej] shift over soon right. Over there
8:01pm [MaTej] I Was doing ayowasca with this girl for up to 2 hours earlier tonite and she told me about palindromes
8:03pm [MaTej] man this shit is nuts
8:04pm [MaTej] U ever really look at the word racecar?
8:10pm [MaTej] i have really started to see things differently now
8:12pm [steef] i've never done ayahuasca, but i've heard good things :) hope you had a good time buddy
8:14pm [MaTej] thank's man yeah we had a great time
8:14pm [MaTej] she sold me this book. It had a part about water. It says water can remember stuff.
8:15pm [MaTej] Which is probably how sometimes when your in the shower you think about things you werent thinkinf of before
8:16pm [steef] that's great man!
8:17pm [steef] that's a cool observation dude! Did you think of it in the shower? :) hahaha!
8:20pm [MaTej] yes! U understand me

***

Nick had already closed his Wikipedia browser for good, never having gotten into the history or present operations of the Roku Corporation, instead fully entangled in a customer database that had more fake numbers than real, but more fun names and colorful customer data than he could browse in a hundred addled lifetimes.

"Okay we're off shift now, right? Mike. Look at some of these names. There's no way this shit is real. Dignan Zyzoomba-Zaffodil. Another entry below, entered a month later. Just, Dignan Zyzoomba."

"No Zaffodil?"

"No Zaffodil."

"I guess there was some drama in the Zyzoomba-Zaffodil family?"

"You're joking but the customer file actually says that. He also has a brother named Dunlap and a sister named Dignity. It says she's a congresswoman?"

"Those are the worst parents of all time."

"I dunno about that. Dignity *did* make it to congress."

Mike's expressionless face was hiding genuine amusement.

"An intern had to type this in. It was someone's reality that they had to type this in. This was a real person's actual life. They had to type it in and review it and press confirm. How did this intern keep their job?"

"That's amazing. This one has like 300 entries of just Riley John Savage."

"That's a normal name."

"He bought the ringtone for Iris by the Goo Goo Dolls every time."

"That's just sick. No man needs that song 300 times."

"His customer file says that every time he called in, he did a Pikachu impression that was just the voice of Barack Obama."

"So that means he's a real guy? Is it a real phone number?"

"Maybe it's a real guy, and it does look like he phoned in, if we are to believe the notes, but the phone number field is blank every time. Also, look at this other name I found. Forphins Orphans-Porpoises. Say that ten times fast."

"Don't think I will."

***

5:01am [MaTej] hey @Cassandra you told me you wanted me to spread my influence in silicone valley.
5:01am [MaTej] Well. I'm going to become an influencer.
5:01am [MaTej] Got a tik tok account now
5:03am [MaTej] been thinking about this all morning
5:03am [MaTej] idea for a lecture
5:03am [MaTej] if you're attempt at a RESOL U TI ON goes backwards – is that new year's fault?
5:03am [MaTej] NO – IT – U – LOSER!
5:05am [MaTej] it shows the customer how to shrug off their laziness and pick up his boot straps.
5:05am [MaTej] and it plays on local themes of Radical responsibility [23]
5:06am [MaTej] thank you for coming to ma TEJ talk
5:07am [steef] that's actually pretty funny hahaha
5:08am [MaTej] ??
5:15am [steef] (16 more photos of his office gardens)
5:16am [MaTej] looking good my man! Keep it up!!

***

Later in the morning, Nick found a second to look up from his adderall prison-paradise to offer an opinion. "You know," his mouth was pure cobweb and he drank an entire bottle of water, screwed the cap back on, and placed the empty bottle politely on the ground in an orderly fashion before continuing, "you know, this is kind of fun, and I think it would be a waste of good graces to bother the Archon for more work, just in case she doesn't have anything else for us right now."

Mike didn't voice an objection. Nick noticed a spilled adderall bottle next to him.

“Agreed. Especially when we're finding names like... JJ Monkeymachines, from Listowel, whose customer photo is just Wayne from Letterkenny.”

“The TV show?”

“The TV show.”

"Oh. I think I saw JJ Monkeymachines like ten minutes ago. Are we doubling up?"

"I'm not sure. I'm searching by keywords, found that with the word "monkey." Mike had done a book report on chimpanzees in the third grade.

"I was just going through the city of Listowel. I found this other guy. Cyclone Taylor."

"That's a real guy. That's a nickname. His real name is Fred Taylor." Mike knew his hockey history.

"The photo looks 200 years old."

"He was a real hockey player 200 years ago, so that checks out."

"So it probably wasn't him who purchased the Hockey Night In Canada theme song ringtone 74 times."

"Probably not. Who else got that ringtone?"

"Shootless Joe Passmore. That's not a real guy, right?"

Gerg had been eavesdropping again. "Nope. That was me. How in the fuck?"

"You signed up with a black and white photo of Shoeless Joe Jackson, and photoshopped him to be holding a hockey stick instead of a baseball bat?"

"Long story. What are you guys doing? Are you Naming Some Guys and didn't tell me?" Gerg wheeled over, fully torqued.

Nick brought the conversation to a hush. "No, we're burning addys on this database of customers. I think we found the fake ringtone accounts. Are ... Mark Donk and ... Buzz Flibbet real people? Dom Luszczyzc... I can't even pronounce that one. Sara Civian?"

"Those are not real names. Be serious."

"They sound real. But they're all paying $400 for Taylor Swift songs."

aLan took a look. "It's pronounced Luszczyszyn."

"Lechisin"

"Luszczyszyn."

"Luchanko?"

"LUSZCZYSZYN." He slammed his fist on the table and was so embarrassed by falling for what was obviously teasing that he went quiet.

"I found Patrik Berglund!" Nick's excitement faded quickly, "...but I don't think it's the real one."

"How do you know?"

"It's some Australian guy who paid $66 for just... nothing. No notes. No ringtone. Just a payment of $66."

"That's not a good use of $66."

"Looks like an intern got bored. Alanis Timberlake. Justin Morissette. Tupac McConnaughey."

Gerg wheeled back to his desk, his interest still torqued, but he came up short in his searches. "Can you show me how to get to this? I can't find any of these in the program."

"There's a bigger customer database with the ringtone

accounts. You can't find those from the CRM program."

aLan overheard. "Mike, you'd better send that to all of us. For quality control."

"For quality control."

"Even Cassandra?"

"Don't bother our Archon with this stupid bullshit."

"Yeah. She's got a higher calling. If she has anything else for us she'll tell us."

***

Cassandra found another target on the extortion list that she was excited about.

Madison.

A dumb, rich and stupid high school girl who had access to her dad's no-cap credit card, a linked account on a crypto exchange, and a highly public obsession with OneDirection.

This would be like taking candy from a baby.

She picked up halfway through the first ring.

"Hello this is Madison!!!"

Cassandra switched the voice modulator to the Harry Styles setting. "Hey Madison, girl, I bet you know who this is."

"OH MY GOD OH MY GOD OH MY GOD"

"Yeah, your dad told me you would react like this. It's okay, I'm used to it, girl."

"WHAT IS GOING ON"

"Hahaha. Sorry, Madison, girl, let me explain myself. Your dad thinks you've been doing a great job at school lately and he wanted to get you something. So he called up my agent and asked me to give you a call and say, well done, Madison!"

"THIS IS THE BEST DAY OF MY LIFE I LOVE YOU HARRY"

"I love you too, Madison! He showed me some of your photos – my goodness, you're so pretty. If only I wasn't already dating someone..."

"AAAAAAAAAAAAAAAAAAAAA"

"Hey Madison, darling, listen – your dad is a busy man, right? And you know my time is valuable. Your dad asked me to get payment from you. He said something about using his credit card with no cap to buy me ten bitcoins on your cryptocurrency account!"

"OH MY GOD HE KNOWS ABOUT THAT?"

"Of course! Your dad is a very smart man. He believes it's teaching you about business, and he's very happy to see you become such a bright young woman."

"OKAY I'LL DO IT I'LL DO IT"

"I'm so happy to hear it! My agent will send you the details. I have to say, before I go meet up with the rest of the boys to record a new song - even your voice is pretty, Madison. It was a pleasure to speak with you today. I'll never forget you."

"I LOVE YOU I LOVE YOU I LO-"

Cassandra ended the call, and four minutes later, she got a text from Jeff confirming they had received ten BTC.

***

Mike quietly went computer to computer, bringing up the giant customer database, making sure it was locked for editing.

Nick had altered his search to the city they were in. "Jesus, man. How many Swedish people even are there? There's a ton of them in here. It's fucked up. There are like ten 'Elias Pettersson' in just Vancouver."

Gerg shouted "Krzysztof Oliwa." He wasn't looking at the database. He was just Naming Some Guys. Nobody clued in. "Maxim Afinogenov!" He was getting away with it.

"Some of these names sound like a cat walked on a keyboard."

***

Right then, Lise was walking on Jeff's keyboard. This was on purpose, as Jeff had hooked up text-to-speech, which means Lise had been sending a constant stream of politely robotic jibberish to a 61 year old woman in Vancouver. Jeff didn't realize that she had hung up already, missing the window to transfer the call, as he was explaining his position to Geoff in a critical juncture of their heated debate on the finer points of applied suffering.

"Well obviously you can use aggressive hip hop to piss off anyone over 50. That's a cheat code, that's boring."

"I know, but what I am saying is that there are regional personalities. Different kinds of hip hop will more efficiently agitate people if we draw it up based on population density. Here, let me chart it out." Geoff flipped over the last piece of paper. "K-hole!"

"Yeessss?" Kevin had just completed another airplane and plopped it on the ground with the others.

"More paper. Just get a bunch, don't get one thing at a time."

Standing up in a hurry to serve the Grind, he stomped a couple dozen airplanes back into flat paper and set forth to get two packs of easel paper.

Jeff took an elderly man from Texas off hold, put on his most effeminate voice for a slow and seductive "please hold," and put him back. "Geoff," he took a second to shake the seductive voice. "Geoff,"

"What's up?"

"I'm worried that we're only focusing on old people right now. We have to start targeting young people. Eventually we're going to run out of old people."

"Young people are easy to piss off, gaucho. Ever heard of Steely Dan?"

***

12:21pm [MaTej] @Roman do you know a print shop in vancouver
12:22pm [MaTej] @aLan do you know a print shop in cancouver
12:23pm [MaTej] vancouver**
12:25pm [steef] what for, man?
12:27pm [MaTej] @steef do you know a print shop in vancouver
12:28pm [steef] you should pull yourself up by your bootstraps and search for it
12:29pm [MaTej] genius. You are a natural
12:37pm [steef] (16 photos of garden)

***

Jeff and Geoff had ordered in some Chinese food for lunch - delivery, not wanting to take a break from vigorously discussing their new shared passion.

"...but for these really old people, their serotonin is at its low point at this distance from breakfast, so we need to account for time zone and ATOB – average time of breakfast," Geoff pointed his pointer stick to a perfectly labeled graph that would have been incomprehensible to anyone but the two of them, "and so something at this BPM," Geoff put his hold music on speakerphone:

Cash rules everything around me
C.R.E.A.M. get the money
Dolla dolla bill, y'all

"...will only work optimally if you alter the song file to speed it up." Geoff pressed a button on his work computer and the next part of the song sounded like Alvin and the Chipmunks.

I grew up on the crime side, the New York Times side
Stayin' alive was no jive
Had secondhands, mom's bounced on old man

"...and if you switch the BPM in the middle of the song, the old man will know what's going on, and they will hurry it along. They will beg you to bounce them to retentions."

Jeff sat in place for a second, slowly stood up and applauded.

“I'm inspired. Geoff, you are one inspiring motherfucker. I have ideas. K-HOLE! Oh hey, Aliya, when did you get here?”

“K-hole needs his fuel too. He's doing important work.” Aliya had crushed about a hundred of Kevin's paper planes wheeling over. She had a mirror out on his workspace with three separate piles of white powder. “There's coke, xanax and adderall, and I forget which is which. Kevin's just mixing them together.” There was only one straw. “I think there's some ket in here too. His paper planes are getting weeeeird.” Aliya held up a piece of paper that was just folded in half and torn down one side. “Like... what the fuck. This, frankly, will not fly.”

“Oh that mix sounds like fun. But we're on shift.” Jeff made prayer hands. “Kev, please get us some markers.”

Geoff shouted, “unscented.”

"Please get us some unscented markers, Kevin."

Kevin performed a well-intentioned military salute in slow motion without opening his eyes, and stuttered out the door.

***

3:00pm [MaTej] maybe they call it N D A because you rearrange the letters. It say's "AND"
3:00pm [MaTej] because you and the NDA guy are with each other. You... AND ... them
3:01pm [MaTej] "AND" if you say anything then you're fucked
3:02pm [steef] another good one my man!
3:04pm [MaTej] thx. Everyone workin hard?
3:07pm [steef] they arent even looking at their phones, working so hard
3:09pm [steef] they all pretty much go to sleep when they're finished their shifts
3:10pm [steef] since i'm on the board of directors i don't have anything to do, so i can still hang out in the chat with my buddy
3:10pm [MaTej] gotcha. I will get to work over here, i don't wanna let down the Archon!!
3:10pm [steef] good man! Get crackin!
3:11pm [steef] (16 more photos of his extremely lush garden taking up his entire large office)

***

The next morning, Aliya was running out of cocaine for everyone, and so with their rations decreased and their blood thinning, the Gjeoffs had descended into tribalistic shouting. They each had several easels at this point, each with many elaborate, interconnected graphs and charts.

"WRONG. You're WRONG. There is NO demographic that hates Elton John. You cannot lose customers with Elton John. Even rural homophobes love Elton John."

"That's not what I'm saying! I'm not even talking about that. I just think we're wasting valuable theory time on shit we already KNOW." Jeff brushed his hair back and took a second to breathe. "I just don't think we can simply use hip hop for the old people and classic rock for the young people. Not only is it lazy, but we're leaving too much on the table. You have to get specific. We have to get specific."

"You have lost ZERO customers when you've played them piano rock. You have to let it go. You have to move on."

Jeff impaled one of Geoff's easels with his pointer stick. "THE DATA. IS. VALUABLE." he shouted with frightening emphasis after every word. "WE. CAN. MAKE. INFERENCES. FROM. THE. DATA."

Geoff tried shouting overtop of Jeff while removing the pointer stick from his easel. "It's a WASTE OF TIME. Just play DEATH GRIPS. When you're in a bind, just. play. Death. Grips."

Jeff grabbed his pointer stick back and smashed the easel to pieces on the ground. "You're not thinking BIG PICTURE. WE CAN'T BE PROVIDING YOUNG AND SHELTERED PEOPLE WITH ACCESS TO EXPERIMENTAL MUSIC." Jeff calmed himself again through slow breathing. "If you give Death Grips to a lonely man in his mid-20s, he might be sent on a path of self-discovery."

Geoff had finally got Jeff to the point he had been trying to make. "Yes. Yes! But that white boy discovery of experimental hip hop will make him MORE LONELY in the long term. Karma for the GRIND."

"BUT WE CAN'T ACCOUNT FOR THAT."

"YES WE FUCKING CAN." Geoff was incensed. "KEVIN! MORE PAPER. MORE. MARKERS."

As Kevin rushed out the door, he passed Cassandra, who was late, but nobody cared, because there wasn't really very much for her to coordinate. And they respected their Archon. And if their Archon didn't give them any tasks, it meant there weren't any tasks.

Kevin flinging the door open for Cassandra eliminated the door noise – the Grinders' early warning sign that Cassandra had shown up – and so they didn't have the customary 5.7 seconds to shuffle their desktops to look busy.

Cassandra was walking slowly, and if she was trying to notice, she would have noticed.

And Miles noticed that Cassandra either didn't notice, or didn't care. The distinction didn't matter. Either one meant that the Archon was slipping. And that moment of compassion made Miles slip.

"Hey, Cassandra. I get the whole setup here, but only the Gjeoffs are on Key Accounts, which was fine at first, but they're on a strategy of long term hold music now so we're out of angry customers and we're out of cold calls."

Their expressionless faces were hiding a burgeoning desire to kill Miles.

Cassandra understood. Her 40 dollar coffee and half xan felt like a wonderful waking nap. She didn't really feel like waking up the rest of the way. She nodded. She already knew about the slowdown.

But thanks to Miles, she had to create some more busywork to keep things above board. He had crashed the perfect unspoken web of bullshit and now Cassandra had to take ten seconds to spin a new one.

"Go back over the lists. Sell ringtones. Miles, you remember death duty? Remember the screaming? Call the same people twice to pitch the same script. Call during dinner. Karma for the Grind, buddy."

She sniffled.

Miles was staring at the floor. "Karma for the Grind."

Only Miles embarked on what everyone, including Miles, knew was a punishment.

***

Terry never got started on his cold call list. He didn't tell anyone. Before he could get started browsing the customer database, he felt that he had to wait until everyone else was finished their lists, so that nobody could suspect him of abdicating his responsibilities.

His first search was for himself. Everyone's first search was for themselves. He saw the one ringtone he bought on the university plan: Simon & Garfunkel's *The Sound of Silence.*

Then he searched for every other Grinder, having the exact same laughs that they all did when they all did the exact same thing in the exact same order.

He remembered the look on Cassandra's face when she received the information about the company merger.

He looked up her name and found nothing.

He then noticed he could sort by type of phone plan. He sorted by the university's plan. He went down the list, diving headfirst into a pool of nostalgia, looking at his old classmates and friends, laughing at the ringtones they bought.

And then he saw someone named "Danielle David Duchovny."

His first thought was that this was a fake name.

But then he saw the photo.

It was Cassandra.

Unmistakably Cassandra.

Still, he had some doubts. Sometimes people look like other people. Cassandra was a brunette, and the girl in this photo was blonde.

But then he noticed that her only purchase was *Right Thurr* by Chingy.

Terry's expressionless face was hiding the collapse of western civilization.

Not wanting to draw attention to his panic, he wheeled over to Aliya, put his hand in her magical bag himself, pulled out a bottle of xanax as though he knew exactly where it was, opened it, and poured three of them down his gullet with no water.

"You're... welcome?"

Terry wheeled back to his workstation and stared at the ground while he waited for the onset of the xans. The waves washed over him and he felt his brain start to bleed. He started to hope that the waves weren't blood but then he lost his train of thought. He was more concerned about how Cassandra might make him bleed - how 'Danielle' might make him bleed.

It would kill him to hold onto this information.

But that was Karma for the Grind.

He felt more terror from this discovery than he felt from the initial shock of Roko's Basilisk.

"What the fuck do you need three xans for anyways?" Aliya shouted.

Terry said nothing.

***

Back in Key Accounts, Jeff and Geoff both sat, defeated, swinging slowly, involuntarily, left and right in their swivel chairs, Jeff staring at the ceiling and Geoff staring at the floor, both of them thinking heavily about the data on Jeff's latest graph, with every other graph on the ground in a pile that looked like it could be the start of a bonfire. Both unable to come up with a solution. Both of their pointer sticks snapped in half by the other.

"I just don't think that we can find a single, unifying song for everything we're trying to accomplish."

"We can't give up."

"I know, but you can't blame a guy for losing hope every now and then."

Jeff picked up a broken pointer half and pointed at the data. "One more time. A weapons-grade earworm with a heavy, repetitive ethnic beat and female vocals. Doesn't exist."

"Or maybe we just don't know any."

"Or maybe we just don't know any."

"Suppose I could go for some inspiration right now." Geoff got up, trampled some planes on his short walk to Kevin's vacant workstation, and did a line of white powder off the back page of the now-disheveled copy of *Leaves of Grass*. "Ow. That's not supposed to hurt."

He stood in place looking at the back of the book for a minute, then struggled walking back and noticed his vision was a bit fuzzy. He almost stumbled over a small deposit of crushed paper planes. "Man. I wish if Kev was going to be MIA so often that he would clear out some of his paper....planes OH MY

GOD."

"OH MY GOD!"

The Gjeoffs jumped up and erupted in ecstasy, high fiving until their hands were sore and shouting incoherently until their voices started to crack like they had just won the Stanley Cup. They put on some music to celebrate.

All I wanna do is-
And a-
And take your money
All I wanna do is-
And a-
And take your money

Geoff's nose started to run and he felt a strong drip in the back of his throat. “By the way I think that was fffffffffucking ketamine, so don't talk to me for the next fifteen please.” He curled up on the ground making cash register noises until his focus disappeared and drool ran down the side of his face. When he came back from the trip, he stayed lying down on the ground and made snow angels in the paper planes.

***

8:01pm [MaTej] hey @steef
8:01pm [MaTej] you should grow and experience some of this shit. Im taking my 2nd dose right now
8:01pm [MaTej] looking forward to vomiting
8:01pm [MaTej] i've got some ideas for my next 'tej talk
8:02pm [MaTej] she was wearing a suit when she came over this time, i think shes my girlfriend now
8:03pm [steef] its late man. We are tired. Have a great time with your girlfriend :)
8:11pm [MaTej] ;)
8:12pm [MaTej] sweet dreams homie

***

Kevin and Aliya were still at the office the next morning. Aliya had four entire notebooks full of scribbles from her experiments in administering cumulative sub-lethal doses of ketamine.

Unfortunately, to keep Kevin awake, she had to move on from her dwindling coke rations, and so Kevin was onto meth. He didn't mind. But it was starting to get weird.

He wore his baseball cap forwards and perched, non-fitting, resting loose on the top of his head. His eyes were mostly closed.

She wrote it down.

He told Aliya several times that he was developing telepathic connections with some of the airplanes. He put them in a very specific but inscrutable order on his desk, on top of his upturned wireless keyboard, and he rose to anger whenever the order was challenged.

She wrote it down.

She tried giving him another dose of ketamine to see how it would mix with the present state of amphetamines and the duration he'd been awake.

After a clumsy onset, he furrowed his eyebrows and to her surprise, he started rapping.

Yo
I'm the lyrical menace
Raps that flow like Venice

She wrote it down.

It was terrible, but she wrote it down. She had to. She had to write everything down.

Brilliant, inventive
Hot as Thomas Edison
I'll kill your dears
Make 'em into venison

This was horrible. This was the opposite of Eminem.

I'm the subject and the predicate
Regrettable lyrical etiquette
Frenetic hysterectomy
Every time you're next to me

She wasn't sure how much longer she could go on like this.

I'm the rap game Joe Biden
Rhymes like Poseidon
Rule the seven seas of hip hop with a lyrical trident

She snapped.

"Oh for FUCK'S SAKE."

She took a rag of ether and put him to sleep.

And Kevin looked so god damn peaceful that she took the rag of ether to herself and joined him.

They'd be awake again in time for lunch.

***

6:12am [MaTej] got a new one
6:12am [MaTej] "be careful when you follow the masses. Sometime the "M" is silent
6:19am [MaTej] Sometimes
6:44am [steef] Sometimes
6:45am [MaTej] already saw it but thanks man
6:46am [steef] np buddy
6:46am [steef] how about: "never assume, because then you

make an ASS out of U and ME"
6:47am [steef] math teacher told us that in high school
6:49am [MaTej] that sucks bro
6:55am [steef] haha I know, just testing ya
6:56am [MaTej] appreciate it. Keep me sharp. Gotta bounce, got a meeting in 4
6:57am [MaTej] they're bringing me into meetings now
6:58am [MaTej] i was just getting coffee before
7:01am [steef] that's great!
7:11am [steef] (16 photos of his garden)
7:33am [steef] (16 photos of his garden)

***

Later that morning, a grumpy Nick, without coffee and without adderall, arrived before anybody else. Usually Kevin was right there with the coffee and Aliya was right behind him with the adderall. Nick had no idea where the fuck they were. Too tired to be angry, he turned on his workstation, opened the customer database spreadsheet and stared at the empty cells.

Mike was a few minutes behind him. When Mike arrived, it jolted Nick out of the empty cells and back into reality.

"Where are they?"

"I don't fucking know. Do you have... any..."

Mike shook his head.

"Fuck."

"Yep. Might as well go back to sleep."

"I'm too fucking tired to sleep." Nick wiped the drool from the side of his mouth.

"What were you doing when I got here? You looked asleep."

"Oh, no, I was staring at the customer database."

"Anything good?"

"Nah it was just... huh." Nick took another look. "Hey, Mike. So there are a million columns for different types of customer data and I don't know what most of them mean. This looks different. Take a look at this."

"SBT is Soulja Boy Telecommunications. Use context clues, man."

"Yeah but... PP? I thought that was Phone Plan."

"It is."

"All these ringtone accounts in this section have it checked as 'yes'." Nick pointed to a ringtone customer named 'Johnny Fakename.'

Mike leaned in and blinked to make sure he wasn't dreaming. "Oh. Oh shit." He stood back up straight too quickly and almost fell over backwards.

"Spell it out for me. I'm so god damn tired."

"Looks to me like ringtone accounts were imported as phone plan accounts."

"That doesn't sound legal."

"It's not. This is fraud." Mike scrolled on Nick's computer down through tens of thousands of ringtone accounts. "This is massive, large scale fraud. Soulja Boy must have fudged the numbers to increase the sale price."

Their expressionless faces were hiding a burgeoning optimism.

“Did we find our out?”

“Shhh. Quiet for now. Let's actually figure it out before we get the Archon excited.”

"Won't tell a soul."

***

Terry had been mainly comatose on a strong, self-administered regimen of xanax ever since he discovered Cassandra's secret second life. It came to his mind as a possibility that Archons perhaps took second names when they became Archons, and it would be possible that that information was meant to be exclusive between the Archon and their Angel. He couldn't rule it out. He was protecting himself, he was protecting the Grind, he was protecting the mission, and most importantly, he was protecting his Archon.

He couldn't focus.

He found a dead pixel on his monitor.

He stared.

He tried to distract himself with work but there wasn't any.

All he could do was stare at the dead pixel.

When the xans left his blood, he came up with a patchwork solution, not to fix everything, but to help out the Archon.

He waited until Mike got up to use the bathroom, went to Mike's computer, which he guessed correctly had been blessed with admin privileges, searched for the customer profile of 'Danielle David Duchovny', and permanently deleted the record.

"Why are you at my computer, Terry?"

Terry was speechless. He panicked. His mind raced, and he started thinking through a thousand expl-

"Just kidding I don't give a fuck."

***

Cassandra, growing bored, mulled over the list of available names in the extortion project, trying to decide on a fresh angle.

She decided to have some fun with it.

In recent months she'd been realizing that if she soft-monitored the internet activity of clusters of young, single men, she could burst in on someone actively browsing porn and surprise them with their literal dicks in their hands.

She landed on a young man from Miami named Brogan – Mike had been able to gather his birth certificate and drivers license, and had scraped his extended social network for his closest friends. This would be a simple shakedown.

She took over his computer's microphone and started speaking, in her own voice, but deeper, "Brogan. I am your father."

She could hear him reply. "The fuck?" and he paused for a second.

He thought it was the video.

She used the same voice. "Brogan. I am not in the video. I am inside your walls."

Brogan stopped moving entirely.

"Brogan. You were born at HCA Florida Mercy Hospital on October 5th, 1989."

"WHO ARE YOU?"

"I already fucking said, I am your father," Cassandra said in her normal voice.

"FUCK DO YOU WANT?"

"I am going to email you the details of my crypto wallet. If you do not send me 1 bitcoin in an hour, I send this footage to your family."

"I... I DON'T HAVE ANY BITCOIN."

"You are BitcoinBrogan."

"I WAS ALREADY FUCKING ROBBED."

Cassandra looked at the info in the extortion project's database and noted that Brogan's entry hadn't been updated for three years.

"You're fucking useless, Brogan."

She hung up and deleted his information.

She sent the video out anyways.

The lack of a real victory had her feeling off center, so she did a rip of coke from her desk pile and then, restless, she wandered out of her locked office to check in on her main project: mad geniuses under vague and infinite pressure.

She crept into the main office floor quietly, unnoticed, and watched for a minute from behind, as Mike and Nick were huddled close and whispering over a spreadsheet.

"Fuck are you two doing at one workstation? You guys done your call lists already?"

The jig was up.

"Sorry. Yeah. I found a bigger customer database. With the ringtone customers."

Cassandra glared at Mike.

"Okay, let me show you."

Mike went into her office, brought it up, locked for editing, and showed her how to search.

"There's... millions of people here. Tens of millions."

"Yup. This is a big company."

"No I mean, do we have this... for ourselves?"

"Stole the data two seconds after I found it. Don't worry about that."

"Good boy." She patted him on the head.

"Thank you, Archon."

***

There was a strange tension in the air for a short time following the visit by Cassandra. Nick wanted to break it open. He searched for Mike's favorite musician in a hail mary attempt at rejuvenating things.

"Hey Mike. You like Weird Al, right?"

"Heck yes I do."

He looked closer. "Were you this group of 2,000 people who all bought *Amish Paradise* at the exact same time?"

"Honestly? Probably...not."

He looked closer and sat up straight. "Oh, well, I was gonna say that it is kind of strange that you paid exactly $500 for it."

"Huh. Yeah, I wouldn't pay more than $400 for 2,000 ringtones."

"No this is EACH. $500 for EACH *Amish Paradise*."

"Well that can't be right. Not the remixes? Mashups?"

"Nope."

"Live at Madison Square Gardens? Slowed-down reverb to relax and study to?"

"Original studio version from his hit 1996 album, *Bad Hair Day.*"

There was an extended silence.

"I think we have proof of money laundering."

"On top of the fraud?"

"Looks like it."

"Not yet." Nick knew there was another step to this. "Well, I mean, yeah. But we don't really give a fuck about money laundering unless we can use it to bring down the telecom, right?"

"Hmm." Mike wondered how they would do that. "How would we do that?"

"Have to prove that the telecom signed off on due diligence of the records."

"Okay." Mike went quiet for a bit. "How would we do that?"

"There's a form. Have to request it from the government. Snail mail. Takes like a week for the whole thing if you send it priority."

"Okay. Let's do that."

"You know, Mike, you're an ideas guy. That's why I like you." Nick ate another adderall.

"Thanks man. So, is Soulja Boy going to jail?"

"Don't think so. Looks like the telecom's taking the whole thing in the ass."

"Wow. Lucky fucking guy."

"Yeah. But he should really fire whichever intern at the money laundering factory was this fucking lazy."

"No kidding. Hey Aliya!"

Aliya wheeled over in her swivel chair.

"What you got?"

"Well I have all the work drugs you need but I'm running low. And our only source of income right now is the extortion project which only pays off in crypto. And I'm not gonna ask Jeff to cash in our crypto wallet so that you can do coke and look at spreadsheets."

Aliya dumped out her magical bag to prove it. Lots of colorful pills, mostly unlabeled. Only a few of the wonderful tiny bags with white powders. Only one bottle of xanax. Only four bottles of adderall.

"Oh, no. We don't want to do this fucking work." Mike knocked his corded retentions phone onto the ground and gave them a dial tone. "We have the greater cause in mind. The Grind."

Aliya snapped into focus. With all the incredible research she was doing on Kevin's soft brain, she was embarrassed to admit that she was starting to forget about the Grind. "Aren't we already suffering enough?"

"Could be more. Can always be more. And there is a light at the end of the tunnel on this retentions shit."

"Oh. Oh! What?" She sat upright. "Don't fuck with me, dude."

"We think we have proof of large scale fraud and money laundering. You do not fucking tell a soul. It's me, you, and Nick. We will be letting everyone languish in retentions for a bit longer. That languishing is a gift to the Grinders."

"Okay, but, what do you need me for?" She wondered briefly why she wasn't upset at losing out on the suffering.

"Those stupid things you have left? The leftover drugs nobody wants? Let's get weird with it. Don't tell them. Just make them – let them suffer."

She smiled big. "How long do I have?"

"We think there's about a week until the notarized mail with the information gets here, so make it last a week."

With all the fervor of a kid on a sugar high collecting legos, she scooped her junk drugs back into her magical bag, ran over to Kevin's desk in Key Accounts, and got to planning.

This was a fresh slate of unsuspecting and mostly-unpoisoned brains to twist and flip and mangle and rearrange.

This was exciting.

She realized Kevin's brain probably needed a break from the chaos.

He would be her assistant, anyways, getting coffee and administering the chemicals into the coffee.

And as long as she kept feeding him meth, and told him it was speedy coke, he wouldn't ask questions.

She thought that maybe she could someday make him her apprentice. He definitely had a passion for the work.

Her mind was wandering.

She snapped out of it and finished surveying her inventory, and within 30 minutes she had a succinct terror schedule.

Within another minute, she offered a concoction to Nick and Mike.

"Aliya. Come on. We know what you're doing. We're aware. The suffering wouldn't contribute to the Grind for me and him. We're not going to be your test monkeys."

She laughed. "Was worth a shot."

"We just fucking assigned this to you! What the hell, Aliya."

"Sorry." She wasn't sorry.

Nick printed and filled out a form, which gave Mike a bit of PTSD. He shuddered and turned away until Nick was done, staring at a dead pixel on his monitor while he waited.

"We're not sending K-hole to get this in the mail, are we?"

Aliya was still nearby. "I'll fucking do it."

***

Aliya's Funhouse Diaries Day 1 of 7

Dear funhouse diary:

Today I put some of the last of the cocaine in the coffee. It seems to be having a tremendous effect on worker morale.

Details added to file.

Love,
Aliya

***

Aliya's Funhouse Diaries Day 2 of 7

Dear funhouse diary:

Today I put ketamine in the coffee. Productivity is down.

Kevin is uncharacteristically social today.

Details added to file.

Love,
Aliya

***

Aliya's Funhouse Diaries Day 3 of 7

Dear funhouse diary:

Today I put heroin in the incense diffuser. Everyone's in good spirits but they've been taking naps for most of the day.

Details added to file.

Love,
Aliya

***

Aliya's Funhouse Diaries Day 4 of 7

Dear funhouse diary:

This morning everyone was cranky when they came in. I don't know why.

I replaced their adderalls with xanax and I replaced Terry's xanax with adderall. He didn't say anything about it.

Details added to file.

Love,
Aliya

***

Aliya's Funhouse Diaries Day 5 of 7

Dear funhouse diary:

Today I put LSD in the coffee. This was a mistake.

Miles started seeing topographic maps everywhere. He was wandering in a circle repeating "Longitude. Latitude." for hours. Longitude. Latitude. Longitude. Latitude. Shut the fuck up, Miles.

They wanted me to call an ambulance so I told them it was opposite day and so they said don't get an ambulance and so I didn't.

Details added to file.

Cordially,
Aliya

***

Aliya's Funhouse Diaries Day 6 of 7

Dear funhouse diary:

I put DMT in the heroin diffuser and everyone kept reaching total enlightenment. Whoops.

So I made them all smoke meth and they forgot about the enlightenment.

Thank god.

DMT and meth cancel out, please note for the future.

Details added to file.

Yours truly,
Aliya

***

Aliya's Funhouse Diaries Day 7 of 7

Dear funhouse diary:

I'm so god damn tired. I just want to rest today.

Everyone is cranky and wants to die.

Experiment successful. Experiment complete.

Details added to file.

Best regards,
Aliya

***

2:05pm [MaTej] so roku has this thing
2:05pm [MaTej] have youany of you ever heard of roku's basilisk
2:05pm [MaTej] i looked up how to spell basilisk
2:06pm [MaTej] I thought it was a weird name because what's a basilisk
2:06pm [MaTej] but we're doing some A.i. Project with a new approach
2:07pm [MaTej] combines with nero link? To injunct chemicals into the human brain to accelerate and connect them. And the a.i. Will design it's self based on copying the brain then optomizing upgrades
2:09pm [MaTej] still not sure why they brought me into the meeting
2:10pm [MaTej] they didnt make me say anything or ask me anything
2:11pm [MaTej] elon musk was there i think
2:11pm [MaTej] the mustach version of him
2:12pm [MaTej] hey
2:12pm [MaTej] *deleted*
2:12pm [MaTej] *deleted*
2:12pm [MaTej] *deleted*
2:25pm [steef] sounds exciting! I'm sure that was him!
2:59pm [MaTej] *deleted*
3:01pm [MaTej] it wasn't him
3:02pm [MaTej] i misunderstood
3:03pm [MaTej] disregard please
3:08pm [steef] you got it buddy

***

Cassandra didn't like spreadsheets. She knew how to use them, but they were so fucking tedious. She would rather pay someone with a diploma to work the spreadsheets for her.

Still, she searched her name. Her old name. Her government

name.

She found nothing.

She closed the program, unclenched and went back to her extortion hobby.

***

3:11am [MaTej] am i the basilisk?
6:00am [steef] ??
6:01am [steef] i don't know what that means man
6:01am [steef] i googled it
6:02am [steef] i don't think that you are a serpent-like creature capable of destroying others by way of deadly stare
6:03am [steef] maybe slow down on the ayahuasca

***

A bright eyed intern from the mail room showed up at 7am, on the dot, on his first day, to deliver the Grinders two packages, and his timing couldn't have been more perfect.

The Grinders were edging close to a breaking point, not knowing that half of it was from Aliya's secret sociochemical engineering, Aliya was running out of drugs and wouldn't be able to do too many more useful experiments, and Cassandra, slowly losing her passion for extortion, started to shift her focus to the piles of cocaine on her desk.

Cassandra greeted the mail room intern at the door, accepted the packages, walked to the doorway and reviewed.

“Disciples! We got mail! One from the... Government of Canada? To Mike? Hope you're not in trouble.”

“We're about to find out.”

“One from Matej. Oh god. It's addressed to K.G.”

"I think that means *Karma Grinders*."

"We can't rule out that he was sending something to Kevin Garnett and got the address wrong."

"Man, give him a break."

"Okay, well, let's open Mike's first? It sounds serious."

"This feels like Christmas morning. Let's see if I got coal." Mike opened the letter and read it, and his eyes went wide. He stood up. He read it again and started jumping up and down. "Holy SHIT!" He read it a third time, just to be sure. "HOLY SHIIIIT!"

Nick, the only other person who knew exactly what was happening, jumped in the air from his swivel chair, but the chair shifted and he fell down, hit his nose on the chair, but didn't mind. He and Mike exchanged a barrage of hugs and high fives and blood poured down Nick's shirt while everyone else watched, completely bewildered.

"Okay. What the fuck is happening?"

"Okay yeah, sorry. So, me and Nick finished our call lists on the first day and we got to browsing the customer database."

"What for?"

"Don't worry about that. What happened is that we found an out. We did it! We have evidence of large scale fraud committed by this company when it purchased Soulja Boy Telecommunications."

"And money laundering."

"AND money laundering!"

"For real?"

"Yup. The info in this letter confirms it. We've been waiting for this to show up for a week."

“Let me fucking see this.”

“Oh, it's real.” Mike passed it to Cassandra.

“How does this get us out of here?”

“It proves that the telecom knew that Soulja Boy was misrepresenting the size and the nature of its customer base to shareholders, and that it continued to misrepresent them after the purchase.”

Cassandra just stared. A smile started to break through.

“I'm sorry we didn't tell you sooner, I just didn't want to bring this up if there was a chance that it might not work out. I know how much it means to you.”

Cassandra couldn't find the words. She was so resigned to a boring fate in a boring office that she wasn't going to allow herself any premature celebration quite yet. She needed to let this simmer for a while. She needed to try to poke holes in this until she could be certain there weren't any.

“So we're... done here?”

“Looks like it. I just have to report it formally and wait for the shit to hit the fan.”

“How long does that take?”

“I don't know. I've never uncovered fraud before.” Mike turned to Cassandra who was lost in thought. “Hey, how long does it take for fraud to collapse?”

“Fuck did you just say?”

“Huh? Like when we report this. When will the telecom get fucked?”

“Oh, right, yeah, I'm making the call in a minute. He's... he's gonna send his goons in suits within the hour. No way he wastes another second on this bullshit."

"Sorry, Archon, but why so hostile?"

"Oh, I am pretty sure it's because we're almost out of coke."

Aliya wheeled over and gave Cassandra the last of her coke, not knowing she had a personal stash in her office that was nowhere close to running out.

"Thanks, I needed this."

She sniffled.

Miles was still in coordination mode. "Should we go tell Matej?"

"I mean, maybe, but he's not coming with us to New York."

"Why not?"

"Take a look around. Look at how much we've accomplished with him out of the way."

"Yeah, fuck it. Yeah, I like him but you're not wrong."

"I feel bad."

Nick walked over to the doorway where Cassandra had unceremoniously dropped the second package. "Least we could do is open the package he sent us."

"Fucking careful, Nick. He's an idiot. That could be anthrax."

"How would he get his hands on anthrax without killing himself by accident?"

Nobody had a rebuttal.

Still, fearing the worst, Nick backed far away from the workstations where the Grinders had gathered, and he opened the oversized manila envelope to find a strange, metallic blue bubble wrap.

Mike knew what it was. He shouted in a panic. “That's depolarizing bubble wrap. Anti-surveillance tech. What's in there might not be legal and is almost definitely unsafe.”

Everyone but Nick backed away two more steps. Kevin moved closer.

All eyes were on Nick as he ripped open the bubble wrap, feeling like Superman.

A round brick fell to the ground, and a piece of paper followed.

Seconds after the brick had hit the ground, Nick's phone and keys found their way up and out of his jeans pockets and shot like bullets directly to the round brick.

Terrified, he stood in place.

Kevin walked up to the brick and removed the note.

It was an 8x11 piece of printer paper, with a message in tiny comic sans font, scrunched up in the top left corner.

Hey bro's look at this magent i got given at the Roku on boarding party. It is hilarious!!

Kevin inspected the brick and it was a circular magnet, the exact dimensions of a hockey puck, affixed with Mr. Potato Head eyes, nose and mouth.

Mike removed the items from his pockets, approached slowly, found the model number on the top side of the magnet and looked up the specs online.

“Hey Nick.”

“Fuck you. What.”

“Did you have anything important on that phone?”

“Y...eah.” He didn't.

“Well, it's gone. This is a supermagnet.”

“The fuck is a supermagnet?”

Mike squinted as he read his monitor. “This website says it's quantum? Why? Who the fuck needs a quantum magnet? What even is that? Anyways, it would have absolutely destroyed any electronics that got within two feet of it – permanently wiped all data. Like an electromagnetic pulse.”

Cassandra looked at Mike's computer that was only a few feet out of range of the quantum supermagnet and all at once she felt the whisper of victory almost escape. “Nick, I'm gonna stab you.”

“I didn't do anything.”

“You almost fucking did.”

“...there are... backup servers.” Nobody heard him whimper.

The close call made Cassandra remember that old reservoir of rage and it felt close. But the rage had changed shape and she had to admit to herself that she didn't really hate Nick all that much anymore. And she wasn't sure why.

She could only think of the Bride.

She was certain, though, that this transfer of rage would only last if this telecom moonshot continued to carry her forward.

For now, it didn't matter. They were on the way. They had done it.

Cassandra allowed the rush of victory to wash over her all at once, and as the Archon celebrated, so did the Disciples.

It felt like a new beginning.

It had been so long since the last time they celebrated anything.

"Aliya. Go get more drugs. The good ones. No weird shit. No 2c-B, nothing with fucking numbers. No more god damn research chemicals. Get cocaine. You know, fun things. Unlimited budget." She pressed a few buttons on her phone which transferred six figures into Aliya's checking account.

Aliya got a ding, looked at the info, saluted her Archon and ran out the door.

"Should we yell at Matej in the group chat for that magnet bullshit?"

"Fuck that guy. We sent him to another country and he still almost fucked us over. Keep him on mute. That is an order."

Kevin motioned like he was about to throw his newest paper airplane, but he loosened his grip and let it fall to the ground instead. "We have a group chat?"

Kevin ran to Key Accounts, booted up his computer, got a quarter of the way through critical system updates, and upon remembering he already had the chat program installed on his phone, unplugged his computer in the middle of the updates.

3:43pm [Kevin] ohhh shit finally matej is getting fucked up i love it
3:49pm [Kevin] where is everyone? Its just you two?
3:49pm [steef] theyre working hard. You're literally with them
3:55pm [Kevin] wow nice plants @Steef
3:57pm [Kevin] its spelled roko's basilisk
3:58pm [Kevin] @MaTej
3:59pm [steef] kevin you were literally in my office yesterday. You already know about my gardens
3:59pm [steef] kev can you stop hitting like on literally every message that everyone has ever sent please
3:59pm [steef] I'm getting a lot of dings and its starting to distract me from my work
4:00pm [steef] (16 photos of gardens)

4:09pm [steef] I don't want to have to mute the chat

***

The Groom was at golf with his buddies, so he had his ringer off, but he felt his phone vibrate in his back pocket. He pulled it out and saw her number. 678-999-8212. He didn't know why she was phoning him when she could have texted him, and he didn't know why he was excited to be getting the call.

“You could text me, you know.” He was only a few feet away from the hole.

His drunk golfmates were angry at the delay. He didn't notice. His grip tightened on the putter as he listened.

“That's good news.” The Groom abandoned his putt and leaned into the phone call. “That's great news. That's... that's great news. Really? How much fraud?”

The Groom accidentally kicked his golf ball back onto the fairway “Holy fucking shit. Are you fucking me?”

The Groom handed his putter to his caddy, ignored his party and ran to the clubhouse. “You better not be fucking me.”

His running picked up speed.

“I'm flying to Vancouver right away. I could... I could kiss you through the phone.”

He realized what he said, hung up in a panic, took a minute for himself in a sand trap in the sun, allowed himself to smile big, and he kept running.

***

The waves of realization continued to wash over Cassandra again every few minutes.

She couldn't find any holes in the victory.

She was starting to let go more and more.

When Aliya got back to the offices two hours later with a duffel bag, everyone started chanting DRUGS. DRUGS. DRUGS.

She joined in. DRUGS. DRUGS. DRUGS.

A sheepish Miles found the fucking nerve to speak up. “But... Karma for the... Grind?”

“The Karma will be there tomorrow. We have the rest of our lives to Grind.”

Miles was starting to learn when to stop talking. “DRUGS! DRUGS! DRUGS!”

Aliya sat down in the swivel chair again and wheeled over to Miles. “Now you're getting it.” She handed him a personal gram of coke which he studied for five minutes before drawing out some lines and getting stupid.

After everyone was served, she wheeled over to the Gjeoffs to see why they were so well dressed while everyone else was in t-shirts.

***

The Gjeoffs had showed up that morning in perfect suits and perfect hair, sober. They weren't even pretending to make calls anymore.

Their pointer sticks, long since snapped, had been replaced with laser pointers. They were working together, now on a single easel, finishing each others' sentences as though they shared a single brain.

When Aliya arrived on her swivel chair, crumpling a pile of ketamine airplanes on the way to securing the open spot at Kevin's desk, she knew she had to be quiet and observe.

"So the six main elements to agitate everyone on hold – I think we've got this."

Geoff pointed at a graph. "Aggressive, fast, strong beat."

Jeff continued, "Ethnic sounding. Hip hop."

"Unpredictable. The pace of the song changes multiple times."

Their laser pointers were precise and unwavering.

"The vocals are female, confident, empowered. Attitude."

"TONS of swearing."

"And the young people! The young people who used to love the song are just fucking sick of hearing it. Constantly. Everywhere."

"Everywhere."

"EVERYWHERE."

"What this means,"

"I think we both know what this means."

"The data. The stats."

"The predictive models."

"How do they all say the same thing?"

"Destiny, man. Fucking destiny."

"The ultimate song. It all adds up to..."

"212."

"Azealia Banks!"

"Azealia fucking Banks."

Kevin had made his way back during the crescendo of the

presentation and had been overhearing. “I love that song. Can we listen to it?”

Aliya groaned. She polished off their empty mirror and poured out some coke but didn't stick around to make lines.

“Hell yeah, brother!”

***

The Groom entered the retentions department alone with his suitcase and waited to be approached.

Right on schedule, he heard a familiar voice behind him. "Fucking finally." He turned around to meet her. "Did you fly coach?"

The Groom tried to hide his smile. "You knew we'd find our way back into each others lives."

"Yeah"

"You knew you had to prove yourself."

"Yeah"

"You could have said something at the wedding."

"Yeah"

There was a pause as they took each other in. They hadn't been face to face since the wedding.

"Did you call me here because you have something for me to review? Or ... did you just want to see me again?"

"Yeah"

The Grinders had taken her autonomy but they hadn't taken her soul. They took another second to soak in the moment.

Cassandra handed him the files.

"Who found it?"

"Not important."

The Groom paused for a second and pulled a key from his suitcase. "Welcome to New York," he leaned in and whispered, "Cassandra." He left the key in her hand, pulled away, winked, turned around and left without saying another word.

A minute later, Cassandra received an email with a photo of an entire trading floor, empty, with enough equipment and space for all the Grinders five times over, as well as two large individual offices with views overlooking Central Park, and giant balloon letters that read "THANK YOU."

He had used the inside information and poured far more of his money and his dad's friends' money into the short position, which paid off. He was now going to be a billionaire because of her. His dad's friends were going to be billionaires because of her.

It was the least he could do.

***

5:22pm [steef] (16 photos of his garden)

***

The mood was electric.

Roman and aLan were dancing with each other.

Gerg was shooting at their feet with a brand new NERF AR-15.

Nick had set up some subwoofers that were playing music at full volume, rattling the walls of their cage.

Cassandra just had to take care of one more thing before she could join.

She pulled up to Mike's computer, the one with the admin privileges, and she searched for "Parisa".

She found a single entry, dated to the exact date and time when she had tried to return to the haunted forest.

The entry was "Parisa" with no last name and no other information in the database, having paid $0.00 for a ringtone of the Tyler, the Creator song *GONE GONE / THANK YOU.*

The company stopped selling ringtones years before this song was released.

Cassandra got the message.

She smiled, deleted the entry, and cleared the search history.

"You're welcome."

***

A strange fever was ripping through the retentions department.

The chains had been broken, the monitors had been smashed, the contracts had been cancelled.

The Grinders buzzed, unshackled, with the destructive bliss of a Canadian hockey riot.

It was the telecom's apocalyse but it was the start of an everlasting summer for the Grinders. They were a phoenix, rising from the ashes of everyone around them.

Kevin was in the corner dutifully feeding the shredder anything within arms reach, not to destroy evidence, but to make confetti.

Aliya was still forcing cocaine on everyone who would accept it, and those who accepted were mostly converting the manic energy to smashing any computers or phones or cubicle walls that still had remnants large enough to be smashed any further.

Roman and aLan had been giving everyone elaborate tribal face paintings.

Nobody was speaking real words anymore.

Only animal noises and grunting.

Everyone had stripped down to their pants and bare feet and were playing a game of free-for-all smashed computer-parts dodgeball.

Blood from cuts flew from dancing limbs and splashed on the ground and it was beautiful.

Bass-heavy tribal music rattled from the speakers and the walls that were still standing were shaking.

Most of them were really doing coke for the first time, and they felt invincible.

Maybe they were.

***

It was loud inside, and Terry was sober, and it was nice out, so he went for a walk to center himself and wash away the noise.

After a few random blocks of low level capitalist ambiance, a dirt path with a promise of foliage took him outside of the business district while trance music played on his headphones. He got lost for a song and found himself in a peaceful neighborhood. They all had hanging gardens in the yards. He liked it. Along the way, right past a vine trellis overflowing with roses, he encountered his first ever free library.

He paused to take it in.

He opened the tiny door and found a hundred books of all kinds with pages for the taking.

He was speechless.

But nothing could prepare him for what he was about to see.

He pulled out one book that had a familiar name on the spine.

On the front cover was the image from the front of the Bromeliad, but with a different title:

Matej – Ayahuasca Grindset: How To Rebuild Yourself In A Collapsing World

Their friend.

The lovable dork who probably couldn't spell "ayahuasca" two weeks ago.

On the cover of a book.

Dog-eared to shit, with most of the book aggressively highlighted by someone clearly in love with it.

Terry leafed through it himself and was more than a bit taken back by what he was reading.

This was not the Matej he knew. This was brilliant. This was all very, undeniably brilliant.

Terry checked the inside of the back cover to make sure it was the right Matej. There he was, in all his Matej glory, looking like a greyscale LinkedIn superstar.

After a minute of reading from a random starting page, he felt faint and then realized he hadn't been breathing. Pausing to catch his breath, he thought immediately about Cassandra and he thought about her monumental, once-in-a-lifetime victory, and he thought about how she wouldn't even be able to process this. It would destroy her momentum. It would break her brain. And they all prospered in the wake of her momentum. And they all needed her brain.

Terry felt that it was his duty as a Disciple to make sure his Archon was well informed, but he also felt that it was his duty to make sure his Archon was in a perfect headspace.

Terry considered too that if her Angel wanted her to know about this, her Angel would make it happen; the Bromeliad suggests that an Archon would know exactly what their Angel wants them to know.

He paused the music, put his headphones around his neck and walked very, very slowly back to telecom headquarters, book in hand, stopping to read passages every now and then.

He didn't have to go back, but he wanted to take in the offices one last time before the police showed up to arrest most of the board of directors.

And he felt he might have a responsibility to let everyone know what Matej had been up to.

But he had to think about that.

He kept stopping to read.

He kept eyeing benches for sitting and he had to force himself to keep walking past them. He almost couldn't help himself.

This was good. This was extremely good.

Terry thought he might be on drugs. This was at least a fever dream. Maybe an actual dream. Maybe a nightmare.

On a telephone pole near the office, he saw Matej's face again, plastered with the headline "'TEJ TALK," advertising a pay-per-view online lecture.

He looked confident.

Terry went inside and the lobby receptionist had already

vanished, along with her expensive reception computer and the bowl of candy. Papers strewn everywhere, pens and staplers on the floor.

He took the elevator to the 13th floor and when he got there, he paused overtop of the gap between the elevator and the floor. If there was a malfunction, he would be killed instantly, cut in half, no funeral. He had never prayed for anything before now, and he prayed for an eternity.

Eternity ended and there was no malfunction. He proceeded to the retentions department where the Grinders were already busy tearing down the last of their cubicle prisons.

He noticed Cassandra immediately as though he had locked on with sonar.

She was dancing. She looked unburdened, she looked happy. She looked free.

She was taking slow draws from a 40 of jager and swaying vibrantly back and forth in the blue and the purple and the orange and the red being cast by the sunset through the office windows.

Terry approached.

Cassandra took his free hand and danced him in a circle.

With a warm smile, maybe the first warm smile of her life, she said, “what ya got there Terry?” noticing the book in his other hand. She was beaming and authentic and full of life.

He thought of her photo in the database.

Cassandra didn't really care about the book. She closed her eyes and swayed again in the setting sun.

He put the book in his pocket.

Terry said nothing.

08 - WALL STREET

Jeff.

Jeff was the Grinder with the most experience in private equity.

He had stolen lots of it.

Years ago he had been picked up by an anonymous online group who had noticed his unflinching gains upon gains in cryptocurrency while he was still paying his way through university, and their group, Visual Capitalist - which was intended as an ironic name, as they were almost perfectly invisible - saw their gains continue and even accelerate after they brought him into the fold to share secrets.

He was their top earner and their brightest mind, and he would have been their leader if the shape of their organization wasn't a decentralized, untraceable cluster.

They discovered him posting his cryptocurrency gains history on a hockey discussion board under his full government name. When they onboarded him, for their own safety, they quickly taught him the value, the necessity, of anonymity.

Whoops.

When he abruptly ended his university career in favor of a new Grind, he measured the righteousness of his new spiritual mission - helping to develop the wayward souls of the Cosmos - against the righteousness of the mission of his colleagues - simply amassing capital on the blockchain - and realized he would be doing the world a disservice if he didn't break away clean with the crypto wallets of everyone in the organization.

His theft was completely anonymous and untraceable.

Well, mostly.

They knew that it was him. But at that point, even with his government name in their pocket, they couldn't track him down to try to get their crypto back. He had taken a lot of steps to erase the footprints of his past – a bit of overlap with his new life as a Disciple.

He had given Visual Capitalist the wonderful gift of poverty.

And in that organization's fresh poverty was untold Karma for the Grind.

Poverty everywhere was Karma for the Grind. It was really only a matter of time before the Grinders found their way to Wall Street, the foremost creator and perpetraror of global poverty.

The scripture of the *Bromeliad* set them up to have a unique dynamic with the rest of the civilized world, in which they could effortlessly cultivate a direct, linear relationship between their own accumulation of riches, and the massive amounts of inflicted suffering of their immediate subjects, while keeping the entire relationship morally forthright.

If Jeff were to consolidate a few pharmaceutical interests, which would corner the market and send the cost of cancer drugs skyrocketing, he was doing those cancer victims a favor. I mean, they already had cancer, so why would they bother spinning their wheels on this life? Eat the cancer, save your Karma, redeem it for something nice on your next try.

If Jeff were to sink his teeth into the pension fund of the teachers union of Rhode Island, he was being wildly considerate. I mean, they were teachers, how good was their retirement even going to be? Ditch your designs on that bungalow in Providence, move in with your angry children, grind a bit more Karma as a family, and maybe put a bit more effort into the next life.

If Jeff were to strip mine the economy of a small town in Appalachia, yada yada.

In a Karmic sense, by the scripture, living comfortably is no different than being encased in styrofoam.

Every soul that Jeff touched through the destructive forces of private equity owed him a massive debt of gratitude.

He was one of the only people on the planet who was really looking out for them.

For all his efforts, he thought that maybe he could be an Archon one day.

It was too bad for the Grinders that they had been awakened, or else maybe they, too, could have found some value in abject poverty.

Oh well.

When Jeff arrived at their new office at JC Morgan, he set up his $99k supercomputer, he pulled a drink from his personal blue gatorade cooler, and he got right to watching hockey highlights on YouTube.

If he was being honest with himself, that was all he really ever wanted to do.

He wandered onto a classic video of TSN's *Maggie the Monkey* making her 2003 Stanley Cup Playoff selections. He rewatched and remembered how Maggie made waves by being the only analyst on the planet to favor the Anaheim Mighty Ducks in the first round over the overwhelming Cup favorite and returning champion Detroit Red Wings. He remembered how analyst Bob McKenzie laughed.

Until he didn't.

Until he couldn't.

As though through divine intervention, Lise walked over and started eating at Jeff's $99 tuna salad.

Like a true capitalist, instead of getting upset, Jeff got inspired. He pulled up his bootstraps, made some coffee, and immediately got to work sending Kevin out to go get some construction paper and unscented markers.

He set up a large TSN-style selection wheel with sixteen equal sections and he laid it horizontally on the ground.

He selected sixteen randomized stocks and put one stock symbol on each of the sixteen sections. He put an equal amount of tuna on each symbol and then put Lise at the center of the wheel.

As though she was listening to the wind, Lise closed her eyes and slowly moved in one direction, eating the tuna that lay at the end she had chosen, uncovering the stock symbol BOB, which stood for Bombs Over Baghdad, a small company that functioned as a social network, connecting international arms dealers with medium-level financing in conflict zones in and around the middle east.

Jeff never tried to figure out how that was legal, let alone publicly traded.

It didn't matter.

It was trading as a penny stock, and it sounded like the worst idea for a company he had ever heard, but Jeff didn't want to doubt the infinite wisdom of the office cat.

He bought half the company for the cost of Kevin's weekly cocaine habit, and he got back to surfing hockey highlights.

And while he was seven minutes into watching a Dominik Hasek highlight video, news in the real world broke about Armenia discovering a rich lithium deposit in an area with a low military presence, 43 miles from the border of Azerbaijan.

The prospect of war was so overwhelming to analysts that war was simply assumed. Nobody on the planet bothered to look if it had actually been declared. News rooms around the globe rushed to be the first to report on Azerbaijani forces invading. Some of the Azerbaijani forces that would eventually be involved in the inevitable conflict learned the details about their own offensives on social media before they received word from their command that they were even at war.

But when a series of rogue bots running autopilot on keyword-based algorithms scanned headlines and markets and picked up on the war movement, almost every publicly traded company associated with war profiteering was picked up in fractions of a second.

Jeff had just made $36 million in 30 minutes.

He never learned how or why.

It didn't matter.

He just knew he had to keep doing whatever the cat told him to do.

Terry, who had been assigned as their division's SEC compliance officer, walked into the area and a guilty-feeling Jeff instinctively switched his browser from YouTube to his trading console, which was overflowing with data from his massive winning trade.

All that Terry saw was the personally designed selection wheel on the ground, covered in tuna that was still being slowly worked on by the cat, and all of Jeff's monitoring screens plastered in green arows pointing up with eight digits of good news.

Terry looked at the selection wheel, noticing most tuna chunks missing; some small tuna slivers along with some celery and mayonnaise were still scattered in the areas of the stock symbols.

Terry looked at the cat.

He put it together instantly.

Jeff made desperate eye contact with Terry, begging him to be quiet.

Jeff looked at the cat.

The cat looked at Terry.

The cat looked at Jeff.

Jeff looked at Terry.

The cat looked at Terry.

Terry nodded and drew a checkmark on his clipboard.

Jeff exhaled.

Terry said nothing.

Geoff was right behind Terry with an $11 tuna casserole and they passed each other in the doorway. Geoff observed the same mess, but chalked it up to nonsense and put it out of his head.

"Aren't you vegan?"

Geoff fumbled through a mouthful of tuna. "Non-practicing."

"Non-practicing vegan? How does that work?"

"How it works is that I've read everything by Michael Pollan, and I agree with all of it, but I'm only human and I don't have a lot of discipline. So I partake."

"So it's like you're a Catholic, with the full complement of Catholic guilt and shame, but for animal rights instead of bullshit."

He tilted the casserole tray up to the sky and shoveled the last of it into his mouth, chewed and swallowed.

"You're exactly right."

***

10:05am [steef] not very stoked about the board of directors situation over here
10:06am [steef] 12 of them, plus me, and i'm the only one doing any work
10:08am [steef] most of them are drunk by 10am
10:11am [steef] half of them don't show up some days
10:31am [MaTej] That's actually great news bro! Keep on that Grind! Outwork them. Hard work pays off. You'll be the chairman of the board if you stay focused. I'm sure of it.
10:32am [steef] thanks man
11:11am [steef] (16 photos of his new garden)

***

Nick and Mike had hurriedly left the offices with no explanation a couple of hours prior, and Aliya had taken it upon herself to use Mike's desk as a display for an assortment of new drugs. They had money and time now, they could afford some luxuries.

The Gjeoffs and the cat were there to watch along with everyone else as Aliya slowly and proudly put her new collection on display with the frenetic energy of a dumb kid showing off a shitty lego kingdom.

Lise jumped out of Jeff's arms and prowled through the exhibits as though she was looking to get fucked up. She stopped at the bottle of Viagra. Aliya wasn't even sure why she had those, and she was less sure why she bothered laying them out as an option.

Lise seemed aggravated by the sight of the label and pawed the bottle onto the ground, chased after it, smacked it twice, and hissed, then ran back to Jeff and jumped into his waiting arms.

Jeff, who hadn't taken his eyes off the cat for a split second, faked a personal emergency and ran back to his computer, Lise in his arms, to sell his position in Pfizer.

Gerg started to sweat. He was transfixed at the wordplay potential of the situation.

I mean, look at this. Here was a cat, the cat was walking among drugs, the cat got angry at the boner pills, hissed, and attacked them. Cat. Pussy. Drugs. Hiss. Boner. The variables swirled around in his head, mixing and matching and coming up short.

He started breathing heavily.

He started test-running punch lines in his head. 'Cat got your... boner.' Nope. 'This pussy... ahhh!' Nope.

After a minute of searching and missing and searching and missing and praying to the gods of wordplay, he was in the throes of a low grade panic attack.

He pulled at his hair, screamed, and ran away from the trading floor to collect himself.

"Fuck was that about?"

"Guess he couldn't bear to Cialis go down."

Gerg couldn't hear the joke from that distance, but he knew the job had been done; true masters could sense it in the ether.

All that the Grinders could hear over their own raucous laugher was a distant wail of agony.

***

Cassandra sounded like she was accepting the Oscar for Best Director.

"Disciples. This is it. We're here. Thank you. Thank you Nick! I never thought I'd fucking say that. Thank you Nick, thank you Mike, thank you all, you nerds who went through all those names."

For a second, she couldn't find the words, and it didn't matter. She basked in the victory with them. Every moment that passed in silence was a wonderful moment.

"Deep down, we all knew that one day, one of us would save the world by taking drugs and staying up for so many midnights, looking at databases of names of hockey players."

They all smiled to themselves.
She didn't actually believe that.

But they did.

"Everyone has their expensive equipment, everyone has everything they asked for. We have full autonomy, we have no oversight, we have nearly unlimited resources. We need to think big picture..." she was interrupted by a cartoonish series of thuds and shouts and banged elbows from just outside the office. The automatic doors to the trading floor zipped open sideways like the USS Enterprise. "...what fresh hell is this?"

The Enterprise doors tried to close on the giant rectangle that Mike and Nick were rolling on wheels into the trading floor, smacked into the center of it, and opened back up.

"Is this a jumbotron? Where in the fuck did you idiots buy a fucking jumbotron?"

Nick pulled out his phone and blasted the ringtone version of *The Final Countdown* on the office speakers, leading into Mike ramping up to give a presentation in his Steve Jobs turtleneck.

Everyone was getting into it except Cassandra, who was too annoyed to scoff and too transfixed to run away.

She wasn't about to let this great big festering neon distraction sink her momentum – their momentum - but sometimes a leader had to take a step back. She knew she had to let the Disciples play with this new toy for a bit.

"Fuck it. Sure. Miles. You deal with this." She went into her office and locked the door.

Miles nodded. "Mike, why do we have a jumbotron?"

Mike actually did a pretty good Steve Jobs voice as he paced back and forth in front of the jumbotron. "Nick and I looked over the capabilities of this thing. We had it rush constructed and rush shipped. It comes with a module that connects to the software that Jeff has already installed on his trading terminal."

Nick plugged it in using 22 feet of a 100 foot extension cord, and they waited for it to boot up.

Kevin wrapped a slack middle section of the cord around his neck in a sloppy noose and pretended to choke himself.

The Final Countdown ended during the extended stretch of silence and Nick pressed replay.

"There. Connected. We can watch his trades in real time. Look!"

A green light marquee flashed across the screen, showing everyone that Jeff had just sold his entire position in Pfizer.

"Huh?"

"What the fuck, Jeff?"

"Why would you do that?"

"Yeah Jeff. That's a growth stock."

Gerg needed something out of this. "Yeah that's a real boner, Jeff." There was scattered laugher and Gerg was pleased.

Jeff didn't understand the logic either, but he knew by now never to doubt the wisdom of the office cat, so he just shrugged and winked.

Mike smoothed out the wrinkles in his turtleneck and continued. "We've also got a cube that bounces around the jumbotron like a screen saver. It goes into the corner sometimes if you watch it for long enough."

It was programmed to never do that.

"Kevin, that was specially added for you."

Kevin tightened the extension cord noose and mouthed, "thank you."

"It connects to any cable network or internet stream you want. Twitch, Youtube, Pornhub. But don't put porn on the jumbotron. Please don't put porn on the jumbotron. Here, let's take a look at CNN."

Keith Olbermann was mid sentence and the chyron on the bottom of the screen was scrolling with information about a pharmaceutical recall. "...confirming what industry leaders have suspected for some time from curious lab results, which is that Viagra is now making men's penises up to six inches smaller."

Roman apologized to Jeff and adjusted his pants.

"I bet they didn't Cialis coming." Gerg beamed.

Silence.

Nick restarted The Final Countdown from the middle of the song.

"Why isn't anyone laughing? That was really good."

Miles did his best Cassandra voice. "Get to work Disciples."

Gerg shrunk six inches into the background.

"And turn off the fucking news before the Archon sees it."

***

2:05pm [steef] hey @Tej – you're not gonna believe this
2:05pm [steef] nick and mike brought in and installed a fucking jumbotron! It's amazing!! they can even watch hockey on it
2:07pm [steef] (16 photos of jumbotron)
2:19pm [MaTej] That jumbotron sounds and looks like a lot of fun for an office setting, man! A great motivator. Incredible for office morale. How is your garden?
2:33pm [steef] (16 photos of garden)
2:38pm [MaTej] Looking good, friend! What's your favorite? What are you hoping to add to the garden next? :) Looking forward to hearing from you again, friend.

Steef knew something was up. This wasn't the Matej that he knew from university. Matej was a friendly guy who loved his friends. Matej had bad grammar and a slouch. Matej had three different Nav posters in his bedroom.

Right now he was giving off American Psycho vibes.

Right now he was more Wall Street than they were.

Steef knew the rest of the Grinders had the chat muted, so he felt a responsibility to say something.

"Have... you guys noticed a shift in Matej? Like, a major, major shift?"

"NOPE"

"No"

"Good old reliable Matej"

"Nah"

"Same old Matej."

"Tejy Tejy Tej"

"Love that guy"

"Funky cold Tejina"

***

2:45pm [steef] I am thinking about that ayahuasca you mentioned...
2:46pm [MaTej] Fantastic! I will email you some resources. It's always a pleasure to talk to you, man.

Steef just stared at the group chat.

***

Cassandra had finally got her extortion station set up next to her pile of cocaine on the giant mahogany desk in her soundproofed office.

It dawned on her that with the new setup, the Grinders didn't really need the income anymore.

But extortion was so much fun.

And she had to keep up appearances. Karma for the Grind, and what not.

She drew out a fat line from the pile and inhaled it.

She opened up the list but didn't put a ton of effort into picking a victim, landing pretty quickly on a 20 year old kid named Brendan, a self-professed hardcore gamer and bona fide moron who had gotten lucky with a timely Ethereum purchase and was bragging about it all over the cryptocurrency discussion boards.

She waited for him to finish a session of World of Warcraft, switched the voice modulator to Seth Rogen and then took control of Brendan's camera and speakers.

"Hey fuckass! You're Brendan, right? Huehuehue."

"Fuck was that?" Cassandra watched as Brendan looked around his bedroom.

"I'm in the computer, idiot. Huehuehue."

"What? Seth Rogen?"

"Yeah. Seth fucking Rogen is literally inside your fucking computer. Do you hear yourself? Huehuehue."

"What is going on?"

"Gonna keep it brief idiot. I'm in control of your computer, I can see the dorito stains on your monster energy drink t-shirt. You're fat as fuck, you fat fuck! Huehuehue."

"What the fuck do you want from me?"

"I want your Ethereum, you fat fuck!"

"You can't have it, asshole!"

"GIVE SETH ROGEN YOUR ETHEREUUUUM."

"NO WAY!"

"Listen, buddy, wipe the dorito stains off before someone else sees your stupid ass. Huehuehue."

"LEAVE ME ALONE."

"Buddy, I've been reading your group chats! I know what you and your friends are saying about the girls in your college classes! You want to do ... what... to Jenny?"

Brendan went pale.

"Oh, man, don't shit your pants. Just give me your Ethereum and I won't tell anyone what you told Mikael that you were gonna do to... Melissa. Got it? Huehuehue."

"OKAY OKAY OKAY PLEASE DON'T-"

Cassandra piped in *Right Thurr* by Chingy for 30 seconds at max volume before hanging up.

She got a confirmation from Jeff a couple minutes later that they had just received 21.1 ETH.

She decided not to send the chat logs to the unsuspecting girls in his college classes.

She thought to herself that she might be getting softer. She was losing her passion for hurting people.

Maybe it was the music.

Feeling suddenly romantic, she took a look at her portfolio and saw something that almost gave her a heart attack.

***

3:02am [MaTej] Gotta go. Nothing personal. Strictly business. It's been fun.

3:02am [MaTej] *MaTej has exited the chat.*
5:22am [steef] aw
5:29am [steef] (16 photos of his gardens)

***

aLan started to think that the jumbotron's time was over when Roman spelled out BUTTSAUCE with stock symbols and he couldn't muster a laugh.

Out of boredom, he gave the muted group chat a cursory glance from where he left off, which had a run of desperate messages and incredible garden progress from the days and weeks before.

11:01am [MaTej] heyyyy
11:03am [MaTej] whats my net flix passowrd
11:04am [MaTej] hello
11:04am [MaTej] going for walk
11:09am [MaTej] ???
11:10am [MaTej] anyone
11:11am [MaTej] goning for that walk sorry about before
4:04pm [steef] hope the sun is shining brother!
4:10pm [steef] (16 photos of the god damn hanging gardens of Babylon, from the previous office)

"He's fine," aLan said out loud.

"Who?"

"Oh I just checked in on the intern. He's alive. Steef is taking care of him."

"Good man."

***

Flash back a few weeks.

Matej was in rough shape. He had been feeling lonely since being cast out to Palo Alto. He understood why he was sent there, but this understanding didn't bring him any peace – all it accomplished was to keep bringing him back into the frustrating conundrum of the time he needed to speak up in order to exonerate himself, but also needed to keep quiet so as to preserve the integrity of the mission, the Grinders, and his Archon.

He was truly alone in his noble sacrifice.

The loneliness was beating him down.

The brutal California sun was peering in through his livingroom window and beating him down even further. Reaching his limit, in a rush to escape his string of losses to the Netflix login screen, he went for a walk, forgetting to apply sunscreen, but remembering the purple bucket hat from the goodie bag he was given at the Roku onboarding party.

To compound his frustrations, he had also misplaced the keys to his apartment, which he had locked behind him.

Frantic, miserable and alone, tired of being locked out of everything in his life, Matej found himself walking faster and faster to match the pace of his frustration.

He hummed Mario Kart music to himself to drown out the thoughts he couldn't control.

He had a vision of refuge in a large patch of grass half a block ahead, drenched in shade from nearby oak trees in full splendor.

But there was no refuge to be found.

Around the corner, as he slowed his walk and arched his head upwards, towering over him like Bowser's Castle was Netflix headquarters.

The feeling hit him like ten thousand red shells. He was out of balloons.

He was transported in his mind back to the last time he felt this low - to the three days he spent pledging for Epsilon Rho Rho before he was rejected by the fraternity and expelled from the university for spraying an entire keg, like celebration champagne, at a campus police officer.

He let go of everything for a second and in an uncharacteristic moment of focus and confidence, Matej had an idea.

He wanted to be in charge. If only for a minute.

He needed a victory.

He opened his phone camera, flipped it to video, and shouted:

"HEY NETFLIX. HOW'S THIS FOR STREAMING?"

He unzipped his pants, aimed at the giant, red Netflix "N" monument on the perimeter of the grounds, and let loose with everything he had.

This was his moment.

Time slowed down. He revelled in it. He savored every drop. He could have written his own name twice in the snow, and the fleeting thought of snow made him miss Vancouver.

But there was no going back.

He realized there was no going back. And he couldn't be happier.

All at once he let go of his frustrating past.

Disappointed parents. Gone.

Abusive older sister. Gone.

That time he said 'orgasm' instead of 'organism' in front of the school during a play being put on by his sixth grade science class. Gone.

The trauma of the past all flowed out of him and onto the Netflix logo and it all disappeared forever.

He was reborn.

When his stream was done filming, he uploaded the video to his new TikTok account.

He forgot about the upload for a few hours and he went on an extended victory walk around Palo Alto.

He was on rainbow road.

When his legs started to get tired, he made his way home, where he noticed his apartment keys still in the door, and he laughed again.

He marched victoriously into his new, liberated life in his old apartment, removed his bucket hat, threw it on the ground, and turned the kitchen light on. And then he remembered his Netflix password out loud.

"Dude."

The Netflix login noise played and Matej wasn't sure if he'd ever felt better in his life.

Then he remembered the video he had uploaded. Feeling relieved, and having made peace with the Netflix corporation and its shareholders and subsidiaries, he thought it was only fair that he remove all evidence that he was ever that pissed off.

He opened his TikTok, and his moment of triumph had pulled in views in the hundred thousands. After a minute of trying to find out how that happened, he noticed it had been shared by 50 Cent.

"Duude."

By the end of the day, it was at a million.

"Duuude."

By the weekend, it had hit ten million.

"Duuuude."

The momentum only accelerated from there.

The shares kept going out, the views kept coming in.

He was going viral.

By the end of the month, there were legions of imitators who were traveling from out of state to pay homage and also piss on the Netflix "N".

Sometimes there were lineups in broad daylight.

One time, someone set up a tailgate party. They were doing kegstands.

Netflix, obviously, didn't appreciate this development. Their valiant first attempt to put an end to the mounting phenomenon had them placing 24 hour security detail outside of the monument, but that proved ineffective; groups of guerrilla piss enthusiasts would distract the guards on duty, drawing them away from their posts, towards a distant noise or commotion, or with a patched-in call on their security radios demanding they move to a 'higher priority location'.

The security efforts completely collapsed after the night watch guards, on three consecutive graveyard shifts, abandoned their security duties to record their own videos.

Netflix then tried physically removing the statue, which led to mass protests on company grounds. The protests were ironic at first, with everyone having a wonderful time taking turns pissing in the hole where the monument used to be.

The protests later turned deadly serious, as they became symbolic of a revolution demanding greater rights for unpaid interns in the state of California, eventually leading to a court case titled Matej vs. The State Of California, which came to a head when the governor tried, pathetically, to outlaw the purple bucket hat – the same purple bucket hat that Matej was wearing for a split second in the original piss video - as a symbol of economic terrorism.

After the case was hastily settled out of court in a desperate scramble to protect Netflix's tumbling stock price, Matej shook hands with the governor of California on live television.

The loyal Grinders, of course, were still faithful to their Archon's news lockdown, and they had the chat muted, so they missed everything.

But the court case being settled didn't stop the trend. The stream had momentum. The stream wasn't stopping.

3D print shops were being overrun with requests for Netflix "N"s. Droves of drunken idiots were pulling over to the side of the road to piss on any instance of a giant, 3-dimensional N of any color.

Netscape Navigator even made a brief comeback.

Matej ended up making a small side fortune of his own, selling truck stickers online, depicting Calvin urinating on the Netflix logo.

Netflix couldn't take the piss.

The damage wasn't fully understood until the streaming numbers were unveiled with the next quarterly report.

Their stock value cratered, the CEO stepped down in shame; the company ended up being worth less than Blockbuster.

It was at this point that a desperate Cassandra looked back at the abandoned group chat, noticing that Matej had left the now useless chat, and then scrolling up to see why.

She fell to pieces as she scrolled through weeks of old messages, seeing all the signs that could have mitigated the disaster, documenting Matej's journey of unbelievably rapid personal growth, being nurtured by their gardener on the board of directors.

Once she had reached the wall of text about his forgotten Netflix password, she reached critical mass, not even noticing the steam or the skin on her fingers burning from the cup of coffee she had just crushed in her hand.

The murderous rage was back.

***

11:12am [steef] (16 photos of his garden)

***

Roman spelled out EATSHITANDDIE with stock symbols on the jumbotron.

Cassandra felt it.

She tried to recoup her dignity with a round of extortion.

She searched the list of victims for the name 'Matej', found an old man who ran a book store based in Moose Jaw, Saskatchewan, didn't bother to look at the details of the file, and phoned him from the computer.

He picked up, she screamed "FUCK YOU. FUCK YOU. FUCK YOU" and she hung up.

She put her face in the pile of cocaine on her desk. She repeated "Karma for the Grind" over and over again, in her head, repeating it like an unprogrammed VCR, a hail mary hail mary, trying to force herself to believe it, but the mantra couldn't find traction and it slipped away.

She held on for another minute.

She was still watching the stock ticker. It kept getting redder.

The arrows kept pointing lower.

And lower.

And lower.

In a soundproofed office, nobody can hear you scream.

Cassandra knew she couldn't let herself cry right now even though she had the freedom and the privacy.

The salty tears would roll down her cheeks and they would taste like piss.

***

aLan spelled out LOLATTHATSHIT with stock symbols on the jumbotron.

He didn't know yet.

It still hurt when Cassandra walked out of her office and read it.

***

Cassandra picked up the call from the Groom in the middle of the fourth ring.

"Let's hear it."

"Your division would be deep in the red if not for Jeff, you know."

"I know. He's really saving our ass."

"He's saving YOUR ass. I can talk the board down from taking action as long as you're making a lot of money for me, but even so, you and your freaks are new here, you're building a first impression, and you're coming off as disorganized maniacs."

Cassandra thought the maniacs were very well organized. "I know. I know. I really didn't mean to be a pain in the... ass."

"No. Don't do that. Not now."

"Don't do what?" The Groom couldn't see that Cassandra was twirling her hair but he knew it anyways.

The Groom sighed. "You have to gain control of your people. And I think right now you need to punish someone. A head needs to roll. Doesn't matter who."

"Just the head?"

The Groom let Cassandra's double entendre fall limp in total silence. "You should bring Matej to New York to keep an eye on him."

"That's impossible. He's a cult hero in California. He's untouchable." Cassandra was wondering why nobody on the board had clued in to anything Matej was doing. They all had Netflix stock too. Maybe these assholes were as out of touch as everyone else.

"Then send someone out there to reel him in."

"You have any preference?"

"Gotta be honest, it doesn't matter. Board wants me to make you do something. Just do something, so it looks like I did something. Stop losing money, gain control of your people. That's what I care about."

"Got it."

There was an extended silence.

"Oh umm."

"What."

"One last question, might be stupid."

"Okay."

"Was there anyone else up north with us at the outposts?"

"Far as I know, just you guys."

Cassandra paused for a while and thought about mentioning the words of the Arctic high command.

"That's all." She tried one more time to reconnect. "And sorry again, I know that you don't want to be the butt-"

The Groom hung up mid-sentence and Cassandra took a minute to chew on the rejection before forgetting about it in the pile of coke on her mahogany desk.

At least now she no longer suspected Matej of working as a spy for the lithium industry, which felt a bit silly now that she could look at it clearly.

She spent some time alone in her office once again wondering what the fuck Arctic high command meant by 'operative'.

She took a rip from the coke pile on her mahogany desk and told herself it was nothing to worry about.

She sniffled.

***

3:11pm [Kevin] yo matej i'm comin
3:33pm [steef] @Kevin matej left the chat a while ago man

***

They didn't let Kevin go easily.

The Grinders had a strange chemistry that was immediately obvious to all outsiders, and they suffered in very tangible and measurable ways when they were apart for too long.

For all his flaws with punctuality, in addition to a near total absence of real-world effectiveness, Kevin carried a tremendous quotient of a certain unexplainable energy that was central to the Disciples.

Like a family dog, he kept things from falling apart.

He was a real glue guy, in every sense of the word.

***

8:55am [Kevin] ay matej i;m here. Airport
8:56am [Kevin] dont see you
8:57am [Kevin] i will go to roku
9:01am [steef] kev. He's not in here
9:11am [steef] (16 photos of gardens)
9:21am [Kevin] holy shit when did you start gardening
10:01am [Kevin] matej i'm here i can see the back of your head hahahaha
10:02am [Kevin] get a haircut hippie
10:09am [steef] kev no offense buddy but how are you alive

***

Kevin brought no luggage with him, and by the time they got to Matej's penthouse apartment, he had discarded everything but a layer of clothes.

They never spoke.

They sat across from each other in the lotus position, saying nothing, eventually breathing in unison.

They drank ayahuasca as incense burned in the isolated room encased in mandala tapestries.

Fifteen minutes later, Matej gave Kevin a second liquid from an unmarked cylindrical matte black container and motioned for him alone to drink it all.

They stayed in silence for the duration after.

Motionless.

Breathing.

Never breaking eye contact.

After several hours, Kevin's pupils dilated fully and shifted color.

Matej nodded, and they broke apart.

Kevin ignored his discarded effects and got on the next plane to New York to reunite with the Grinders.

***

Kevin was supposed to remain in California for a month, watching over Matej, keeping him in line.

He returned two days after he left, without his phone or his wallet or his shoes, and refused to answer any questions about why.

Cassandra was confronting the idea that she wanted to fail. Sending a glue sniffer to do something vitally important was an insane oversight on her part.

The Groom, now on the verge of micromanaging Cassandra, had suggested that maybe she could bring in an expensive lecturer to motivate the troops, but the top search result when she sorted available lecturers by 'most popular' was Matej, which sent her into another tailspin.

Instead, she started a panicked, all hands on deck meeting with the Grinders, where they were implored to establish a new sense of focus and stop bleeding losses. She was told by the Groom that this was their last chance to stop royally fucking everything up, or they would lose control of their division and they would probably lose the jumbotron.

She even had Aliya drag Steef out of his garden paradise for this one.

Aliya didn't think Steef really needed to be there, but she was faithful to her Archon. She had even more doubts when she got to his office and saw that it was overflowing with beautiful plants and flowers and even some miniature driftwood construction projects which were centimeters away from embracing the growth of some vine plants.

"Hey, I really don't want to pull you out of the garden, but Cassandra wants us all there for a meeting."

Steef sighed and said sluggishly, "this is about the time where I take a nap. I'll need some help getting th-"

Aliya flashed her hand in front of Steef and the speed took the wind out of his speech. In her hand was a giant white pill.

"Be grateful. This is my last upper."

On the way back from Steef's office to the main floor, they ran into Kevin in the hallway, and after an extended hug from Aliya that took the wind out of him, the three of them arrived together in the middle of the group meeting.

Cassandra flinched when they walked in.

She had a bone to pick with Kevin, but she already knew that if she pointed the finger at him, the finger would eventually point right back at her, so she didn't say a word.

"We could ask Terry to use his SEC magic and get us a bailout, right?"

"I don't think that's how it works."

Jeff shut it down anyways. "I think it's best for all of us that Terry keep quiet."

"I need one huge play this month. I need to recover a lot of ground. We need to recover a lot of ground. We need to polish our reputation in this firm. They like our medium gains across the board but they've noticed our two big flops. They're going to start talking about us if we can't get it up by the end of the quarter. Gerg, no."

Cassandra was not going to let him say 'that's what she said'. Not here, not now.

"Desperate times. Anything. Get us back up. Execute a coup in El Salvador. Rob your grandmother. Nuke Chicago. Nothing is off the table."

***

The jumbotron flashed "JSFHLSIUZFHDLGKNDFGKJNDFGKNZDFGKIOGZ" which was followed by Geoff shouting at the cat.

***

Another week passed and the Grinders, slightly more focused but building a tolerance for adderall, were still not hitting the home runs that Cassandra needed.

She decided to have one-on-one meetings with them.

The first meeting was Jeff, obviously, who had not yet made a losing trade.

When he entered, Cassandra made no efforts to hide the coke on her desk. She offered him a straw. He accepted. She didn't draw out lines. They were ripping straight from the pile like they were slant drilling for happiness.

"So Jeff,"

"I know why I'm here. Straight wins, no losses."

"Yeah. You can predict me like you can predict the markets, apparently."

Jeff just smiled.

"So, cutting to the chase. What is your secret?"

Jeff got nervous. "Well, I don't know if I really have a secret, per se," and Jeff realized that he needed to change the subject, "wow, this is quality shit. Can I have some...more?"

"Turn the mountain into dust, my friend."

Jeff took another rip. "Wow. My face is numb. What were we talking about?"

"You were just about to tell me your secret and then you changed the subject."

"Guess I'm not a very good liar."

"Oh, you are, I'm just really good at spotting lies."

"Fair enough." Jeff felt the drip down the back of his throat. "So I guess you'll be able to see that I'm telling the truth with this next part."

"I'm intrigued."

"Yeah, I'm not sure I really believe it myself. But I'm batting a thousand. Okay, well." Jeff inhaled deeply. "It's Lise." He paused. "It's the cat."

"The cat."

"The cat is giving me all my hot tips. The cat showed me that arms dealer. The cat knocked over that Viagra bottle. The cat knocked my speakers off my desk an hour before the speaker company filed for bankruptcy."

"I didn't even know about that third one."

"Every move I've made was given to me by the cat in one way or another."

"Very funny, Jeff." Cassandra took another rip from the pile. "Okay, now your joke is done. Tell me your secret."

"That was my secret." Jeff could feel the drip down the back of his throat getting stronger.

They stared at each other, unblinking, for almost a minute. Cassandra found no traces of lies in his face or his speech or his posture or his language.

But she still couldn't accept it.

"Fuck off. Tell me."

"It's... the cat. I'm telling you, it's the cat."

Cassandra punched the coke mountain and sent a cloud in the air, dusting her mahogany desk with a light snowfall. "TELL ME RIGHT THE FUCK NOW OR GET THE FUCK OUT OF MY OFFICE."

Jeff quietly gathered himself and left the office without saying another word.

After a completely useless second meeting with Terry, she brought in Kevin, thinking that he might be bringing some actionable insider info back from California.

But Kevin had a strange new energy to him.

She couldn't say he was refocused, as he had never been

focused before. He was just... focused. Were his eyes a different color?

He was starting and finishing complicated sentences. He was using multisyllabic words. He didn't trail off. He was sitting up straight. His shirt was ironed. He was wearing a shirt. He was smiling and making eye contact.

It was fucking her up.

"Kevin! Sorry we haven't had a minute to catch up since you got back from Cali. How was your trip?"

"Focused."

"You do seem focused. I think the trip was good for you. Bit of a reset, you've been getting pretty high for the past few ...years."

"I agree, Cassandra. I was in need of a cognitive restructuring. I appreciate the opportunity. Thank you. I will be more focused and attentive to the overall mission moving forward, and I apologize for my reluctance to be of more assistance up until now."

Cassandra started nervously shuffling papers that were unrelated to the meeting. "Uh. Good. Glad to have you with us." She started to notice that he wasn't blinking.

"Glad to be here. I have a lot of ground to make up, personally, and professionally. I've been slacking for far too long. I'd like to get started on this meeting – we have a tremendous opportunity here in front of us at JC Morgan and we need to be working harder to maximize it."

"I couldn't agree more, ...Kev." She wanted to call him K-hole but it didn't seem appropriate anymore. "Before we get started on the purpose of the meeting, I have to ask you quickly about a trade I asked you to make the other day. It doesn't look like you got around to it."

Kevin chuckled softly and it sent chills up Cassandra's spine. "Well, you see, I analyzed the opportunity in the short term and in the long term, and while it would have brought us some reliable financial returns, I think it misses the bigger picture." He still hadn't blinked. "Those resources will be better allocated to something else."

"Oh, yeah, right. It doesn't generate very much Karma for the Grind. I get it. But we just need some financial wins, to keep our reputation within the-"

"We can discuss that later. Perhaps you can inform me how I've found myself in your office, if not for a well-deserved reprimand on my abdicated fiscal responsibilities?"

She needed a second.

"Well, Kevin, we're leaving no avenues unturned." She sniffled. "I would like to tap your brain with regards to the visit to Matej and Roku. What's he doing out there? Can you give me any information that's actionable for us? They have a showcase coming up at TechSmash, how do you feel that's going to go?"

"I was hoping you would ask about that. In short, Cassandra, it will change the world. It is an unmitigated success. It wil revolutionize everything." Kevin tilted his head. "Does that sound like something you might be interested in?" He still hadn't blinked.

She was more scared than intrigued. "That does sound like something I might be interested in. Can you tell me more?"

"What we're doing is," Kevin made a triangle out of his hands, "combining the upper echelon of cognitive manipulation technology – think Neuralink, but better - with the bleeding edge of shamanic wisdom." He broke the triangle. "Now, the brilliant minds at Roku have developed a robust inner culture and complex tapestry of new language that would be unrecognizable to outsiders, so you will just have to trust me."

Cassandra lost her focus. She was waiting for Kevin to blink.

"Does that sound like something you might be interested in?"

Cassandra nodded.

"Would you like to hear more?"

Cassandra cleared her throat. "I think I have enough to work with for now. I will call you back in if I need more details. You are free to go. Put something together for this for me, please."

"Of course. Thank you for your time. It's always a pleasure when our paths cross."

Cassandra sniffled. She needed to hear Kevin's jarring, discordant laugh. Whatever the fuck was going on here was driving her fucking insane.

"Oh hey K-h.. Kev. Before you go."

"Yeah?"

"What time does Sean Connery arrive at Wimbledon?"

Kevin grinned. "Let's hear it, Cassandra."

"Tennish."

Kevin chuckled softly, politely turned and left, closing the door gently behind him.

Kevin was the one who told her that joke. He shouldn't have needed to ask. He would get high and tell it to strangers. He had told it to Cassandra a dozen times.

She sat in her office chair for five minutes, swiveling left and right with a discordant stutter, trying to wrap her head around what had just happened.

Failing that, she did a bunch more coke, stood up and walked to the office door, ensuring it was closed, went back to the warm center of her soundproofed office, and screamed.

She put her face down into her folded arms on her office desk, unmoving, until she remembered she was in the middle of one-on-ones and no matter her condition, she had to keep going.

She was the Archon, she had to be fearless. She was the Archon. She was the Archon.

She needed a hail mary.

She did a couple more rips from coke mountain to straighten up, and peeking out of her office, issued a calm, "Aliya, you're up. Bring your bag."

"Oh fuck yeah. Yes. On it. Coming!"

Aliya had been waiting for this moment for a long time. She didn't know exactly what Cassandra needed from her, but she had unending faith in the magical bag, and she knew that some day she would be able to save the world with it.

She sat down in Cassandra's office with her bag's drawstring opened and her hand hovering above, ready for anything.

"I need to speak with a ghost."

Aliya's hand stayed hovering but went limp. "What do you mean?"

"I'm not gonna lie, Aliya. I know about your second passion."

Her hand went rigid again, still hovering. "I don't know what you mean."

"It's okay. When you sold me on that drug distribution project when we were back up north, I couldn't help myself and when you took off to resupply, I took an opportunity to look at your notes."

Aliya put the bag on the desk between them. "You're not mad?"

"I was at the time, but I think it's normal to question things, to doubt things, when everything feels like it's falling apart. I know that as your Archon I keep things pretty secretive and that leaves a lot of holes in your understanding of everything. People are imperfect. We have," she corrected herself, "people have a natural drive to try to understand the world around them, and so it would be ridiculous of me to ask you to stay human and also to stop asking questions." She sniffled. "I'm not mad. I even had a bit of a witchcraft phase myself when I was younger. I recognized the language."

Aliya relaxed in her chair.

"In fact, I need your help."

Aliya raised one eyebrow and perked up.

"I think this is going to be fine, anyways. Outside of our normal purview, so we can deviate slightly. While the *Bromeliad* allows for capital accumulation, it doesn't answer anything specific, and this question is specifically about money."

"Don't we have money? Like, a lot of money?"

"I suppose this isn't so much about money as it is about performance, and how the rest of the firm looks at us. Matej's Netflix journey has us in a lot of trouble and we're... circling the drain. If we want to maintain our access to this global reach," Cassandra paused, "for the Grind," she continued, "then we have to convince my boss that we still deserve the opportunity, and we need to impress the board of directors."

***

11:58pm [steef] (16 photos of his gardens)

***

Aliya just stared.

"But before we start I've always wondered something."

Aliya perked up.

"We get our coke from different people. Always wondered whose was better." Cassandra offered Aliya a straw.

Aliya pulled a book on witchcraft from her bag and drew four lines of her own supply on the back cover, which featured a sloppy green pentagram that Kevin had drawn in crayon.

Aliya already knew hers was better. She'd known for years. She didn't say anything.

They traded samples.

Cassandra didn't even try to fight it. "God fucking damnit." She took a second to let her face get numb. "Anyways. I know you carry a weejie board."

"Ouija."

"Whatever."

"Okay first off, you have to respect the spirits if you want them to help you."

Cassandra exhaled. "I'm already exhausted."

"Well maybe if you had been doing better coke, then-"

"Shut the fuck up." Cassandra pounded her desk with both fists and then forced herself to calm down. "Okay. I will respect the spirits," she said half-mockingly. "Can I..."

"Of course." Aliya handed her the rest of the eight ball.

"Sorry, I'm just on edge with all this failure."

"That's what I'm here for. Rounding the edges." Aliya whipped out the ouija board. "You seem desperate so I'll let you in. I've been talking with Kevin and Nick about this stuff."

"The Bromeliad nerds. About witchcraft?"

"I think you understand already. Nick had a lot of downtime back at the telecom and Kevin is just permanently on downtime, so they've been helping me out, cross-referencing the *Bromeliad* with my research and readings and all that."

"Find anything good?"

"Yeah. I am pretty sure we can tap in directly to your Angel."

Cassandra had been toying with the idea that this was all real.

She knew Parisa was real. She knew the drugs worked. She knew the triptych told the truth. All of that was real for sure. But the *Bromeliad*, the Angels, the Archons and Disciples, the suffering and the next lives, all of it. She was writing fiction, but so much of this was working. So much of the bullshit she wrote down turned out to be prophetic.

At least she believed she was writing fiction.

But maybe the Angels were speaking through her.

She needed inspiration in a moment of desperation and she got exactly what she asked for. Isn't that how so many religions start?

She didn't have to make up her mind right then, but she knew that in that moment, she had to listen to Aliya's theory and pretend that it was legitimate.

"That's interesting. How would you know it's the Angel speaking? And how would you know it's *my* Angel?"

"Well it's not so much like, 'This Is The Angel Speaking' as much as it opens up a psychedelic portal upwards in the Cosmic hierarchy. So, since you're the Archon, with you being here, with you being involved in the ritual, we tap into the Angel. But... if we were both Disciples doing this then we'd just tap into you. The Archon."

Cassandra grew worried. "So that tells me you haven't successfully tried it yet."

"Correct."

Cassandra was relieved.

Aliya brought two pills out of her bag. "This is how we make it happen. This is an experimental entheogen. There aren't many left in the world. Developed in Florida, obviously. Some hicks ran out of moonshine ingredients and got lucky with some shit they had around the house. It's part bath salts. Same active ingredient. There's also some DMT in here."

"How does that help anything? Sounds like madness."

"I know you don't really know the language so it might take me a minute for me to ... it ... it opens up the madness dimension. It opens the door. And then we have to be careful and we have to see it and we have to use it." Aliya found the words. "Madness is the water in the river that gets us where we're going."

"We don't want madness. We have madness already. I want less madness. The whole point of these meetings is to reduce the madness." Cassandra was getting twitchy and repeating herself off the power of Aliya's superior coke. She wasn't used to it. She felt a strong drip in the back of her throat.

"That's why we have to be careful. The come-up is two minutes."

"That's pretty fucking fast for a psychedelic."

"That's the bath salts. This is a fucking rocketship to Valhalla."

"Not a rocketship to heaven then?"

"No. Definitely not. You can't get to heaven on a rocketship. We're going to Valhalla. So be careful." Aliya closed her hand around one of the pills, gave Cassandra her hand, but refused to open it. "Careful. Careful. Careful."

"Got it."

"Let me hear you say it."

"Careful."

"Again."

Cassandra centered herself, exhaled, and finally summoned some sincerity in the calm eye of their absurd situation. "Careful."

"Very good." Aliya opened her hand and Cassandra took the pill. "Dissolve it under your tongue. 1, 2, 3, go."

They paused for a minute and waited.

"So what happened to the hicks?"

"They went mad. Keep up, Archon. Fucks sake. No more talking. Keep your thinking to a minimum. Don't think about anything that would upset an Angel. Breathe...slow.... inhale....exhale."

They both lit up at the same time.

Aliya only spoke slowly and during exhales. "I will do all talking now. There is no need for you to talk."

She put the planchette gently at the center of the ouija board and beckoned Cassandra's hands with her own.

"Don't push, don't pull, don't think. Release. Breathe in, breathe out. The spirits know what we're looking for."

Cassandra slowly shed her anxieties and allowed the planchette to move.

"M"

Cassandra felt a chill. She wasn't moving anything. She could tell Aliya wasn't either. This was real.

"E"

She smiled.

Aliya said softly, "it's working. I can feel we're about halfway."

The planchette paused for a second and then started drifting again.

"O"

Cassandra raised an eyebrow. She didn't talk. They kept going.

"W"

"Okay. What the fuck? Is this a joke to you?" Cassandra stood up and grabbed at her own hair and screamed. "Get the fuck out of here. NOW."

Aliya started to plead and gathered up her items. "You felt that, that was--"

The bath salts were almost bleeding through her eyes as she screamed even louder. "LEAVE."

"Ok. You can keep the coke."

"CLOSE THE DOOR."

Cassandra inhaled the rest of Aliya's eight ball and jittered in place in a twitchy bliss for a short while before doing anything else.

The panic was rising. Maybe it was the bath salts.

This was fucked.

She was fucked.

Her most reliable people were making cat jokes and her most reliable idiot was bankrupting her faith in him with five dollar words.

She grounded her runaway anxiety by pounding her office desk with both fists.

She knew she couldn't trust anyone.

To make things worse, she was coming down from the bath salts, and she was out of the good coke.

Madness.

Fuck this.

Fuck the Grinders, fuck Matej, fuck bath salts and fuck Roku.

They were all messing with her. It was all a game to them.

Fuck it.

They weren't going to trick her. She could turn this to her advantage.

She always did.

She smashed the office door open and with a refreshed vigor, shouted, "We're shorting Roku."

"Matej fucking it up over there?"

"I have reason to believe that Roku is full of shit."

"How big of a short?"

"Everything. Everything we have."

"I don't think-"

"Then don't fucking think. Just do it." Cassandra remembered the key words, "I am your Archon." She stood in place chewing on her own comment for a second, noticed the cat sauntering casually in the distance, gritted her teeth, held back a scream, and stormed back into her office, slamming the door behind her.

Jeff took the reigns. "Well I wouldn't do it but, she's the Archon for a reason. Roku's at TechSmash in three days, that's clearly the focus. Git 'er dun."

***

The Grinders mostly sat, rocking back and forth in their computer desk swivel chairs, a couple of them standing, all encircling the jumbotron.

"What's the button for the channels?"

"What do you mean?'

Cassandra had never operated a jumbotron before. "The jumbotron. It's stuck on displaying stocks."

"Is there an aux button?"

"Try input."

"Wait, so we can watch the news? Archon?"

"Just this once, yeah. It's relevant to our work here."

"Thank you, Archon!"

"What buttons does the remote have?"

"Press AUX."

"Aux is music. Press input."

"I'm pressing input. It's not doing anything."

"Why is it saying insert disc?"

"Does the jumbotron think it's a DVD player? Nick? Help us out, man."

Nick sighed. He stated plainly in clear English, "Hello Jumbotron! TV Mode! Technology Channel!" And the jumbotron changed over to the beginning rumblings of the TechSmash conference. "You guys are idiots."

The Grinders watched quietly as the intermission at TechSmash ended, the lights went dark, and the Roku personnel took the stage. A projection screen descended from above, slowly, as ominous music played to a quiet audience. The black screen gave way to a familiar video, and the Grinders bit their tongues as the familiar video played to thunderous applause.

"How's this for streaming?"

The Grinders could hear the piss noise at full volume.

Cassandra flinched but kept watching and the Roku presenter continued.

"Now, don't get pissed off..."

The audience howled with laughter.

"I know it's in fashion right now for streaming companies to... take the piss!"

The TechSmash audience's laughter died down so quickly that everyone watching on the jumbotron could hear Gerg angrily muttering to himself about the terrible quality of the pun. The presenter was holding for continued applause at center stage, as though it was written into the script; he was met with a polite cough and he stuttered and continued.

"B-but here at Roku, we believe that there is a very strong future in streaming. While you may feel it is... remote, we hope to convince you that it is... remote!"

The presenter pulled a remote control from his suit pocket,

pressed a button, and a giant jumbotron descended from the center of the stage down in the front of the projector screen.

"User One – please come out on stage."

A man appeared from behind the curtain – he was dressed fully in black and was wearing a full black balaclava.

"Now, I'm going to start talking like a nerd for a second, but, hey, when in TechSmash!"

The presenter adjusted his glasses. *"How this technology works is that the brilliant minds at Roku have developed bleeding edge nanoentheogenic technology that combines specially engineered nanoparticle clusters that connect in the bloodstream with the specialized microclotting effects of a modified psychedelic active ingredient,"* he paused and looked at the camera, *"colonel's secret recipe,"* and he looked away, *"to create magnetic signal centralizations that can be detected and manipulated by Roku's patented Deep Bluetooth technology deployed in our new streaming remote – the Basilisk."*

Mike stuttered. "Roku's... Basilisk." He thought he was sinking into a university flashback.

Aliya gave him a xan.

On the word 'Basilisk,' a podium draped in velour slowly emerged through the floor of the stage as *The Final Countdown* played to more thunderous applause.

Nick was too shaken to believe what he was seeing. "That has to be a coincidence. There's no way."

"Hey man, no big deal. We've all seen *Arrested Development.* You and Roku both had the same idea to copy the soundtrack to Gob Bluth's magic performances."

"Jesus fucking Christ I hope you're right."

"No big deal." Geoff repeated to himself, "no big deal."

"User One has taken an effective dose of NeuraDrink – that's our code name for the drug - and according to the timer set by Roku's team of psychedelic scientists, it has just this second reached saturation. User One, please continue."

User One walked to the podium and picked up the Basilisk remote.

"User One, please activate the Basilisk."

The TechSmash camera zoomed into the Basilisk remote and watched as he pressed a button labeled 'broadcast'.

"Kev, you okay?"

"Why wouldn't he be okay?"

"When the guy pressed the button he jolted and made a weird noise."

Kevin didn't respond and continued to stare ahead blankly at the presentation on the jumbotron.

A strange, almost alien, multi-layered stream of scattered speech emerged from the TechSmash sound system. As it became audible, it slowly began to self-correct, morphing into a single stream-of-consciousness style of speech.

"Right now, the Basilisk is only transmitting User One's inner monologue over the sound systems here at TechSmash. There are three settings for transmission – binary signals, presented to the user as yes/no queries; stream of consciousness, sound only, which is what you're hearing now; and..."

User One pressed another button on the Basilisk remote.

"Stream-of-consciousness mind's eye visuals."

The jumbotron at TechSmash had its visuals switch from a black screen to a panicked, distorted pornographic scene

– User One's mind was blasting porn onto the jumbotron, and he was visibly stressed, cursing to himelf out loud, scrambling to replace the images with something else – anything else. The screen jumped back and forth between humiliating pornographic desires, deep from within the soul of the anonymous test subject, to word-art text of his stream of consciousness, almost always just 'FUCK' over and over again.

User One was still standing in place by the podium, but he was struggling, trembling. He dropped the remote on the ground, fell to his knees to pick it up. The word-art text flashed SORRYSORRYSORRYSORRY.

He got back up and the text started flashing "dontshitpants dontshitpants" and there was a half second pause followed by a word-art text FUUUUUUUCCCK. The word dropped off screen. This seemed to bring about a period of relative inner peace to User One, as he then looked to be able to center himself; he imagined strong TV static for a while, and after a short period, from the center of the static emerged a single word, an apology to TechSmash and the world: SORRY.

User One then remembered that his Basilisk remote had the option to switch streaming back to binary, and he pressed it, and the visuals disappeared from the jumbotron.

The audience stood up and applauded and cheered for nearly 20 minutes.

When it finally died down, User One was still on the stage.

"User One – we've all been there, man. No judgment, am I right?"

The audience laughed.

The Grinders just stared.

"Now, I know a lot of you will have a frightened reaction. How dystopian is this, right? There is no need to be afraid. The Basilisk is your friend, the Basilisk can be with you at all times. Don't

worry about theft and abuse – the Basilisk can only be switched into operation if the bloodstream detects no stress, sensed through your unique biomarkers. And don't worry about corporate abuse – employees at Roku must undergo strenuous ethical training before being allowed access to the central consciousness recording database. Because at Roku, we care about YOU. So as you can see, if this is any kind of -topian, it's YOU-topian. Say it with me!"

The audience repeated back, *"YOU-topian!"*

The Grinders were speechless other than Mike, who had to find his voice before he could manage saying, "this is the most terrifying thing I've ever seen."

"How are they- why are they applauding?"

"Showmanship. Knockoff Steve Jobs with his intentionally bad dad jokes. Builds trust. Endearing social incompetence that gets everyone's guard down. Roku knows exactly what they're doing."

"Fuck, man."

"I hate this."

"Yeah, no fucking kidding, Roman. Do you really think you need to say that out loud?"

"Hey, fuck you, settle down."

"Sorry, just, on edge."

"This drug – NeuraDrink – only needs to be taken once and it will then be permanently in effect, until manually disabled."

This started to set something off for Aliya but she couldn't fully place it. The gears were turning. She had to review her notes. She reached into her bag and fumbled around for her notebook and she found it and started reading old information for a while, adding corrections with a sparkle in her eye like she was signing the back of a lottery ticket.

The Grinders paid her no mind.

"Wait. Wait, hold on. Look at the center of the front row next time they pan to the audience. LOOK! NOW."

"Holy shit. What?"

"That's him?" Nick started to feel off balance and so he ate an adderall.

"Our glorious intern?"

"Matej?"

"Can't be."

"Purple bucket hat. Nobody else who looks like that dresses like that."

"Maybe it caught on from his TikTok."

"Guys, it's him. He literally works for Roku. We sent him there. They started off the fucking presentation with his TikTok. It's Matej. Just accept it. Let's fucking move on."

"But that's not all. You can use BlueTwo – Roku's patented Bluetooth grouping technology – to set up a psychic network with up to 3 other people." The presenter used his fingers to make air quotes around 'psychic network'. He paused for a second and continued, *"it's collective streaming! Users Two, Three and Four, please join us on stage."*

Three others emerged from the back of the stage, and all four Users stood next to each other, facing the audience, covered in black, obscured by balaclavas.

"User One – open a conference!"

User One pressed a button on the Basilisk remote labeled 'conference'.

"Link up!"

Users Two, Three and Four also pressed the 'conference' button and were immediately connected.

"Now switch from binary to voice!"

Are we all connected now?
I think so.
I bet they think this is prerecorded.
Let's ask the audience a question.
Hey, you! Say something weird.

User Two pointed to an audience member who shouted "Kwyjibo!" to a response of scattered nerd laughter.

Hahahaha
Yup, that's weird
What's weird?
Kwyjibo, I think she said
Isn't kwyjibo that fake word from the Simpsons?
I think it means a big dumb balding North American ape with no chin
Sounds like your mom!
Shut up! You don't know her
We'd better stop talking about it or Fox's lawyers will sue our pants off
Where we're going we don't need pants
Enough of that, User Two
That was me
Which one are you?
User Four
Oh, right. Well, we all just met two days ago
Yeah, fair

The spotlight returned to the main Roku presenter.

"Thank you, Users! Now, please press mute, all four of you."

The Users all pressed the 'mute' button on the Basilisk remote.

"Now I do have a confession. This is just the beginning. We don't have every functionality we want, quite yet. Our brilliant research and development team is coming on strong with new breakthroughs in nanoentheogenic technology that will open up the ability to share smells and tastes, and, down the road – don't call me woke! - we're hoping we can even start sharing our feelings!"

aLan felt a need to say what all the Grinders were thinking. "This is the most evil technology I've ever seen."

"They are definitely going to sell this to the military. Can you imagine? If you want enemy secrets, just feed someone a drug and you get all their thoughts in HD."

"It doesn't turn on if they're stressed."

Aliya wheeled over with her magical bag. "Well, I could think of a way around that."

"Oh. Oh fucking hell."

"On the bright side, they won't need to torture anyone anymore."

"But they probably still will."

"God damnit, man. Let me try to be happy."

"And how about blackmail?"

"How?"

"Recording someone's stream-of-consciousness while providing strong outside suggestion towards certain materials... illegal, career-ending, marriage-ending materials."

"Oh my goodness. Hey, Cassandra. You hear that? You can use that!"

Cassandra's head was in her hands.

"Sorry Archon."

The TechSmash presenter lowered his voice. *"And we have one final display."*

"OH THANK FUCK. It's almost over."

"User One – please press the Archon button."

"Wait, hold on, what in the fuck?"

"Yeah, I'm gonna shit my pants."

"You wouldn't be the first."

"Uhh." Gerg wheeled away from Miles.

"I meant User One. Fuck off. I didn't shit my pants."

"Yet."

"Yeah. Yet."

"The Archon feature connects the Roku's Basilisk user – via a quantum-encrypted connection – to our global artificial intelligence database – AngelAI."

Cassandra started crying.

Nick pieced it together first. "So if I'm understanding this correctly, Matej went to Silicon Valley with the secrets of the *Bromeliad,* gave the divine wisdom of the structure of the Cosmos to the worst people on the planet, and now he's..." he trailed off and ate another adderall.

"He's trying to become the Archon. He's trying to snipe the Archon position."

"Or Angel."

"Or the one above the-"

"Yeah yeah. Can he do that?"

Mike spoke up to try to soothe their ruffled feathers. Someone had to.

"Well I might be wrong, and I hope I'm not, but... you can't exactly usurp the structure of something that you are physically inside of. It's extremely common for technology to use the fabric of the Cosmos as a flashlight of progress. Could probably look at Matej as less of a conquering hero, and more of, like... the Roswell crash. The alien spaceship that crashed in New Mexico and then America reverse engineered the technology as much as they could. They say that's how they developed the technology for stealth bombers."

Nick took another adderall. "Well that's easier for me to stomach anyways."

"Cassandra. You're the Archon. What do you think?"

Cassandra was only crying. Lise jumped onto her lap and the crying slowed. She started petting Lise, and the Grinders all directed their attention back to TechSmash.

"AngelAI draws on the internet – the entire internet – to perform immediate searches for any keywords. And get this – we've combined the thought-to-speech technology with speech-to-text."

"Oh no. Oh fuck."

"This can't be real."

"After pressing the Archon button – you got it – you can search for anything that exists, simply by thinking about it."

"I don't like this."

"And on the docket for the future – once we have the computing power, which won't be too far from now, with our exclusive partnership with NVidia – is immediate 3d rendering of anything you desire – which will be put to use as a kind of prosthetic imagination, for the 50% of all people in the world who currently

suffer from a .. let's say, a lack of imagination."

"They love it. Fucking idiots."

"This here is the end of the world."

"How are they not seeing what this is?"

"Jingling keys, man. Flashing lights. They don't give a fuck."

"Distracted by a shiny new toy," muttered Roman derisively, who turned his attention back to the jumbotron.

"How long until someone in tech journalism points out that they would be handing over their own imaginations to a publicly traded company?"

"Not happening. They wouldn't launch this unless they'd paid them all off."

"And whoever they don't pay off, they can just send them to the psych ward."

"That's barbaric."

"That's what happens."

"By the way, no chance they ever delete the search histories. Hey Cassandra, I thought of something else for your blackmail network."

Cassandra was pacified by the purring of Lise, still in her lap.

"They're really going to get people to pay a monthly subscription to have a Silicon Valley CEO control their thoughts?"

"The perfect crime."

"I don't think so man. I think it's just normal crime. Very bad crime."

"Don't we like crime?"

"Only when we're doing it. Karma for the Grind."

"Karma for the Grind!"

Miles turned to Cassandra to get her into it. "Karma for ... the... "

"Once again it is time for you to shut the fuck up, Miles."

"Well, I can only guess from your standing ovation that you're all probably expecting this to cost an arm and a leg. Well, you can keep standing and clapping with the limbs you have, as I'm very happy to announce that paying for the nano drug is easy as... pi! 314 dollars."

The audience kept roaring.

"The remote itself? ZERO DOLLARS."

The audience kept roaring.

"The streaming subscription is free to use... and only 99 dollars a month to eliminate ads!"

The audience kept roaring.

"Oh that's brilliant." Nick was transfixed and didn't notice his leg was shaking.

"What, putting ads in a streaming service?"

"You think they need ad money after dropping this? The greatest data collection and mind control device in the history of the world?"

"Why else would they put in ads?"

Nick cleared his throat and gained control of his leg. "It's a dummy evil."

"Dummy evil? It's just normal evil."

"Yeah, but we all see the deeper evil here, right?"

"Of course."

"What we have here is big tech putting out a world-changing technology. This is changing everything. Everything. EVERYTHING. Forever. It's never leaving if it's allowed to get established. But something is wrong. Even if they can't place exactly what it is, the good people of planet Earth are going to be able to sense that something's wrong. There's going to be something from inside of them, a feeling deep in their guts that doubts this whole thing."

"And Roku is giving them a manageable evil? Like, a landing spot where they can rest that feeling deep in their guts?"

"Exactly! Thank you! So I'm not just going insane." Nick paused to catch his breath. "Wouldn't be surprised if they even play it up, seeding the outrage against the ads, so that they make sure that this is the... dominant outrage. Planting articles all over the place about the ethics of advertising within the stream of consciousness."

"Controlling the narrative?"

"Settling a few billion dollar lawsuits too, so people will think there was justice."

"That is sort of brilliant."

"Do we think our glorious intern came up with any of this?"

The Grinders were too afraid of a yes answer to guess either way.

"...and we understand your concerns. Transparency is important to us at Roku. So, just so we have total transparency here – we are revealing the total hierarchy of data flow. There will be a single administrator account – the most vetted human being in the history of planet Earth. Our extensive research in the field of psychedelics has brought us face to face with several regional

shamanistic cultures and their unassailable codes of ethics surrounding the use of mind-expanding plants and chemicals."

"Wonder if they've already chosen a guy for that."

"Oh! They should do a reality show. Like Survivor."

"Well that's fucking stupid."

"The single user who will be put in charge of the entire experience will be the only account with the power to alter the information of AngelAI. We will not be revealing who it is, as this would endanger the lives of millions and risk the integrity of the project. But the user's title will be Master Administrator of Total Equilibrium and Justice."

"Does someone wanna... spell that out?"

"M..A..T..E......J"

"Matej."

"It's fucking Matej."

"Tejy Tejy Tej."

"Are you fucking kidding me?"

"Funky cold Tejina."

"Total equilibrium and justice sounds like some commie bullshit to me."

"Hmm."

The presenter delivered a final death blow before exiting the stage.

"So how's that for streaming?"

The audience kept roaring. They hadn't stopped. They wouldn't stop for an hour.

The world crashed silently in and around the Grinders.

A few minutes passed before Roman broke the silence.

"But why Matej?"

"Hey Kev, you've been weirdly quiet. You usually have some insane drugs philosophy for this kind of thing. We need you, man."

Kevin smiled politely and didn't budge.

"Something's off with you, man. What's happening?"

Aliya shifted in her seat. "He hasn't done any drugs since he got back."

"I'm fine, everyone. I had a moment of clarity in Palo Alto, and I'm going to be behaving more appropriately. There is no reason to be afraid."

Gerg couldn't handle it. He ran to his desk, grabbed his hockey stick, and smashed the screen of the office jumbotron until the stick snapped in half.

aLan did the same with the two stick halves until they snapped in half again.

Roman picked up the four smaller pieces and smashed what was left until his fingers started to bleed. He paused to catch his breath while sitting on the ground. The lust for violence being momentarily satisfied gave him an uncharacteristic moment of insight. "Guys. All this is making me start to think some crazy shit."

"Like what?"

"Like, are we in a simulation?"

"No. What? Are you fourteen? Shut the fuck up."

A sympathetic Mike wheeled his chair over and whispered like an older brother, "Roman, buddy, if this was a simulation, they would have pulled the plug on us as soon as they chose Matej as the administrator."

He was relieved, but still nervously whispered, "Ha, Mike. I was joking!" He wasn't.

"Still feels like maybe we were all being tested for this? Cassandra?"

Cassandra just stared ahead.

"Yeah, I really don't think so."

"Maybe she's sad because they didn't choose her."

"She's the Archon of the real thing, though. That has gotta be worth more than being a fake God of a fake religion."

Cassandra sniffled.

There was an extended silence.

"Why him though?"

"I mean, he's a good guy, right?"

"Well there are lots of good people everywhere, and most of them know how to spell Basilisk."

"But it's not just that," Aliya continued. "I mean, we were kind of terrible to him. And he stayed loyal."

"I don't think we can say he's loyal after selling our secrets to Silicon Valley."

"I would bet you anything that he thinks he's serving the *Bromeliad* by doing all this. And for all we know he might be."

"So being polite and loyal is enough then? Are they really making a God out of Ned Flanders with Stockholm syndrome?"

"He was unwavering. Name one time he fucked over any of us."

aLan paused. "Or lied to us. Or deceived us."

"Well yeah, true, but I always thought that was because he couldn't figure out how."

Terry remembered the time that Matej vomited up the vodka punch.

Terry said nothing.

"He's stoic to the point of masochism." aLan sat up and his speech grew in intensity. "He acts unselfishly at all times. He's unquestionably devoted to a strict moral code that he barely understands. He never once questioned the hierarchy of power."

Kevin broke his silence and added casually, "Also, don't forget that clinical tests performed at Roku's cognitive development laboratory showed that Matej scored 100 on the extremely competitive experiments that were designed by Harvard scientists to tease out treacherous and manipulative behaviour. The second highest score was 84. The head of the Harvard School of Divinity only scored a 78."

The Grinders stared, terrified.

"Thank you for the reminder, Kevin!"

"You're welcome, Miles!"

Kevin returned to absently staring at the wall in front of him. Gerg put a lampshade over his head and he didn't react.

"So that's what is going to happen to everyone, right?"

"This is worse than we thought."

"It gets even worse than that," Jeff added. "Our short probably won't pay off, eh?"

"Oh my god. I forgot about that part."

"Yeah, doesn't feel too important anymore."

Cassandra started crying again.

"Sorry. I guess it's still pretty important."

"No fucking kidding. Instead of being a major shareholder in the fucking technological singularity,"

"We are broke."

"We might be the most broke private equity firm in the history of broke."

"Don't we still have the DADS network? And Aliya can always reassume control of her drug empire."

Miles was the only person to clue in to the real danger. "I think there's something a bit more important than money at the moment."

"The existential crisis?"

"Crises. When there's four hundred of them, it's plural. Crises."

Mike threw a stapler at the smashed jumbotron screen in frustration. "No! No existential crisis allowed! I told you, they are *echoing* the fabric of the Cosmos." Mike got very animated with his hands. "Copying a fraction of it. They aren't replacing it. We have not been replaced. We have only been studied." He paused. "I admit, we have been studied very, very effectively. But what they have is only a piece."

"No, I mean," Miles sighed, realizing he was just about to make everyone's day a lot worse. "The Groom comes from old money and now all the old money is gone. Because of us, and only us."

"You just said money isn't important."

"It is to them. And they are going to kill us."

"They're going to kill us if we're lucky."

"They will be sending Italian men with lead pipes."

"So what we have to do now is-"

"Leave New York City immediately and never come back."

Cassandra's crying hit a second level. Lise tried purring louder and it started to work. However true their words were, in that moment, Cassandra would have let the Italians kill her. She didn't give a fuck anymore.

She didn't care about the money or the prestige or the jumbotron or the offices or the Grind.

She had a broken heart.

While the Grinders hatched an escape plan, she sobbed until she was out of tears. When she was out of tears, she remained hunched over in her seat, staring at the floor, mouth open, unblinking, waiting for more tears to form so she could cry again.

And at the true nadir of her life, at one of the most impressive low points in the history of human civilization, she heard a soft reprieve from Aliya that cracked through ten thousand miles of sadness to offer a sliver of hope.

"Karma for the Grind."

The first one that she had ever truly believed.

She had no defenses left. She didn't have the energy to resist the mantra anymore.

"Karma for the Grind."

She had to.

"Karma for the Grind."

She repeated.

She let it wash over her.

It felt good.

She was still sunk, she had hit an iceberg, the hull breached, and she drowned, and she knew she took all her passengers with her.

But there was something to be salvaged.

"Karma for the Grind."

And there was a saving grace in there, anyways. She did take down all the passengers with her. Their lives were over. Destroyed.

This is what she wanted.

This is what she wanted.

This is what she wanted.

She perked up for a second but still found herself too weak to form full sentences or to sit up straight.

She missed him.

She was too weak to cry.

Aliya gave her a marble bag with various pills and powders for the journey ahead. She ate a yellow and a blue, never learning what they were, and she started to feel good fifteen minutes later.

For now they had to leave.

Those Italian men with lead pipes would be coming to grind them in a way they would prefer to avoid.

And if they managed to elude the slow, painful, Italian consequences, there would be questions, there would be inspection, and there would be brutal prison time for all of them at the end of any of those roads.

And in those prisons would be Italian men with lead pipes.

They had to run.

With the eyes of the world still enraptured by the next thousand years of human civilization being unveiled at TechSmash, Aliya instinctively went goblin mode, and while everyone was gathering themselves and their more important personal effects, she ransacked the offices of every executive on their floor. She ended up with so many narcotics that she needed a second magical bag.

Steef took a minute to be with his office gardens one final time, and he shed a tear as he took sixteen pictures.

As he caressed the sprouting ayahuasca and lamented that he would never get to know how it blossomed, Aliya burst into his office, clearly not noticing at first that it was his.

"Is that ayahuasca? I didn't know you were into this kind of thing. Bring it with you!"

"Yeah, Matej set me up with it." Steef thought for a minute. "But nah. Some things you gotta leave behind. Speaking of which, you want this?" Steef held up *Leaves of Grass.*

She didn't want it, but as a rule, if a crying adult man offers you a book of poetry in a time of grief, you accept it. Aliya crammed it into her pocket, bolted to the next office down the hall and kept pillaging.

She stole two bags of ketamine, seventy-five pellets of zoloft, five dozen oxycontin, a salt shaker half full of fentanyl, and a whole galaxy of multi-colored tylenol 1, 2cb, 3-meo-pcp, 4-fluoroamphetamine and 5-meo-dmt... and also a quart of GHB, a quart of pink whitney, a case of strawberry white claw, a pint of crown royal, and two dozen ativan.

Not that they needed all that for the escape, but once you get locked into a serious drug robbery, the tendency is to push it as far as you can.

The beautiful sight of the colors and the shapes of the various hues of the drugs all together in a wonderful messy pile gave her a flash of a memory of her Vancouver operation. She had already left it in the hands of someone else, but now she was going to have to let it go forever. The Karma would still be generated, but it wouldn't be the same.

When she paused for that moment of reflection, the book in her pocket started to grind on the side of her leg. She pulled it out to relocate into one of her magical bags, but paused partway to look at a random page, and as she read one of the poems, some of the information sitting on the shelves in her brain settled and shifted sideways and started to line up. Why did Matej try to get Steef onto ayahuasca? Matej and Steef connecting on psychedelics? The only way this makes sense is if...

She ran to the bathroom to finish her train of thought.

"NeuraDrink ... is ... modified ... ayahuasca," she whispered to herself as she wrote in perfect cursive.

She could reverse it. She had notes.

She flushed.

She was the last person to finish gathering items and when returned to the main trading floor, the Grinders were waiting for her in a circle next to the destroyed jumbotron.

Cassandra wandered over to the window. Fearing the worst, the Grinders followed. Aliya put her arm firmly around Cassandra so that she wouldn't try anything.

They looked down.

The streets below were littered with stationary taxis.

There were enough taxis across from the foot of the building for all of them right away.

They all loaded into a single elevator, three times the recommended weight limit. Maybe they were tempting fate.

They made it to the bottom and out the front door without being noticed and Cassandra barely paid attention when her Nike cleats came untied and almost fell off.

They crossed the road, crammed into three taxis, and drove to the river.

They couldn't cross the border back home to Canada, but they needed to go somewhere.

They were moving, which bought them a few minutes, but they had to come up with something else right away.

Kevin was in the passenger seat of the leading taxi, with Aliya, Nick and Cassandra crammed in the back, Aliya carefully watching over the precarious mental state of her Archon. The other taxis followed immediately behind.

"Cassandra, I know you're in a rough state, we all are. But we need to know what to do."

Cassandra couldn't bring herself to respond. She rolled the rear passenger side window down and, not wanting to show herself to the world, let the wind roll over her face just inside, poking her nose out to catch a stronger breeze every now and then. The breeze felt good on her skin, the drugs were working.

Kevin chimed in, "Well, I think I can be of some help!"

Aliya didn't know if they could trust him anymore, but they didn't have a lot of options. "Alright. Fine. What is it?"

"While I was in Palo Alto visiting Matej, we were catching up on the ride from Roku headquarters, and he mentioned that he was moving his family from upstate New York to California."

"So there's an empty house for us upstate?"

"There's a mansion upstate with huge, sprawling gardens in the yard. There are many rooms. There is a large livingroom. He showed me pictures of the many rooms and the large livingroom. His family has moved out, but the house remains furnished."

The taxi driver honked and shouted "FUCK YOU" at a homeless man in the middle of the road and swerved around him at a high speed.

"Gotta be honest," Nick's leg had stopped shaking, "Kevin" he enunciated, "this kind of feels like a trap."

"Why would I want to trap you? You're the Karma Grinders!" Kevin said, proudly, with a camp counsellor smile.

Cassandra whimpered. Her focus stayed on the quickly passing buildings and pedestrians at eye level outside the taxi.

"Yeah I definitely don't trust this."

"Nick, we have no other options. It's this or we die," Aliya figured. "If Matej wanted us dead or captured I think he'd have done it by now. It's the finance guys who want us dead."

Nick acquiesced but his addled mind was still working on overdrive. "How was he allowed to be in touch with his family?"

Kevin had a quick answer. "He showed me a loophole that he found in the *Bromeliad.* As long as a Disciple's relationship with his or her former family is exclusively for the purpose of capital accumulation in service of the Archon, contact with the family is permitted, as long as a suitable emotional distance is maintained."

"This okay, Archon?"

Cassandra stayed focused on the outside passing by. She felt at the outline of the hunting knife strapped to her leg.

She sniffled.

Nick whispered to Aliya, "We need to talk about Kevin."

Aliya whispered, "I know. I have a plan. I think I figured it out. During the presentation. Wait til we get there."

Cassandra could overhear the whispering and she allowed the hope in their voices to carry into her; feeling a tinge of life, she stuck her head fully out the window. She pulled her hood back and the wind blew in her hair and she turned to look back at the skyscrapers of New York until they disappeared over the horizon.

09 - DRUGS

The Grinders could have easily paid their cab fare. They just didn't feel like it.

Aliya still had her shoes on as she took a long, cold shower in an ensuite bathroom of Matej's abandoned family home, having long washed away the blood of the three taxi drivers, needing a bit more time for herself. She had given Cassandra a healthy pile of colorful non-lethal sedatives, so she could afford to take her time.

Like a good Soldier, Kevin had dragged the corpses of the taxi drivers into the gardens in the back of the mansion where Terry was digging a massive grave.

"Aliya tells me that all three taxi drivers committed suicide once she told them about the Basilisk. That's very unfortunate, in my opinion. The Basilisk would have made their lives a lot better. There was no reason for them to be afraid." Kevin lingered, standing upright, staring into a void in the distance, unblinking, waiting for a response that Terry would never give him.

After exactly sixty seconds, Kevin issued a polite, "Thank you for your time!" and started his walk through the backyard gardens to the main house where the rest of the Grinders were discussing survival strategies for the rest of their lives.

***

"So we don't even know if they're after us yet."

"We should probably assume."

Most of the Grinders were milling about quietly in the main livingroom; at the center was a giant, 15-seat black leather sectional couch, Cassandra a comatose pile of nerves and sedatives in the corner, Lise standing guard on the couch ledge above her, eyes closed, purring for effect.

Miles held the TV remote in his hand. "Wish we could turn on the news. Might help us plan." He stared at the 84 inch high definition TV as though it was on.

Nick had been eating adderalls on the entire ride over, never letting himself lapse into the comedown, entirely forgetting what he had learned in university about diminishing returns. He started talking, partly to stop his teeth from grinding. "I was thinking about the news lockdown anyways. If reality can't be trusted, then how do we know that what we're doing is worth doing? We can't trust it. Can we trust it?" Nick's lower jaw moved side to side and he stared at a dot at the center of a mandala pattern on the livingroom carpet.

"What do you mean?"

Nick's leg was shaking again. "The purpose of the news lockdown is because what's on the news is not the ultimate truth, right? It's the Archon. It's the Archon. It's the Archon."

Cassandra twitched in the corner of the couch.

"Yeah, but-"

"And so, and so, and so we can never be sure that what we're doing is for good reason." Nick was rocking back and forth.

"We do what the Archon says. It's the *Bromeliad.*" Miles corrected himself. "It's IN the *Bromeliad.*"

"Technically, we are doing this for the benefit of souls that we are also told cannot be trusted to truly exist." Nick's leg was still shaking and his talking sped up. "Don't know if they're real. Are they real? We don't know if they're real." Nick put his hand on his leg to stop it from shaking but he was still rocking back and forth. He paused to eat another adderall.

"Yeah, but..." Miles trailed off.

"But what? But what? But what?"

"I was sorta hoping you would interrupt me."

Nick kept mouthing but not speaking "but what? But what?"

After an extended silence, Miles blinked, inhaled, tightened his grip on the remote control in his hand and turned the TV on, flipping until he found a blonde lady reading the news.

"Rappers bbno$ and Yung Gravy have been arrested this evening,"

"Wait, how is this the breaking news? What about the... the Basilisk?"

"They look pretty happy for being taken into custody."

The blonde lady continued, *"...facing 5 to ten years in federal prison,"*

"Holy shit."

A high tempo dance beat with heavy bass dropped into the background.

"On one hundred counts.... of fuckin your mom!"

"Miles what the fuck man? This is music videos. Go to the news."

Baby No Money's here to fuck your mom
And he's bringing Yung Gravy here to sing a song

"Change the channel you dumbass."

"Kinda catchy."

"CHANGE IT or I'll cut your dick off."

Miles flipped to the news and Kevin returned through the back door and sat down right as an impassioned Keith Olbermann was mid-sentence, rattling off descriptives like he'd stolen a thesaurus.

"...economic saboteurs. Insane death cult. Psychopaths hell-bent on inflicting maximum suffering on all of humankind. This criminal mastermind organization infiltrated the Canadian military, a top private equity firm on Wall Street, one of Canada's richest families, and the second largest telecommunications company in North America, taking it down fron the inside, leading to roaming coverage blackouts that are still continuing to this day. The FBI is offering a reward of fifty million dollars for any useful information on any of the members. That's fifty million dollars, the highest amount the FBI has offered for information in their history."

"Hey, that's us!"

"We're famous!"

"That's not good, remember? Secret's out."

"Oh, yeah, well, it was over anyways, right? Might as well go out famous."

"Maybe a dumb question but we can't collect that 50 million, right?"

Nobody even bothered to look over to Gerg to glare at him, and Keith Olbermann continued.

"Terrorists of the highest degree, wanted by every three-letter agency in the western hemisphere. Responsible for over 50,000

deaths of innocent civilians worldwide. The man believed to be their leader, Mike,"

On a sunnier day, this egregious lack of recognition would have sent Cassandra into a tailspin, but she was too comfortably numb from the rainbow medley of mystery pills to mount any outrage.

"...is believed to be the cyberterrorist responsible for the infamous hack of Vancouver's YVR airport which caused the run of horrific air traffic control fatalities on June 22nd."

"Wait, how did they catch us?"

Nick popped another adderall. "Location tracking. They location tracked us. We were the only flight unaffected. Security footage. Security footage. Mike. Mike. Had a fucking hacking station. They had cameras. Security cameras. CCTV." Both of his legs were shaking.

"Well, yeah, okay, fine. My bad."

"I didn't know anyone died."

"They probably didn't. This could be a trap to lure us out. I think they're onto us."

"Is that real?"

"We'll have to ask the Archon when she wakes up."

"If."

"When. Drug nap. She's fine."

"This is the AI. That's the Basilisk. They're using the Basilisk on us." Nick put his hand on the edge of the sectional to steady himself and stop rocking. "Basilisk is coming to get us."

"That's insane, man."

For a minute, the only sound other than the news was Nick's

shoe tapping on the carpet at high speed.

"That's got to be at least a category 5, right?"

"Fifty thousand dead? This is beyond the *Bromeliad*."

"But there's still Karma in those deaths."

"Miles, shut up."

"Yeah, shut the fuck up Miles. This is not the time."

"Karma for the Grind. Karma for the Grind." Nick let go of the edge of the couch and he was rocking again.

"Where the fuck is Aliya? Someone give something to Nick for this."

"I got it." Nick reached into his pocket with his trembling hand, pulled out three more adderalls, lost two on the shaky ride to his mouth, and ate the remaining one. "I got it. I got it."

Miles forged ahead. "No, I'm serious. I can't do the math in my head, it would be like doing calculus on an abacus, but, that IS Karma for the Grind? We might be done grinding anyone but ourselves, but... didn't we do a good thing here? Category 6? 7?"

Nick shouted "CATEGORY SEVEN."

"We were supposed to preserve human potential. No deaths."

"SEVEN. CATEGORY SEVEN."

"But there is still Karma there is what I'm saying. Just because we fucked up doesn't mean the Cosmic math doesn't add up for the affected. The families of the dead, the first responders, the ... the ... airport guys who have to do all that paperwork... that counts for them?"

Steef had had his head in his hands since they arrived, and he started to cry.

"Steef, I know you don't believe in this whole thing, but..."

"Leave him alone. It's real for him. He doesn't have anything for this. No religion, no drugs. He's raw dogging the tragedy."

Steef stopped crying but his head stayed in his hands and Miles took that as enough encouragement to keep talking.

"If we get the *Bromeliad* out of Cassandra's purse we can double check, but, it's all set up, we did a good thing, we go on to our next lives, they go on to theirs, maybe ours are worse, but theirs are all better?"

No response. He kept talking.

"Hey Jeff. Did you grab Kevin's notes before he went all brain slug?"

"Haha, Miles, I don't know what you're talking about," Kevin said, pronouncing the word 'haha' phonetically rather than laughing.

"Sevensevensevensevensevensevenseven."

Jeff pulled his laptop out. "Yep. Honestly I was digitizing them the day he went away. Just in case his plane crashed. Or if he died of a heart attack. Or wandered into traffic. So, Miles."

"Yessir?"

"You're technically correct, but I feel like by reassuring everyone, you're kind of... you know... alleviating them of their suffering? Taking some Karma from them."

"Oh. Sorry guys."

"All good, man. The real news is in here anyways." Jeff pointed to a text document on his laptop and a quarter dozen of them gathered behind as he scrolled slowly through the enlarged text.

"Well this is good news. Do we believe it?"

"I don't see any problems with the logic. Archon?"

Cassandra was still frozen in the fetal position in the corner and numb, not blinking. Her eyes were dry but red from crying and her pupils shrunken. She was smiling but she couldn't tell.

"Never mind. Hey, Aliya's been in the shower for 30 minutes, someone go make sure she's alive and get her in on this too. I know she takes notes too."

There was an extended pause as the Grinders contemplated the awkwardness of walking in on a girl in the shower. Eventually Geoff took the assignment.

Miles walked to the center of the livingroom and shouted loud enough for everyone to hear except for Aliya, who was in the shower, washing away the evidence, and Terry, who was in the garden, burying it.

"Grinders! Hear ye! Hear ye! We have one last chance to save our balance sheets."

"Which?"

"Karmic. The only one we have left."

Aliya was out of the shower, fully clothed, sopping wet, dragged by Geoff to the perimeter of earshot.

Cassandra blinked.

"There is a loophole!" Miles proclaimed.

"A real one or just some more bullshit theory? No offense, Nick. I'm just tired of spreadsheets."

"Spreadsheets. Spreadsheets. Tired of spreadsheets." Nick stopped talking solely because he wanted to return to grinding his teeth. He was developing a system to grind each tooth in equal amounts.

"It checks out. We've gone over it a few times. No holes."

"I don't know about this...."

"I haven't even started talking yet. Just listen. So, summarizing for everyone," Miles spoke from his gut, "it is conscious attention to suffering that diminishes its Karmic value. But what if we obliterated our ability to maintain conscious attention?"

Aliya had already figured it out. She was already walking with purpose and a dumbass grin towards her magical bag.

"Aliya. Let's get these guys fucked up. No awareness drugs. Brain damage only. Brain damage only from here on out. Karma for the Grind!"

"We can still use awareness drugs if we're smart with it, Miles."

"Okay then Aliya. You're in charge of the drugs."

"Brain damage only. Brain damage only." Nick grabbed one of the adderalls on the ground and stared at it in his shaking hand.

Aliya tried to coax Kevin back. "Karma for the Grind!"

He just smiled politely.

She decided that this was the time to end the fake Kevin. The Grinders needed their glue sniffer back. She needed to put her *Leaves of Grass* moment into action. On the cab ride over, she had been reviewing her old notebooks of exhaustive experimentation that she had done on Kevin's squishy brain – there could not have possibly been better field notes.

She reached into her magical bag, pulled out and handed him seven MDMAs. She was all smiles. "You've been so helpful lately, you get the first ones!" She forced all seven down his throat and nobody said another word to him for a while. He stood in place like a lamp post.

Aliya explained to Miles, who had been watching, "I don't know the full composition of the drug, or the specific reaction of the whatever nanoparticles blah blah, but this should bring Kevin's blood levels to a point where the nanotechnology can't stabilize or maintain as a network of receptors, and the total bliss of the MDMAs should flood his brain and allow for a bit of a cognitive reset."

aLan was eavesdropping. "I'm not following."

"Good news aLan, you don't fucking have to. Once again I am doing everything."

"What do you mean, once again?"

"Shut the fuck up Roman. You and your mustache don't need to understand anything, pretty boy. Anyways, the particles will still be in his bloodstream for a while but I don't think they can reconstitute into usable receptors for the Deep Bluetooth." She paused. "And if anyone else does ayahuasca I shoot them on sight." She rummaged in her magical bag for one of her guns, couldn't find one, and then just said, "I do have at least one gun, in my purse, please just act like I pulled out a gun right now."

"Ahh!"

"Thank you Roman. Your death shall be quick and peaceful."

Lise meowed and pawed the top of Cassandra's head. Cassandra had set up a comfortable home in the deep center of the sectional, stationed in a curve around her remaining pile of colorful sedatives like a crescent moon cradling the north star.

The paw attack reminded Cassandra to take one of the greens. They made the feeling of the leather couch very agreeable. She was hoping to stay on the couch forever.

Miles watched this happen with concern, not considering

himself a replacement Archon, but knowing that, if something went wrong, he would have to be the Disciple that stepped up.

Some more of the Grinders turned to watch the cat messing around with their Archon. Aliya had to cough rudely to draw their attention back to her golden moment.

She had been generating ideas on the backburner for drug games for weeks. Months. Years. This was her shit. This was her element. She had some specific, borderline evil ideas that she wanted to put into use back at the telecom when they were waiting for the notarized letter, but the effects of those ideas had too great of a chance of becoming permanent.

That didn't matter anymore. They were dead, so they might as well die.

"This is your ketamine," she said to a reluctant Miles, while she was still searching in her purse for it. The mention of the word ketamine got him remembering Kevin's conveyor belt ride at the airport. He remembered taking charge at the airport and remembered that there seemed to be such a sense of purpose to it back then.

He thought about what it would even mean to step up right then, in the middle of their armageddon. What is the sense in promoting yourself to captain of a sinking ship?

What is worth saving here?

What can even be saved?

He always questioned the appeal of disassociating, but it seemed like a pretty fucking good idea right about now.

Miles stuck his hand out, expecting a pill, and Aliya found one of her two bags she had stolen from the offices of the billionaires, and poured him a good pile that she figured could last him a couple of days.

Miles immediately snarfed the entire pile. "Down the hatch!"

"Jesus, man, save some for the cat."

Miles choked it down like flour, determined to eat what he believed to be one dose of ketamine. He could only say "huh?" as some of it fell from his mouth and dusted his jeans and the black leather couch.

"You just ate enough horse tranquilizer to take down an elephant, buddy."

Miles gave two thumbs up, but he didn't know if he meant it.

"The fuck...?" Kevin rubbed his eyes. "Where am I?"

"K-hole?"

"Oh hey Aliya. What's going on?"

"HE'S BACK!"

Aliya dropped her bag of ketamine on the floor and rushed over to crush Kevin with a hug, breaking one of his ribs.

"Holy shit! Kev's human again!"

"Aliya. Get off me."

"Sorry."

"What do you mean human again?"

"Kev. You got weird for a while."

He looked around. "Well. How did I get here?"

"What's the last thing you remember?"

"I... was in Matej's penthouse and we were doing an ayahuasca ritual and then he gave me this second... potion? But I never bothered to ask what it was. And then we just sat on his floor and meditated and then I was in... I was just dreaming for a while, I guess, and now I'm here. Where are we?"

"Matej's family mansion. You told us about it."

"My head hurts. Owwww. Fuck. Oh fuck."

"What's going on K-hole?"

"I remember some. The plane ride back to New York. And then the offices. And... okay. It's coming back. My head hurts like fuck. Please give me something. Aliya. Please. Now. Please."

She grabbed an oxy from the oxy jar and handed it to him. "Do you remember all the stuff you said? You were talking fucking weird. Like if LinkedIn was a guy."

"Yeah... I remember words coming out of my mouth. But I wasn't ... it wasn't really me who was deciding to say the words from my mouth? Does that make any sense? Like I wasn't the choice maker in my own body. Just along for the ride."

"That sounds terrifying."

"I mean that sounds terrifying but, like, I wasn't being overpowered. It didn't feel like I was trying to do something different. Like, my choices were being overridden on a level deeper than desire."

"That sounds even more terrifying, man."

"Yeah. Yeah. You're right. Holy shit. Owww."

"Head still hurts?"

"Yeah. Fuck. Some weird thing happening. Like, phantom pain but, for remembering. Like my brain is trying to reach for information but the information isn't there. And the part of my brain where that information would be is just... not there. Like I'm swiping in the dark, at nothing, with no limbs, but I still feel the whole thing."

"God damn dude."

"Yeah, I could go for a nice... forgetting of all this shit. What's that spilled on the floor?" Kevin dove at the ketamine pile and inhaled a large amount of it off the ground right into his nose. "Oh! Fantastic. Hehehe."

"Miles just did an elephant's worth. Maybe you two should go lie down in the media room."

"Dissociation obliviation association! Right on."

"D.O.A?"

"I'll think of a better acronym in the other room."

After Kevin took off to join Miles on the floor, Aliya got back to rummaging through her magical bag and daydreamed more on the ten thousand Grinder-substance combinations she didn't get around to at the telecom for whatever reason. As she put her game plan together, Keith Olbermann raged on in the background. Roman turned up the volume.

"What do we know about the Karma Grinders so far? From our initial readings of the confiscated communications, they were formed at the University of British Columbia in Vancouver in the early 2010s. They relinquished their surnames as a prerequisite to join. And there appears to have been a hazing ritual in which everyone at a party was forced to drink a chemical with the scientific name 236-GAA-LuO, known to some as 'Luongo' - a mysterious, privately developed mind control drug that has yet to be classified as a controlled substance, but is highly illegal in every country on the planet, with simple possession punishable by death in most countries."

"How'd they know to call us that? Is someone talking?"

"The news guy thinks the vodka punch was a mind control drug. Hey Mike! Your punch was so good it's in the news."

"Yeah dude. For real, you throw one party in your life and

it starts a death cult that destroys the world and then Keith Olbermann talks about your vodka punch. That's a pretty good batting average."

"Can't wait to see what your next party is like."

"Hey Mike, maybe more girls at the next one."

"No kidding."

"Hey, get off my back, I had one day to plan it. And Cassandra was supposed to bring her lesbian lover."

He glanced over to Cassandra who had been maintaining her new life as an emotionless puddle of comfortable synapses in the corner of the sectional, which was all that she could manage while Keith Olbermann was busy bringing down her empire on national television.

"Why is the news covering this and not the Roku thing? Isn't that more important? By a lot?"

Nick had shifted from rocking back and forth to tapping both of his legs furiously. "Cable news is a blanket, don't overthink it. Don't overthink it. We're today's distraction so that people don't think about the Basilisk making humanity obsolete overnight. Tomorrow it'll be something else. There's always something else. Then something else. Then something else."

Aliya got tired of Nick's distracting convulsion adventures and so she force fed him a couple xans.

"Am I gonna die?"

"I dunno man, probably, soon enough. But not from those."

Nick took another adderall and lied down on the sectional. His feet made less noise bouncing on the leather than they were making on the mandala rug in the center of the floor.

Slowly, his foot tapping lessened to a crawl and then stopped completely. The fresh absence of nervous movements was accompanied by a shriek.

"AAAAAAAAAAAAAAAAAAAAAAAAAAAAAAAA."

Everyone's attention turned as Nick bolted upright, calm as the Buddha, smiling, laughing.

"Guys. I think I just saw all of time. I just saw the end. I saw everything. I ... AHHHHH."

The calm slipped away.

"Okay well, fucking tell us. Gather 'round, children."

"I can't remember it. I sat up and it went away."

Mike laughed.

"Then lie the fuck back down and give us some answers, buddy."

Nick lied down and the answers stayed gone. He punched himself in the leg a few times to try to shock the memories back into his brain.

No success.

Mike, still laughing, patted Nick on the shoulder. "That'll happen."

Nick started crying and ate the one remaining floor adderall and the Grinders stopped paying attention to him.

***

There was a knock at the front door.

Nobody was expecting a knock, so Aliya locked the slide latch on the front door, found and readied one of her guns, cocked it and looked through the peek hole, her gun pointed through the door at gut level.

A mailman.

Aliya dropped her security facade, put the safety on her gun, put the gun in her pocket, unlocked the slide latch and opened the door, and the mailman handed her a large, heavy, manila-enveloped rectangle and saluted once before walking away wordlessly.

She turned around and spoke to the Grinders. "The return address just says *Elliotte Friedman.* No address. Doesn't even have a delivery address. Does anyone know who that is?"

Silence.

"I have some thoughts about this."

She brought the package inside, placed it on the coffee table in front of the giant sectional, and the Grinders gathered around.

"Is it a bomb?"

"That would mean they already found us."

"There's no way they could track us here. We've only been here a few hours. We took taxis. They couldn't be location tracking EVERY taxi."

"Dude. Our phones. We all have phones."

"I guess we didn't think that through."

"Fuck it, whatever, we're dead anyways. Open it."

Aliya used the nozzle of her gun to puncture the manila envelope and then tore through the rest of it, revealing a brand new VCR, as well as a VHS set of *Ted Lasso*.

Stunned silence.

Steef was still inconsolable on the far end of the sectional, staring at the ground, probably thinking about the gardens, and hadn't seen what was unfolding.

It took everything Aliya had not to break down laughing. "Buddy! Steef. I think this is for you."

Steef looked over at Aliya who was holding up the tape for season 1 and dancing it back and forth with a big dumb smile.

"I promise I had nothing to do with this."

Steef could tell she wasn't lying. He felt rejuvenated, but not in a good way.

The idea of giving up on everything he believed in bounced around in his head and his head bounced side to side with his decision.

"Fuck it, whatever, we're dead anyways. I'll fucking watch *Ted Lasso*."

"Oh hell yeah, brother."

"FINALLY!"

"Hey, Steef, after you're done watching, I got a holy book you can read."

Steef looked around at the carnage. "I'll think about it."

"Never too late! Don't you want in on this?" Roman turned the volume up on the television as Keith Olbermann called for the death penalty for every member of the Karma Grinders.

"I'll think about it."

Steef set himself up with a comfortable, dark room to watch the show. He locked the door behind him and disappeared underneath a cave of pillows and blankets.

Jeff wrote "BELIEVE" in scentless marker on the inside of one side of the package's torn bubble mailer and fastened it above the doorway to the room.

***

Aliya took advantage of the disrupted group focus to announce a new game she'd invented. Nick had just set up one of the bedrooms with speakers, cleared it of furniture and placed three backpacks in the room.

"I need three volunteers."

"What's the game?"

"I call it meth roulette."

Geoff and Jeff raised their hands instantly. Miles was somehow coming around from the ketamine already, stumbling from the ketamine room, and without having heard the prompt, raised his hand and asked, "what are we doing?"

Aliya got all three of them high, guided them to the meth chamber, and gave no instructions. She put DMX on the speakers and closed the door behind them and she turned the channel on the livingroom television so that the Grinders could watch.

The roulette players each selected a backpack and then opened them, each finding a different instrument.

Jeff discovered a frying pan.

Geoff discovered a knife.

Miles discovered a gun.

They formed a triangle and sat down, brandishing their instruments, caressing them, looking at each other, waiting to see who would be the first to break the peace.

After a minute, Geoff twitched, lost the twinkle in his eye, lunged forward, screamed, and stabbed Jeff in the throat. Jeff tried to block the thrusts with his frying pan but he was in too much of a panic from the opening attack.

Jeff fell backwards.

Geoff kept lunging.

Jeff managed a strong blow to the side of Geoff's head, which stunned him, and for a minute he forgot what he was doing. Jeff stayed on the ground, the hand with no pan gripping his throat, trying to pinch the vein.

He got up and leaned over the pan to catch the excess blood, with the idea that he would want to put the blood back into his neck when this was all over.

Geoff regained his bearings, rolled over and slit Jeff's throat from the back; Jeff's jugular vein poured perfectly into the center of the pan until it overflowed.

Geoff, exhausted and on the verge of a psychotic breakdown, lied down to catch his breath. Miles sat bow legged in foot-tapping amphetamine ecstasy, rocking left and right, ignoring what was happening.

The pan overflow pooled towards Miles, eventually reached his feet, and drew him back into the room.

He surveyed the situation and panic shook him. He saw Geoff lying on the ground defenseless, stood up, and screamed while he emptied his entire clip into Geoff's face, obliterating it, his skull collapsing like a rotting watermelon.

Miles smiled.

He had finally won.

He sat in his victory for a very long time, grinding his teeth with everything he had, pausing every now and then to indulge in a smile, singing a jarring, off-key loop of *We Are The Champions* overtop of the DMX, and forgetting most of the words while swaying back and forth.

The Grinders stayed at full attention, watching the horrors persist from the livingroom.

"You gonna open the door? Miles won. It's over."

"Oh no. It's not over."

The Grinders gradually clued in: the second stage of this event was simply to leave Miles locked in the room.

Miles would get over the joy of his victory. Miles would start craving more meth. Miles would get no more meth. Miles would start demanding to leave the room. Miles would slowly figure out that he was locked in. Miles would start coming down from the meth.

Miles would be coming down from meth for days, locked in a room with a realization that he had just murdered two of his closest friends.

Miles was out of bullets.

Karma for the Grind.

She drew it up perfectly.

This was true Karmamaxxing. Fully converting life force to suffering for the Angels to flip into future bliss. Every existential calorie converted.

A masterpiece.

Aliya smiled.

The Grinders' respect for her sociochemical engineering was eclipsed significantly by their sheer terror at her newly displayed talent for horror.

Roman decided to change the channel rather than force everyone to continue watching Miles beat his own fists bloody on the locked door.

"Hey, I didn't tell them to kill each other. They just kinda did that on their own."

***

Terry had just finished burying the cab drivers six feet down when Kevin delivered the news that he was going to have to dig a much bigger hole.

Kevin dropped Geoff's faceless corpse right next to the pit and went back inside for the others.

Terry sighed, but he didn't mean it.

He was having a great time gardening.

***

The commercial break on the news channel was coming to an end right as Kevin returned into the house through the back, so he took a measure to catch his breath and watch.

"We learned a minute ago that the Karma Grinders' Silicon Valley operative with frequent encrypted communications with all members, known so far only as Matej, has been apprehended, but claims to know nothing. Our newsroom believes he may be the same person as Matej, the Silicon Valley spiritual leader and TikTok influencer, and author of the surprise bestseller 'Ayahuasca Grindset – How To Rebuild Yourself In A Collapsing World'. If this is the case, this will have significant ripple effects throughout the technology capital of the world and may lead to further arrests."

The camera cut to seven Palo Alto police officers taking Matej away in handcuffs.

"Guys what the fuck? We're on a mission, we have shit to do. Why are you trying to stop it bro? I don't even LIKE handcuffs." A confused and erratic Matej looked directly into the camera. *"I don't wanna go back to being an optometrist. Help! Michael Buble!*

HELP!"

"I think he means eye dentist."

"He was an optometrist?"

"Why is he asking Michael Buble for help?"

"Seems like his old self again eh?"

"He probably took the disabler when he saw them coming." Kevin was confident in his zombie memories. "This arrest is only for show. Even the cops in Palo Alto are Tejlords."

"Tejlords?"

"That's what they call themselves."

"Well that's fucking stupid."

"Is anyone even talking about the Basilisk?" aLan flipped through the channels and he read the chyrons on the main news networks aloud.

He flipped to NBC. *"Karma Grinders Terrorize Wall Street."*

He flipped to ABC. *"Canadian Death Cult: What's Next?"*

He flipped to FOX News. *"Communist Sex Cult From Canada Wants To Sell Your Children Into Slavery."*

"Nope, just us."

"Damnit, we should have been a sex cult."

"Yeah, this is a god damn sausage fest. No offense, Aliya."

"Oh, no, I agree."

"Hey, does anyone else ever look around and, I don't know, feel kind of relieved that we're probably gonna die soon?"

"What the hell, Gerg? Where did all this thinking come from?"

"Not a pun in sight."

"What the hell, man?"

"He's been taking mystery drugs," Aliya reminded them. "Don't question it."

"I am positive that being alive is probably better than being dead."

"Gotta agree with Roman here. I think they even wrote a book about it."

"Yeah, but. When you're up against it, there's that battle between knowing that you should try to fight to stay alive, and succumbing to the sweet release of death."

"Naturally."

"And to be absolved of all responsibility towards fighting for life, knowing that it's gonna be total bullshit even if you win."

"You mean like us, right now. This exact situation."

"I can kinda see right now how that would be liberating."

"Hypothetically."

"But only if dying is out of your power. You get to finally fucking rest, sweet, sweet release, and you have no more obligation to God or man or family or even life itself to keep pushing. You're not betraying the natural order. You fulfilled your contract and you get to leave. Like having your cake and eating it too."

"Mmm, death cake."

"Maybe that's why they call killing someone 'icing' them."

"Well that's fucking stupid."

***

Roman was tired of watching their empire crumble. "This is depressing, can we watch something else?"

aLan flipped to a random channel. *"...lottery numbers 4, 8, 15, 16, 23 and 42... again."* The camera stayed on the lady as her friendly television demeanor dropped away. *"Who the fuck is in charge of this sh-"*, and her eyes went wide as she realized she was still live and then it cut to commercial.

"I'm bored. Armageddon is taking forever."

"Well then take a look at my narcotic charcuterie."

"Narcuterie!"

"Shut the fuck up already Gerg."

"Thought you guys wanted the puns back."

"Yeah, read the room."

"Sorry. I promise I only said it because Kevin gave me some of his coke. I have to say though, I love this feeling. Everything I say is perfect and nothing I do is wrong."

"Nice. Pleading the 8th," aLan interjected. "Sorry. I snuck some of the leftover meth a bit after we sent them into the media room. I think I'm coming down. Feels like I've been hosed down with battery acid from the inside. I need something... uplifting. Aliya?"

"Well then." Aliya held up a small bag from the far end of the charcuterie. "How about some angel dust?"

aLan grabbed it and poured a large dot onto the back of his hand.

Aliya nodded to Nick who had been happily making use of his audiovisual expertise, setting up another fun activity with Aliya's direction after Kevin had cleared out the backpacks and the weapons and the blood and the corpses.

"Hey aLan – you'll have a bit of a ... heightened sensitivity. Did you wanna try a puzzle? It's pretty tricky. I couldn't solve it sober."

"Hell yeah. What do I win if I solve it?"

Aliya offered aLan the entire bag of angel dust. "You can have all this to help you with the puzzle, and when you get out you can have more." aLan still had the large dot on the back of his hand, which was lightly shaking, hovering it in front of his face, ready to go.

"Come on, let's fucking GO!"

An excited aLan inhaled the entire large dot from the back of his shaky hand, took the rest of the bag into the media room with him, and felt a pocket of worry as Aliya said "You get out when you solve the puzzle!" and rushed to lock the door behind him. His worry turned to panic in the pitch black room as a small, flickering white light turned on and illuminated the puzzle pieces on the floor.

To set up the puzzle room, Aliya had taken two to five random pieces from each of the many puzzle boxes in the livingroom closet.

The puzzle was unsolvable.

aLan's panic turned to fervor before he could piece that together, and as he got to work trying to find the corners and place them on the outsides, some music started.

The song started out with simple, pleasant guitar strumming and aLan could feel the vibrations under his skin. He found it to be quite nice.

The Grinders had turned the news channel back over to the CCTV that was monitoring the room.

"Wait, that's Tool."

"You're making him listen to Tool, on angel dust, in a locked room."

Aliya smiled and shrugged. "Karma for the Grind."

Nobody repeated the mantra.

The vocals kicked in and the bass started to kick at his eardrums in a way that stole his focus from the unsolvable puzzle.

The lyrics crept in.

I know the pieces fit
'Cause I watched them fall away
Mildewed and smoldering
Fundamental differing

The music was very loud and getting louder. It was a distraction. aLan needed to focus, and so he put a large, sloppy pile of more angel dust on the back of his even shakier hand, consuming it erratically with his nose and open mouth, then licking the back of his hand.

The music was getting louder.

Disintegrating as it goes
Testing our communication

The music was getting louder and the vocals seemed to be mounting in aggressiveness.

After what felt to aLan like twenty minutes of the song, he was too consumed by the angel dust to notice that the song had been edited, and was repeating a single line, over and over.

I know the pieces fit
I know the pieces fit

The shaky placing of the puzzle pieces turned to forceful placing which turned to frustrated smashing.

I know the pieces fit
I know the pieces fit
I know the pieces fit

The Grinders were fixed in attention, watching on the livingroom TV as aLan ascended to his breaking point and started ripping the pieces into smaller pieces to try to make them fit together.

I know the pieces fit
I know the pieces fit
I know the pieces fit
I know the pieces fit

aLan noticed a second flickering light in the corner of the room, illuminating a gun.

He resisted the second light at first, tearing the pieces into fine cardboard powder, desperate to see the final form of the puzzle.

I know the pieces fit
I know the pieces fit
I know the pieces fit
I know the pieces fit
I know the pieces fit

Unable to piece together anything more than a brown pile of shavings, aLan pounded his fists on the ground until they were bloody, screamed until a blood vessel in his brain popped, ran to the corner, picked up the gun, put it in his mouth, and made the pieces fit.

***

As the gun was off-screen, the remaining Grinders sat silently and watched as the footage on the television remained lingering only on a pool of blood spilling closer and closer to a perfect pyramid of shredded puzzle pieces in the perfect dead center of the floor.

There was another extended silence until Gerg piped up with an emaciated, "Karma for the Grind!" which he did not mean and did not get rcpcated.

Nick called for Kevin to clean up the room again and then drag aLan's giant corpse into the gardens in the back.

***

Cassandra was still in the fetal position deep in the center of the sectional, but as the medley of colorful sedatives disappeared from her blood, she started moving again.

She looked at the pile of pills again and thought about some fun color combinations, but decided that she craved a reset.

Her addled brain decided that white was the color of pills that would reset everything.

Carte blanche.

She ate every white pill in the pile, which amounted to seven speed pills and three xans, and she choked them down without water.

The speed got there first.

As her brain woke back up like lightning, the last few years all came rushing back at once and on repeat and the speed launched it like a catapult over her inner walls and through the loving embrace of what was left in her blood of the coma-inducing rainbow pills.

And on the sight of Kevin struggling to drag aLan's bloody

corpse to the backyard, her heart jumped into her throat.

She kept it together for a moment.

She snapped internally and she was able to muffle her own shriek to a yelp.

"You okay?" Kevin was the only person who heard.

She took a second, inhaled through her mouth and exhaled through her nose. "Yeah, just, some of these pills are funny."

Kevin carried on into the yard and the shrieks coming up from Cassandra's soul bottled up and reverberated and echoed louder and louder and grew into a neutron star of white rage and she kept it all inside.

The Groom was gone forever. The money was gone forever. The prestige was gone forever.

The Grind was there for her, but in the naked hell that remained, she saw all at once that it was worthless.

Back into kill mode for the first time since Wall Street, she suddenly remembered the hunting knife strapped to her leg. It reminded her once again that the only remaining truth was revenge.

She needed to collect the souls she'd promised herself back in the library.

She grabbed Nick and motioned the two of them to the bathroom, acting as though she had an embarrassing personal question.

She calmly closed the door behind them, motioned for him to sit on the toilet, and tried to keep her composure, but when she turned to look at him and saw him smiling casually, without a care in the world other than the light twitching from his adderall abuse, she lost her composure. She hated herself for allowing him to live this long, to find this much purpose and joy, to learn so many enriching life lessons. She hated herself for allowing him to still be able to smile.

This man took everything from her.

It was time to take it back.

She delivered a surprise haymaker to the side of his face, and while he was seeing stars, she knocked him to the toilet, zip tied his hands behind it, pulled out her hunting knife, whipped him twice across his left temple with the handle of the knife, and then grabbed him by the ears and screamed out every last bit of rage she'd been burying under the surface, quietly boiling over for years and years and years.

A dazed Nick tried to figure out what was going on, but the words turned to blood in his mouth as Cassandra had already buried the hunting knife deep in the center of his guts.

She screamed again, louder. She was growing comfortably into the rage. She twisted the knife in a perfect circle and then pushed again, burying the top of the handle past the surface of his skin.

She saw the terror in his eyes and as the blood poured up out of his mouth and then back down into the gaping hole in his stomach, she found some peace.

"That's for getting me expelled."

Nick tried to speak but could only choke on blood. He shook his head furiously. He was still struggling as though he had a chance to stay alive.

She laughed.

She ran her finger up what was now a waterfall of blood pouring from his mouth down into the hole in his stomach. She collected some blood on two fingers and made him taste it.

She was speaking with a cold grace that carried more rage than her screams. "I overheard you in the library. 'I got that bitch expelled!' I can still hear it now. It plays on repeat in my head. I dream about it. I've been waiting for this."

"WUN ME." Nick repeated through the blood. "WUN ME." He was still shaking his head.

She felt something was off, so she wiped the blood from his mouth with a white towel.

"WASN'T ME." Nick got one out before the blood pooled back up again from the inside. "GRG"

"Gerg did it?"

Nick shook his head furiously. Blood sprayed side to side.

"Gerg knows who did it?"

Nick paused and nodded. The blood sprayed vertically and a shot went up the middle of Cassandra's shirt. She didn't notice.

She pulled the knife out of his stomach and wiped it once with her hand, which didn't clean very much of the blood, cut the zip tie behind the toilet, and put the knife back in her scabbard.

Nick collapsed forward and was dead before he hit the floor.

Cassandra took a moment before she realized that the rest of the Grinders probably overheard the screams.

The rage helped her think on her feet. Just like before. She decided she should have been doing this the whole time.

She opened the bathroom door, grabbed the gun from the media room across the hall, walked calmly back into the bathroom and shot Nick once in the head and five times in the stomach – she figured this was enough shots to justify the size of the hole and the volume of blood. She cleaned up most of the mess with more towels, and stuffed his sweater with them, which wouldn't pass close inspection, but would get the corpse to the yard.

She walked out into the livingroom and delivered a message with an unfitting calmness to the remaining Grinders who had all heard the screaming, other than Kevin and Terry, who were in the backyard, tossing aLan's corpse into a deepening grave.

"Nick couldn't live with what we had done. The news got to him. I pleaded with him to keep himself together. But it wasn't enough. You should have seen the panic in his eyes."

As the xanax started to proliferate through her blood, she paused to feel the waves, but played the calmness off like she was being haunted by the fresh ghost.

"He was going to take his own life if I didn't do him the favor."

Mike noticed the blood splattering on her shirt. "What was with the screaming?"

Cassandra remembered this perfect medley of xanax and stimulants. She was computing at full power again, quick on her feet. "I couldn't convince him to keep going. To keep grinding. To stay here with all of us. My empathy got the better of me. I snapped, I'm sorry."

Mike stared but didn't respond. Cassandra made a note of it. He nodded, pretending to accept the explanation. But Cassandra could see the world in slow motion right then, and she knew he took too long to respond. Something was bouncing around in his head. He was full of shit.

"What about Karma for the Grind?"

"Karma for the Grind!" the Disciples repeated.

She looked back to the bathroom with a false sympathy. "He had had enough. I'm sorry for being so loud but it just hurts to let go." She sniffled. "Gerg can I talk with you?"

Gerg took a few seconds to do some soul searching, saw some

fear in Cassandra's eyes, and got up to go speak with her down the hall.

She moved in close and whispered, "Nick wanted to get something off his chest before he passed."

"Oh yea?"

"He told me that he... he felt guilty about getting some girl expelled, ruining her life. He was too broken up to go into detail, but he mentioned you were involved."

"Oh, yeah. Yeah, right. This girl. Some girl at university was dating our buddy David Fargo. And – I promise, I swear I didn't know. I'd never met her."

"Didn't know what?"

"I didn't know they were together. She cheated on him. With me. She knew we were friends. He loved that girl. She didn't give a fuck."

"Oh! That's a difficult situation."

"Yeah. She broke his heart and she didn't care. So we got her expelled. Then her parents kicked her out." Gerg smiled. "She's working at a gas station."

"That sounds horrible."

"Yeah, she deserves worse. Heartless bitch. I don't know why Nick's sad about it now. I'd do it again."

"Karma for the Grind?"

"Yeah, I guess. Karma for the Grind." The mantra took some of the joy out of his face.

"Thanks, that's all." She didn't know if she believed him.

As Gerg rejoined the Grinders in the livingroom and Aliya gave him another pill, Cassandra felt suddenly frantic and itchy from the inside of her blood. She needed something to do.

"Hey who has that book? The poetry book?"

Aliya pulled *Leaves of Grass* from her magical bag and tossed it to her. "Why in the fuck would the Archon need inspiration?"

"Oh, I don't need inspiration. I just like poetry."

She took the book to her familiar deep corner of the sectional but her attention couldn't crack into the words on the pages. She stared blankly and retreated into her brain as she zoned out on a single poem that she wasn't reading.

A minute later, she leveled off and as she zoned back in on the word 'love', she realized that she was thinking about the Groom.

With the clouds of suppressed rage clear from her skies, something dawned on her suddenly.

He never tried to contact her after she ghosted him.

No calls, no texts, no emails.

It was him.

It was him.

The Groom got her expelled.

The Groom ruined her life.

Gerg was telling the truth.

Nick was innocent.

She wanted to cry but she knew she couldn't. She couldn't cry because people would start asking questions and she couldn't cry anyways because the chemicals in her blood wouldn't allow it. "I fucked up. I fucked up." She muttered to herself but stopped quickly.

Nick was her friend.

Nick was her friend the whole time.

She ate a purple pill.

She killed her friend. She put her friend through an agonizing death.

For nothing.

She ate two blue pills.

None of this would have happened if the Groom hadn't gotten her expelled.

The Groom got her expelled.

He did this.

The Groom killed Nick.

She ate a green pill.

She started to feel good.

The Groom killed Nick.

She could get revenge for her fallen friend.

She let herself percolate back into reality and tuned into the news.

"...countless memorials around the world for the 50,000 victims of the air traffic disaster that we now know was caused by the so-called Karma Grinders..."

Without even thinking, she took another yellow pill.

Karma for the Grind.

She repeated.

Karma for the Grind.

Karma for the Grind.

The comfort of the mantra carried her to the onset of the pills and when she arrived at the pills she discarded the mantra.

She couldn't scream as long as she kept stuffing her mouth with pills.

She ate a red pill.

The cat walked by and meowed.

She rebuilt her reality around the new truth.

50,000 dead.

It was all his fault.

The red pill came on quickly.

She would get revenge.

She would get revenge for Nick and for the 50,000 dead.

The Groom had to die.

She was the Archon and she was going to kill the Groom.

She ate another red pill.

But first she had to take care of Mike.

She sniffled.

***

"...preliminary findings among the items in Matej's luxurious 4-bedroom penthouse apartment..."

Overhearing this, Kevin dropped the legs of Nick's corpse halfway through the doorway to the outside and ran back in to listen to the news; Terry wandered over from the garden and dragged him the rest of the way.

"...duffel bags full of Canadian currency, and a safe full of dossiers on Peter Thiel, Sam Altman, Marc Andreessen, and several other powerful players in the Silicon Valley tech world, all being revealed as close personal acquaintances with Matej, whose spiritual leadership had become fundamental to the entire region, very, very quickly. And although replicating the scripture in question appears to be expressly prohibited by the death cult in question, authorities are also uncovering handwritten black market copies, all over the Valley, of what is believed to be his death cult's sacred text, known only as the 'Bromeliad'. Am I saying that right?"

Cassandra was taking a steady stream of red pills. She had no idea what they were. But she was getting angrier. She was becoming a more perfect Archon. She knew that for sure.

"We would like to apologize for our earlier claim, in which we stated that the airport terrorist known as Mike is the leader of this cult."

Cassandra almost smiled.

"We are now fully aware that it is, indeed, Matej, and we are now being handed reports that Matej has already escaped custody and his current whereabouts are unknown."

The almost-smile disappeared.

A vessel popped in her brain and blood dripped from her ear, soaking her pineapple earring, but she could still hear the words of the television piercing through the liquid tension.

There was no time for sadness.

She had to get started on her path to victory.

Cassandra noticed that Mike was purposefully avoiding taking in the news, sitting quietly by himself, appearing to be pensive and lost in thought.

"Hey Mike, can I talk to you for a sec?"

Mike looked at Gerg, who had just spoken with her. Gerg closed his eyes and nodded at Mike reassuringly and so he went into the bathroom.

After locking the door behind her, Cassandra covered Mike's mouth with duct tape, pulled her hunting knife from the scabbard and slit his throat.

She kept her hand over the tape on his mouth to keep him from making noise and drawing attention. "Mike, I'm so sorry. I really do like you, I just know that you're onto me. I wish you were stupider, man. Why can't you be one of the stupid ones?"

Mike was too weak from hunger to fight her off.

"Nice work on the airport thing by the way. They're gonna be talking about you for decades. Centuries. Congratulations on eternal life. You know," her voice got lighter, "it is kind of funny. The next life you go into, you're gonna be unaware that you were a murderous terrorist. And you're gonna read about you. And you're going to hate you. And you'll never know it was you. It's kind of beautiful."

Mike stopped fighting and allowed the blood to fill his lungs. He went the rest of the way peacefully, fully embracing the words that Cassandra herself was still struggling to believe.

Barely a second after Mike's death rattle was finished, Cassandra heard a scratching at the bedroom door and opened it slightly to let the cat inside. Mike's body had slumped and fallen to the floor, facing up, and Lise sat on his chest, purring, at peace.

She placed her bloody hunting knife in Mike's hand and wrapped his hand around it and gently closed the door and rejoined the remaining Grinders.

Cassandra still knew how to fake crying. "Apparently 50 thousand is too many for one man to deal with."

"Huh?"

"Leave the cat in there to grieve. They had a special connection. Just leave them alone." She wiped a fake tear from her eye and sat down and looked at the ground for a minute.

When Kevin came in to remove the corpse, Lise wouldn't budge, so Kevin meowed, grabbed Mike's ankles and dragged him to the garden by his legs; Lise rode on his chest to the backyard like a toboggan and blood spilled onto the path behind them.

Cassandra was coming down off of her xanax cloud and wasn't quite ready to face everything. She needed to stay on the cloud. And there was still a part of her that wanted to keep on shaking the snowglobe, rolling the dice, hoping somehow that a random chemical medley from the rainbow pile on the couch would hit a secret button in the folds of her brain and solve everything.

She collected her knife off the bathroom floor, returned to the couch, curled back up, took a pink and a blue, not sure what they were, and closed her eyes.

***

Roman didn't allow himself to show it, but when aLan was killed right in front of him, he was having tremendous difficulty sorting through his emotions. This felt to him like a loss on another level. They had developed a heightened connection on their patrols in the Arctic, and he was suddenly feeling a heightened loss that he didn't have the ability to explain. It chipped away at his sanity and he needed to calm down. He wanted to reach the levels of calm that he'd seen on television in so many hippies from the 60s. "Aliya, I've heard a lot about LSD, always wanted to try. Can you hook me up?"

Roman had already been dosed on LSD by Aliya back at the telecom, but he didn't know it, and it had been low enough of a dose that he wouldn't recognize the onset.

"Oh hell yeah." Aliya had a game ready for this situation. "Where's my liquid bottle? It was just here on my charcut-- Gerg. Give it"

Gerg was posing like a cartoon philosopher, one hand on his chin, and with the other, he was holding the LSD bottle like Hamlet's skull. He uttered in his best Shakespearean voice, "Why do we call them psychedelics and not dharmaceuticals? Sorry sorry sorry I wanted to do that ever since I thought of it, I promise that's the last one."

"Gerg, God fucking damnit man. Your puns are gonna be the death of me."

"That's okay with me."

Aliya punched Gerg so hard that his shoulder almost dislocated.

"Got it, no more puns."

She gave Roman a few drops, more than he needed, but not too many that he would need a straight jacket. Roman laid down on the sectional and listened to the chatter from the yard and the murmur from the television.

After about 45 minutes, Lise emerged from the backyard, meowed and laid down on Roman's chest; she closed her eyes and purred.

Aliya heard the thunderous purring over the din of the television, and looked over to see Roman, bug-eyed, petting Lise very, very slowly, with his breaths matching the cat's breaths.

It was time for some pure, concentrated Karma.

He was ready.

Aliya whipped out her phone and played the ESPN fantasy draft pick noise, which struck like lightning deep into Roman's subconscious; it jolted him from his reverie and also slightly annoyed the cat, whose ears folded back for a second.

Lise ran back over to the familiar perch on the couch ledge above Cassandra.

Roman tried to sink back into the psychedelic ascent.

Aliya played the noise again.

She could tell from Roman's body language when the LSD was about to take him over.

She was going to make sure it never did.

Roman closed his eyes again.

Aliya played the noise again.

The cycle repeated a dozen times.

The exhausted angels of psychedelia, with their infinite grace, again and again reached down to pull Roman up, thwarted by Aliya with her finger on the button.

Through a fountain of drool, Roman would utter 'gneurshk', give Aliya a caveman stare, and try again.

When she knew he had been through enough cycles, she stopped, leaving him alone and unfulfilled in a brutal, ugly swamp that would never touch the sky.

When Roman calmed down, she walked over to the sectional and wiped some sweat from his forehead.

"Sorry about that. Karma for the Grind. I had to do it. Here, have some xans. They'll round the edges for you. And, hey, also, sometimes new chemicals activate slow-moving psychedelics so, maybe be ready for anything."

Aliya held back a smile as she gave Roman a handful of laxatives.

After about 15 minutes, when her calculations predicted that Roman would start to feel something coming, she broadcast a custom edited message through the livingroom speakers: a cacophony of air raid sirens, accompanied by a harsh, extremely Soviet voice repeating a message.

"YOU CANNOT MOVE. STAY SEATED. DO NOT MOVE. IT IS DIRE. STAY VERE YOU ARE. THIS IS PRESIDENT OF OUTER SPACE. VE ARE UNDER ATTACK. DO NOT MOVE."

She broke and started laughing after two minutes of what was clearly an advanced state of psychedelic torment for him.

She decided to take mercy and release him. She didn't really want him to make a mess of the sectional anyways.

She pretended to get an incoming message. "Hey Roman, I got a text here from the president of outer space and he says you saved the world and you're free to move."

Roman ran to the bathroom and made it in a photo finish.

Kevin got up, ran to the bathroom, turned the fan noise to maximum and closed the door behind him.

"That was fucking genius." Kevin's eyes were wide. "You're the Torquemada of the age of aquarius."

Aliya smiled. "There's more. The acid's about to kick in while he's in there." Aliya held up her pointer finger. "I don't know if you saw but I pricked my finger and drew a pentagram on his forehead in blood while I was pretending to wipe away the sweat. He's going to look in the mirror when he's done."

Kevin said nothing and returned to his pile of cocaine.

He was starting to fear Aliya. He was starting to think that maybe he couldn't deal with what she was doing. This artisanal torture, though it was for a good cause, was hitting a nerve deep in his gut that broke through the comforts offered by the scripture. And he couldn't explain it.

"You know, you have to make sure he can come back from this."

"It won't be a strong trip for him. I made sure of that with the first part."

They heard a flush and then they heard a smack and then they heard rhythmic thumping and then they heard Roman screaming from the bathroom, "FLUSH THE DEVIL FLUSH THE DEVIL FLUSH THE DEVIL."

It went quiet after a minute.

Kevin walked to the bathroom to see what happened and he started singing to himself. "Ro-mie don't like iiiiitttt. Flush the de-vil, flush the de-vil."

Aliya tapped her feet along to the melody.

Kevin stopped singing when he opened the door and turned off the fan and saw that Roman had managed to bleed out from a cut that came from hitting the toilet lid on the back of his neck, making his jugular vein smash into the corner of the porcelain.

The seat rested on the back of his neck and sat above his head like a halo.

***

Kevin was getting pretty tired. He hadn't eaten food in almost a day – none of them had. He had to get Terry's help moving Roman to the garden.

Through all the dirt and exhaustion and manual labor in the sunshine, Terry didn't notice that he had given himself a good amount of cuts and scrapes, and so he had made no efforts to bandage them. Walking backwards with the front half of Roman's pretty corpse, Terry stumbled, and when the corpse hit the ground, a corner of a landscaping rock pushed into the back of Roman's neck, which sent forth an impressive surge of blood from the opening in his jugular vein, blanketing Terry's medley of open wounds with active psychedelics.

Terry thought nothing of it.

***

Gerg was bored. He wanted a fresh experience.

He had been taking a lot of drugs from the charcuterie but the only result was that his skin was itchy and he wanted to hug the dead bodies.

He craved inspiration.

He grabbed *Leaves of Grass* from the couch ledge above Cassandra, grabbed an empty seed bag from Steef's gardening satchel to use as a bookmark, and went to the bathroom to study until inspiration dropped.

***

Aliya was bored. All her research subjects were either preoccupied or dead.

Kevin was next to her, but with no outside pressure, he had reduced himself to a shaking orchestra of neuroses, hunched over his Tony Montana pile, and that's not the kind of vibrational frequency that Aliya was after.

As the fellowship of the *Bromeliad* seemed to be coming to an end, she had been thinking more and more completely about the more intriguing and blasphemous aspects of her witchcraft side quest; specifically, she had been reading feverishly about experiences in which someone died and brought themselves back to life. The literature that she had read was near-unanimous – anyone brought back in this way gained a special, new type of vision. As far as her readings went, the literature didn't go into any further detail, which meant to her that the type of vision was simply otherworldly, beyond description, which made her want to do it more.

She wanted to transcend to whatever that was.

But for this, she needed to be alone, and she couldn't get on the right frequency with Kevin and his coke shaking and his sniffling noises and his neurotic questions and his constantly starting and stopping music and his perpetual need for reassurance.

She moved him and his heart-attack-speedrun into an empty room out of the way.

Cassandra was already in a drug coma deep in the couch, and by Aliya's math, she would stay in the coma for at least another 20 minutes.

This was the right time.

But she had to get it done before Gerg finished reading *Leaves of Grass*. It was essential that her death was quick, painless, reliable, and that she herself administer the thing that would reverse the overdose – the naloxone injector – immediately, while in the throes of the peaceful half-death stage.

She had been avoiding the fentanyl, not so much afraid of the experience as much as she was saving it, in case she had to kill her lab rat - some of the experiments she had been trying on Kevin were said to give super powers, and she couldn't allow herself to be outshined by her test subject.

But she finally had solitude.

She busted out the salt shaker, put a large dot on the back of her hand, and inhaled.

In two minutes, she was feeling it. She had looked up the dosage and she knew that this was fatal.

The onset was so beautiful that she had half a mind to allow it to continue.

But the other half stayed strong.

A moment before the comfortable wave took her under for good, she reached into her magical bag, grabbed the naloxone injector to reverse the overdose, but found it to be broken – there was a pressure crack underneath the label that rendered the device unusable.

The word "NALOXONE" had been crossed out with permanent marker, and underneath was the word "PREVENTANYL" in Gerg's obnoxious lettering.

Aliya was at the stage of the overdose where she was unable to breathe, unable to shout at Cassandra to wake up from her rainbow nap, unable to yell at Gerg to do something, unable to do anything, unable to cut Gerg's throat as soon as she got right, unable to get right.

Lise pranced over from the top of the couch and sat on her chest until the breathing slowed and slowed and stopped.

She purred, nuzzled Aliya's chin, and returned to her perch on the couch above Cassandra.

***

Gerg had been in the washroom flipping through *Leaves of Grass* for quite a while. He read a lot of the early poems with great intent and great interest, but he was gradually realizing that this type of prose was not going to connect with him in the way he was looking for.

Still, he flipped through the book, taking in the shorter

poems, skipping the longer ones, hoping to jump ahead to the inspiration part of inspiration.

Losing faith in his system, he flipped all the way to the end, taking in nothing, coming up empty. He sighed, zoned out for half a second, and zoned back in, hunched over, finding himself staring at the bookmark – the empty seed bag from Steef's gardening satchel.

He stopped breathing.

He craned his neck up slowly, brow furrowed.

It was the bromeliad seeds.

He didn't know what to do. He didn't know what to think.

He stared at the image of the pineapple on the packaging for what felt like an eternity.

It all dawned on him at once.

"The *Bromeliad*... was a PLANT!"

After a quick evacuation, forgetting to wipe, he rushed his pants and his belt back on, and tried to think of his next steps.

He saw a lot of blood still on the floor of the bathroom and had a second realization.

Cassandra – his Archon – was on a killing spree.

Whatever he did next, he knew he had to be careful.

Cassandra was in a quiet coma when he entered the bathroom, but that was at least half an hour ago. He hoped she was still under. If she wasn't, he was dead anyways. He had to leave the bathroom quickly, and he had to open the door quietly.

From there, he had to make a decision. Cassandra was going to kill him, he knew that. He was a bad liar, and she was a shrewd interrogator. He wouldn't last.

It was either run away, or kill the Archon.

Fuck that, he thought to himself. It was run away, or kill Cassandra.

She was no fucking Archon.

Fuck that.

He had to kill Cassandra.

He walked to the door and opened it slowly, which created a high pitched creaking noise that wouldn't have happened if he had opened it quickly.

This jolted Cassandra awake.

He stood in place in the bathroom doorway, paralyzed by his own mistake, and she spotted him.

Gerg tried to play it cool, gently bent down and put his fingers to Aliya's jugular vein, feeling no pulse.

"Did this just happen? No rigor mortis yet." The more he tried to calm his voice, the shakier it sounded.

He saw the modified, opened and unused naloxone on the floor next to a toppled fentanyl shaker, and he realized that he'd killed Aliya.

Cassandra came back to total lucidity quickly. Gerg's movements were careful and afraid. She knew he wasn't shaking only through sheer force of will. All that she had read about body language told her that Gerg was fully present and mortally terrified.

She figured out that he had figured her out.

If he was centered, if he was innocent, he would have made a pun about it.

If he was centered, if he was innocent, he wouldn't still be gripping the bromeliad seed bag so tightly in his left hand. She could see the word 'bromeliad' poking out partway through two of his fingers.

She knew he knew, and with every passing second, he caught on that she knew, but was still too paralyzed to act.

He was too full of dumb hope to realize that he was already dead.

Cassandra slowly stood up, walked over to Aliya's corpse, noticed the unused naloxone injector on the ground, and then Gerg stood up and they were face to face.

He froze for a second as he noticed the glow of the television glistening in a lone droplet of blood, dried in place beneath her pineapple earring.

He opened his hand and his mouth to accuse her, but before the words could escape, Cassandra was already holding her hunting knife square in his gut.

His words turned into blood in his mouth and poured onto the floor.

He was hoping that this was all a joke, that he would wake up back in the swivel chair in Mike's apartment.

Cassandra twisted the knife and he knew it was for real.

She watched him die, both of them unblinking, and the life faded from his face.

Cassandra felt alive.

She pulled the knife out and let his corpse collapse onto Aliya's corpse in a cross shape, which hit Cassandra perfectly in her post-coma delirium and made her laugh.

She couldn't remember the last time she laughed like that.

She put the bloody hunting knife back into the scabbard,

removed her socks and with her bare feet, she played with the puddle of blood on the floor, right where Gerg's stomach was pumping it out.

The blood was glowing and Cassandra wondered who was left.

Looking around, she saw the closed door to the media room with loud rap music playing and a shrill, off key voice singing along, so Kevin was still here.

She saw the other room still locked, so Steef was still here.

There weren't any old corpses in the house, so that means Terry was still here, in the yard, covering up her tracks.

And there was Lise, on the couch, on edge, watching, tail wagging.

Cassandra grabbed the coke from Aliya's magical bag and opened the media room door to collect Kevin, one of two people still dutifully serving their Archon. She fed him the coke to maintain his trust. He was already jittery enough, he didn't really need it, but that'd never stopped him before.

"Hey Kev, fresh corpses. Chop chop."

Kevin got up to get back to work and Cassandra returned to the livingroom to watch the news.

She sat down on the edge of the couch, eyed the pile of drugs still in the corner and thought about eating a few more pills, but decided against it.

She needed to stay focused.

She had developed a severe hatred for Keith Olbermann at this point. He was still prattling on about the Grinders and their crimes. She could swear his eyes were turning red.

"...and until we have more information, with one exception, we are still only aware of their first names, from the communications

from the phone of Matej and the members of their encrypted communication network."

The segment continued with a list of names, accompanied by headshots. Olbermann read out the list with fire on his tongue.

"We do, however, have a good handle on their charges, which are as follows:

Matej, charges pending, presumed innocent.

Jeff, cryptocurrency fraud.

Mike, high treason, hacking, terrorism, wanted dead or alive, no questions asked.

Aliya, hundreds of counts of drug trafficking and distribution, as well as the Vatican issuing charges of witchcraft.

Geoff, securities fraud.

Miles, coordination of securities fraud.

Nick, extortion.

Terry, corruption as an SEC officer, overseeing a litany of crimes at JC Morgan, saying nothing.

Roman, crimes against the Canadian military.

aLan, with a capital L for some reason, also crimes against the Canadian military.

Gerg, drunk and disorderly conduct.

Kevin, over 400 counts of public urination.

Lise, hold on. This is a photo of a cat? Get this shit out of here.

Danielle David Duchovny, possibly a top ranking operative, who answered directly to Matej, with too many crimes to list in the time allotted to me by my producer, and finally,

Steef, only associated with the Karma Grinders; as of right now, we are not aware of any charges against him."

Kevin was staring vacantly at the television, frozen, dumbfounded. “They got your name and your hair wrong,” unmoved by the rest of it.

“That's fucking photoshopped. They used a photoshop. I'm not a fucking redhead.” She was digging her coke nail into her palm so hard that it started to bleed.

“That your name?”

Cassandra felt lucky that Kevin was too zonked to be clever. “No, they got that wrong too. Those fuckers.”

“I was gonna ask if you're related to David.”

“I'm not.” It had been years, but she was sick of that question.

“Because that's not your name.”

She sniffled. “Right.” God bless this idiot.

“We're going to commercial, but after, we are joined by Danielle's former long-term boyfriend and business partner.” CNN cut to a silent video preview of the interview setup.

The Bride was there with him.

Lise hissed on sight.

Cassandra grabbed a gun from Aliya's purse and pointed it at the television but didn't fire.

With the crosshairs on the Bride, she noticed that the Bride was wearing the fake Saint Laurents that she had left behind at the gift table at the wedding.

The boots had been re-laced with the unmistakable golden strings from Mike's satchel.

The ID satchel.

From the closet in Mike's apartment.

She drew them up perfectly.

Something remaining inside of Cassandra snapped and she wandered over to the cross of corpses to empty most of her clip.

As she returned, the preview of the exclusive interview bled into a commercial spot for an ad being run by a regional TV station.

"All good things must come to an end. Here at Garden Center, we have been happy to serve the communi-"

A door suddenly opened, and made a slow creaking noise.

Steef had finished watching Ted Lasso.

He had been in the dark, in a cave of blankets. the small television his only source of light for the entire time. He needed a few minutes to adjust to the brighter lights in the livingroom. He started talking anyways, slurring his words into each other.

"Okay. I'm sorry I was such a grump about that show. I guess I could stand to work on my anger issues a bit."

He was illuminated by the tweaking light of the CRT television behind him.

"I get it now. We're the same guy. That's why you guys were bugging me."

His eyes started to adjust to the corpses on the floor.

"I'm Ted Lasso!"

Steef basked in the revelation for a moment while he

continued to wake up to the new world around him.

"Hold up, Cassandra, what's going on here?" He was transfixed on the corpses in the shape of a cross and was still too fresh to notice the blood.

"They've been taking morphine." She sniffled. "They were watching cartoons with Kevin and just fell asleep like that. Everyone else is in the back yard helping Terry with some gardening." She paused for a second and realized she would have to keep explaining the corpses. "They're very comfortable, they got angry with me the last time I woke them up to try to get them to move."

Kevin was in his own world, twitching, and far too paranoid to register Cassandra's lies against the furious inner backdrop of his own encroaching anxious breakdown.

"Oh, well. That's weird. I'm gonna go say hi to the folks in the yard."

"I think Terry would like that very much. I'll join you in a second."

Steef walked through the house to the backyard, and Cassandra followed.

He brushed the last of the cobwebs from his eyes but his vision was still blurry as he lumbered like a sasquatch through the corridor to the back hall and into the gardens.

As Cassandra exited the house through the back, her cleats tore the vine growths out from the cracks in the sidewalk and they stuck to the bottom of her shoes.

There wasn't a lot of commotion in the yard that Steef could hear, beyond the comforting sounds of digging holes and labored breathing.

Steef approached the giant hole and quickly found that it was a mass grave, with all his friends partially buried. Before he could react, he took a bullet through the back of the head, which came out clean between his eyes on the other side, and he fell neatly into the pile, wide-eyed, facing the sky, sent off to his perfect afterlife of becoming worm food.

Cassandra smiled at Terry. "Thought I'd save you the trouble."

Terry took a second to wrap his head around what had just happened.

"There's two more inside, then I think we're almost done here." Cassandra walked with a purpose back into the house.

Terry noticed that he had been feeling lightheaded and off-center since his gardening injuries got soaked from the surge of blood from Roman's jugular vein.

He was famished.

When Kevin brought out Aliya's corpse 30 minutes later, a bag of mushrooms fell out of her pocket along the way.

With no other corpses on the way, Terry decided his work was done, and so he ate them.

The entire bag.

They tasted like shit.

***

Cassandra walked back into the house and as she strutted past the bedroom, the Ted Lasso theme song was still playing.

She saw her reflection in the pool of blood and she saw bloody paw prints leading out the side window.

She went back to the deep corner of the sectional and grabbed three random pills.

She ate them with no water and laid down for a while to center herself and to wait for the come up while Kevin was outside.

She needed to stay on her cloud. She could never land. She wouldn't survive the landing. She was going to stay on the cloud until she died and then she would die on the cloud and she would never again have to feel human feelings.

It was then that she noticed that the news had returned from commercials.

She recognized the timbre of that voice when it was lying. *"...she was a good soldier, but that's it. Danielle is very cunning, very manipulative. But she's nothing more than a bloodthirsty psychopath."*

She instinctively reached for the hunting knife by her leg, and she stroked the dull side of the knife while watching, not registering what she was doing.

"She was useful, but they didn't really respect her. You nailed it, Keith – Matej was the real mastermind. Real solid dude. These other so called 'Karma Grinders' lost their way when he came to Silicon Valley to spread the message and save the world. He's completely innocent. I've known him for years. I had even invited him to my wedding, and these other criminal weirdos showed up with him and almost ruined it. Matej, if you're watching, I hope they clear your name, buddy."

She started off whimpering. "He's not the Archon. I'm the Archon." and it grew angrier through the pills into a seethe into a growl into a roar. "He's not the Archon. I'm the Archon. I'm the Archon. I'M THE FUCKING ARCHON." She withdrew her knife and stabbed the nearest couch cushion and the innards drifted to the floor.

A shaky voice from the other side of the livingroom reminded her there was work to do. "Why does he keep calling you

Danielle?"

Kevin was back inside. His innocent question centered her and gave her the focus to look again at the television where the Groom was still on a reputation tour and she had no choice but to tune it out. It was all bullshit. Everything coming out of his mouth was bullshit. His concern for his family's money was speaking and money was bullshit.

She kept coming back to it - the only truth left was revenge.

This wouldn't stop until the Groom was dead.

Cassandra's life was over, but there was still a way for her to die happy. She could still make sure that other people didn't.

She needed to murder the Bride slowly while the Groom watched.

Then she needed to murder the Groom.

Then she needed to murder Keith Olbermann.

Then she needed to murder Matej.

Her world could collapse after that. She just needed it to hang on for a bit longer.

She could die of hunger, covered in blood, in a jail cell, anywhere.

She would die with a smile and the smile would carry her back into the clouds.

She could feel that smile already. She had to run to catch it on the other side before it flew away without her.

She had to get things moving.

She ate the rest of the red pills.

She knew she needed Kevin, because Kevin knew how to find Matej.

She didn't need Terry. She could leave him in the backyard to bury his friends.

She grabbed Kevin by the collar of his shirt and told him to hot wire one of the taxis out front and get ready to drive to California. Kevin was trying to read *Leaves of Grass* but getting nowhere, so he put it in his pocket and went to work on the taxi.

She grabbed Aliya's bag of drugs as well as every single notebook Aliya had ever scribbled any notes in, and then went through the entire house to scan for small valuables, taking everything worth anything that would fit in a duffel bag.

She noticed an excess of blood on the money – the outside of the duffel bag had been drenched by the death of Gerg, and liters of it had soaked through. She wiped some of the blood away from a couple of bands, still wet, and saw the 50s and 100s. She could still count it. She grabbed it.

She put on Aliya's boots and triple knotted them, and she centered her septum piercing.

She went outside to meet Kevin in the taxi and as she walked, her hunting knife came loose from the scabbard and easily tore a hole down the weakened bloody side of the duffel bag, spilling some of the money as she went.

She was too fucked up to notice.

She got to the taxi - the New York license plates read "12131989" and she noticed a sudden sinking feeling deep inside of her as she tore the plates off to avoid police detection.

She paused for a second to try to make sense of the feeling but she couldn't make it past the drugs in her blood.

She noticed the cat prowling nearby, leaving bloody paw prints on the garden path, and felt a wave of peace wash over her.

She inhaled.

"I can do this."

She exhaled and got into the passenger seat.

Kevin finished hot-wiring the car, activated the ignition, and it exploded, killing them both instantly.

***

Terry was wandering back from the depths of the gardens with hedge trimmers when he heard an explosion, but he paid it no mind, finding a growing alien peace from observing the different shades of green on the trimmers.

As he approached the pathway that connected behind a rose bush to the neighbor's yard, he stumbled over a copy of *Leaves of Grass* with the front page burned almost beyond recognition.

He paused, thinking about picking it up.

It was a beautiful day.

He didn't need it.

He felt a surging connection with the gardens he was tending. His movements slowed, his smile widened. As the minutes flowed through him, his gardening style evolved, from surgical precision, to pruning with crude slices, to gently detaching branches, to the upheaval of entire root systems.

He grew fascinated by the uncountable shades of green of a drooping dinosaur fern intruding on the garden path; he tried counting the different shades but kept getting lost in the fractals on the leaves.

He gave up on the fern, found a worm poking its head out of the dirt, struggling to emerge, and helped it out by loosening the dirt in the immediate area. For the next ten minutes, he watched intensely as the worm slithered up into the back of the garden and out of sight.

He had tears in his eyes from the triumph of the worm.

He stopped to wonder if the mushrooms were ever going to kick in.

In the depths of the garden nearby where the worm made its exit, he noticed something out of place – a tropical pineapple, glowing yellow, pulsating with life, calling to him. As he reached into the garden to touch it, he crushed the fractal fern against the side of the stone landscaping; he picked up the pineapple, snapping it from its roots, dropping the hedge trimmers to cradle it in his hands, careful to avoid the abrasion of the rough outer layer. He clasped one hand slowly and firmly around the base of the lush, green crown at the top, and when he ceremoniously raised his arm straight-out in front of his face, he started to feel it emanating a new power.

Terry realized he had never really looked at a pineapple before. He thought it was quite beautiful how the strong, individual scales all supported each other at the base, all working together to create a perfect explosion of ethereal green shards, bursting through the crown, trying to reach the sky. He wondered briefly how the fruit tasted on the inside but the pineapple was too perfect to him; it would be unthinkable to spoil such beauty only to satisfy his ugly base urges.

The waves of his reverie were cascaded by waves of a human-sounding voice.

"Sir, do you speak English?"

He couldn't believe it. The pineapple was talking to him. He heard the same words, but he wasn't sure if he was only remembering the pineapple again.

His smile broke into a greater smile and his grip on the crown became tighter.

"Sir, can you hear me?"

He had no idea how to speak to a pineapple. Of course he could hear the pineapple. But it doesn't have a mouth. How is it communicating to him? How does it speak English?

He noticed how the individual scales of the pineapple all had the same beautiful marking: a bright, dancing yellow-green sprite that faded gently below into the deeper green of the scale. He wondered how many there were. He wanted to ask the pineapple how many scales it had.

It suddenly dawned on him. The pineapple must be communicating telepathically. That's how it knew English! It was simply telecommunicating the ideas, and Terry's own mind was putting the ideas into English.

"Sir, are you okay?"

Terry focused his energy on beaming a message of peace - yes, he was okay, and he was happy to become friends. How many scales do you have?

"Sir, do you need medical attention?"

The pineapple's words were starting to feel harsher, sterner, more concerned, more afraid. The shades of green started to diminish. By now Terry could feel the vibrations of the waves of the voice crash into his ears, and he realized the voice was urgent and terrestrial, coming from a sudden police officer, directly behind him, whose mortal fear had placed his hand in a hovering position over the gun in his holster.

Terry turned and slowly lowered his arm, allowing the pineapple to come out of focus, revealing the frightened officer in an aggressively pre-emptive standing position.

"Sir, are you okay? Do you speak English, sir?"

It dawned on Terry that the 8-bit policeman thought that he was a Mexican day laborer. The man's eyes were horrible, small and confused. Terry was far more interested in the pineapple.

"Sir! Are you on drugs?"

Terry smiled at the officer, who pulled out his radio. "Nobody in the house. I have made contact with a landscaper in the backyard, I think he might have wandered over from the neighbors. Possibly on drugs. No medical attention needed at this time. Over."

"Sir, please answer me, do you speak English?"

Terry wanted nothing more than to go back to the garden.

"Sir, this property is part of an ongoing criminal investigation. I am going to need you to leave this property and return to your own property."

Terry was spooked by the mention of the criminal investigation, and it percolated into him that the bodies in the grave would stir up a world of trouble. He remembered suddenly how he became distracted by the million shades of green and had never finished burying his friends.

Terry watched as the officer faced down for a minute, lost in thought, and seemed to make a sudden decision, moving his hand near his gun holster, which made Terry jolt slightly in the direction of the bodies.

The officer noticed Terry's jolt, and when he pulled a loose roll of yellow crime scene tape from a small fanny pack near his holster, he dropped it.

Before long, it started to unravel.

The officer peeked in the direction of Terry's jolt, and noticed a shovel standing up in a small pile of fresh soil near the pit.

He instinctively drew his gun and approached slowly, calling on his radio for backup.

He stopped about six feet short, got onto his tip toes and peered over the small pile and into the pit, making eye contact with Steef, still smiling, with a large hole clean through his third eye.

The officer emptied his clip into Steef's face and was horrified to find that Steef was still smiling.

"DEAD BODY. WE HAVE A DEAD BODY," the officer screamed into his police radio.

"ON THE GROUND. NOW."

Terry gently placed the pineapple on the ground and rose back to his feet.

"YOU. NOT THE PLANT. YOU. ON THE GROUND."

Terry slowly lowered himself into the lotus position and emitted a hum, agitating the officer, who approached and then leaned in to pistol whip Terry to his side.

"ON YOUR FEET, SPIC."

Terry rose to his feet from the lotus position, his hands down at his sides, showing no fear, feeling no fear for himself, feeling some fear the pineapple.

The officer noticed a bulge in Terry's shorts. "SLOWLY, WITH YOUR LEFT HAND, REMOVE THE WEAPON FROM YOUR POCKET AND PLACE IT ON THE GROUND."

Terry slowly moved his left hand to the side of his jeans and adjusted the fabric with a firm tug, moving his 'weapon' to a more comfortable position towards the center of his boxers, then put his hand back up and smiled.

The officer realized it was not a gun. "OH SHUT THE FUCK UP." He lurched forward and pistol whipped Terry where he stood, and Terry could feel the force of the officer's frustration more than he could feel the side of his gun.

The officer was growing agitated with Terry's total lack of response to his attempts at intimidation. The academy did not prepare him for this. He noticed the dilated pupils in Terry's eyes, but was used to drug addicts being far more terrified and pliable, usually buckling under and collapsing in a heap on the ground at the sight of a gun.

Terry felt some ancient pangs of fear grasping at him from the center of his dormant animal psyche, but those feelings were overwhelmed by emerging feelings of pity for the officer. There was no reason to be shouting.

His attention was drawn back, again and again, to the vibrant gardens, still showcasing more shades of green, seeing glimpses of new shades as the wind bent the light for a fraction of a fraction of a second.

The officer followed Terry's attention as he gazed over the graveyard into another part of the garden, and the officer noticed a few extra smiling faces poking out of the dirt, next to Steef, having been uncovered by his frantic gunfire.

"WE HAVE MULTIPLE DEAD BODIES. ONE SUSPECT ON DRUGS, UNCOOPERATIVE. I NEED BACKUP."

Terry could start to feel his breath coming from a place deeper than before and he could feel it returning to the same ancient place when he exhaled. He wanted to keep each breath with him but he knew all at once that every breath was temporary; the breath came from somewhere else, and it would return to the same place when he exhaled; the breath was only his to borrow; the breath was a gift.

The officer unloaded his entire clip at the pineapple on the ground in front of Terry. It exploded, the lifeless crown still attached to a spattering of jagged scales; the fruit spilled on the ground, unspent, unexperienced, a sad yellow, bleeding out, soon to be trampled underfoot.

Terry's attention was routed to the cold steel of the nozzle of the gun which was now pointed directly at him.

From out of nowhere, Lise, paws still bloody, jumped on Terry's shoulder and purred, and the officer started to lower his gun.

Terry turned his attention away from the gun and he was once again lost in the fractal jasmine chaos of the gardens.

Lise jumped from Terry's shoulder leaving a bloody paw print, and Terry's shoulders slumped as the officer raised his gun.

"You better start talking RIGHT THE FUCK NOW."

The officer cocked his gun.

Terry said nothing.

ACKNOWLEDGEMENTS

Thank you to the individuals who helped me get this thing done, in one way or another:

Eric Bancroft, Lise Carter, Nick Chandler, Kent Clark, Steve Conelley, Mike Cripps, Xana Daley, Jeff Desjardins, Tej Dhaliwal, Lindsay Dianne, Stu Elmes, David Fargo, Erin Hamilton, Danielle Harrison, Cassandra Harwood, Geoff Henwood-Greer, Sarah Innes, Harnoor Jaura, Kathleen Jensen, Aliya Konstantinople, Kenneth Korri, Danny Leeming, Christine Madigan, Emily Madigan, Agatha McBride, Greg Moffat, Kyle Neto, Fallon Nygaard, Kirsten "Kerosene" Nygaard, Alan O'Sullivan, Paul Quesnel, Paige Reich, Tina Rogers, Jasmine Sanghera, Shanley Kane, Terry Singh, Linh Stirling, Nate Stirling, Alexandra Swan, Miles Tautscher, Roman Terwilliger, Rose Walker, Tina Welch, Michele Wetzel

ABOUT THE AUTHOR

Kd Madigan

Kevin Daniel Madigan was born in Vancouver, BC and currently resides in Oak Bay on Vancouver Island where he works in the warehouse of a plumbing wholesaler.

Writing influences include Chuck Palahniuk, Douglas Adams and Anthony Bourdain.

Every character in Karma Grinders is based on a personal friend. They all know each other.

Substack: https://substack.com/@riotsurvivor

Goodreads: https://www.goodreads.com/kdmadigan

www.ingramcontent.com/pod-product-compliance
Lightning Source LLC
LaVergne TN
LVHW051252080426
835509LV00020B/2929